# Contents

# Cox on Cox

## *An English Curriculum for the 1990s*

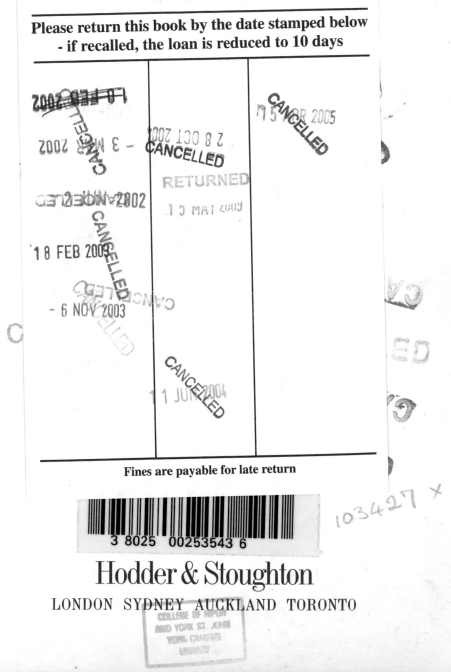
## Hodder & Stoughton
### LONDON  SYDNEY  AUCKLAND  TORONTO

For the English Working Group:

Mrs Di Billups
Ms Linda Cookson
Dr Katharine Perera
Mr Roger Samways
Professor David Skilton
Mr Brian Slough
Professor Michael Stubbs
Dr Charles Suckling

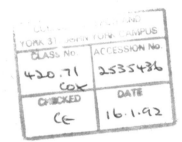
**British Library Cataloguing in Publication Data**

Cox, Brian
  Cox on Cox: An English Curriculum for the 1990s.
  I. Title
  420.7

  ISBN 0-340-53792-2

First published 1991

Typeset by Rowland Phototypesetting Ltd,
Bury St Edmunds, Suffolk
Printed in Great Britain for the educational publishing
division of Hodder & Stoughton Ltd,
Mill Road, Dunton Green, Sevenoaks, Kent by
Clays Ltd, St Ives plc.

# *Preface*

The National Curriculum English Working Group submitted its final Report, *English from ages 5 to 16*, at the end of May 1989. It was welcomed with enthusiasm by teachers, and helped to foster a consensus in the profession about what constitutes good practice in the teaching of English. Its recommendations apply only to England and Wales.

Copies of the Report were sent free to schools and appropriate educational establishments, but it was not published in the normal way, and cannot be obtained in bookshops. Many teachers of English have barely glimpsed the Report, and as battered copies disappear it is in danger of becoming unobtainable. It has never been seen by parents. The attainment targets and programmes of study, in their final form, have been published by HMSO (*English in the National Curriculum*, 1990), and these are printed at the end of this book. In addition, the National Curriculum Council has published non-statutory guidance for English in the National Curriculum. But the crucial chapters 1 to 14 in the original Report, on which my Group worked so carefully, and which explain our rationale, are no longer easily available to teachers and new entrants to the profession. Almost all this material is printed in this book.

In preparing the Report for this publication, I had to edit it in many small ways, for it was originally prepared for the specific purpose of putting proposals before the Secretary of State. All the substantial sections which drew so much praise from teachers have been retained. At the same time I have added my own commentary, telling something about the political machinations behind the scenes and explaining the Group's thinking. In particular, I have considerably extended the chapter on literature, which many teachers thought too short. I hope this book will be of great help to teachers as they apply the National Curriculum recommendations in the classroom.

I have dedicated this book to the members of the Working Group. Many paragraphs were originally written by one or other of them, although we all took part in revision and redrafting. I am very grateful to all of them for their loyalty and their lively participation in our discussions. I take responsibility for the commentary and editing of this book. They take responsibility for the great success of the original Report which, I am sure, will be remembered and discussed and consulted for decades to come.

I am grateful to all those who helped with the typing and preparation of the manuscript, particularly Miss Maxine Powell, Mrs Mary Syner and Mrs Sara Finestein.

Brian Cox

# The Political Context

In the late 1980s the British Conservative government set up two powerful committees to advise on the teaching of English. Their two Reports, popularly called Kingman and Cox, were not welcomed by leading right-wing Conservatives. The Kingman Report was not liked by the Prime Minister. When Professor Kingman discovered that his Report's recommendations might be rejected, he used the Robert Robinson factor to cajole the civil servants. Robert Robinson, the popular and skilful host of the TV language game, *Call My Bluff*, was a member of the Kingman Committee and signed its recommendations. Would the Prime Minister really find it advisable to appear in public in opposition to the famous Mr Robinson? When my Report was submitted to Mr Kenneth Baker, Secretary of State for Education and Science, he so much disliked it that he insisted that it should be printed back to front, starting with chapters 15 to 17, which included our recommendations for attainment targets and programmes of study, and relegating the explanatory chapters 1 to 14, which he thought unnecessary, to a kind of appendix. The creation of a National Curriculum in English was influenced by several bizarre incidents of this kind.

How did it come about that the Conservatives chose committees whose Reports disappointed their hopes? Why did both Kingman and Cox so offend the Conservative establishment? What arguments and manoeuvres went on behind the scenes?

## THE CHOICE OF COMMITTEES

The Kingman Committee, of which I was a member, was appointed by Mr Baker at the beginning of 1987. We were asked to recommend a model of the English language as a basis for teacher training and professional discussion, and to consider how far and in what ways that model should be made explicit to pupils at various stages of education. The Committee's Chairman, Sir John Kingman, Vice-Chancellor of Bristol University and a mathematician by training, submitted his Report on 17 March 1988, and it was published on 29 April. On

26 April I was summoned by Mr Baker to his office at the Department of Education and Science, and asked if I would chair a Working Group to prepare proposals for English in the National Curriculum. We were asked to 'build on' the work of the Kingman Committee. I was not consulted about membership of the Group, and with the exception of Dr Charles Suckling, a member of the Kingman Committee, I met the members for the first time when we assembled in London for our opening working session. The National Curriculum English Working Group was formally set up on 29 April 1988 by the Secretaries of State for Education and Science and for Wales to advise on attainment targets, programmes of study and associated assessment arrangements for English in the National Curriculum for the period of compulsory schooling. English was defined as including both language and literature and we were to take into account relevant aspects of drama, media studies, information technology and information handling. The framework for the National Curriculum was set out in the Education Reform Act 1988.

The Kingman Report was not well received by right-wing Conservatives because they wanted a return to the traditional teaching of Latinate grammar, and the Report came out firmly against this. Many politicians and journalists were ignorant about problems in the teaching of grammar and about the status of Standard English, and simply desired to reinstate the disciplines of study typical of schoolrooms in the 1930s. In chapter 2 I discuss the Kingman recommendations on the teaching of grammar, and describe their influence on my own Report. Because Kingman was deemed unsatisfactory, my Working Group was chosen carefully by Mr Baker, with the assistance of Mrs Angela Rumbold, Minister of State at the DES, to reflect a more conservative stance to the teaching of English. I was well known as the chief editor of the Black Papers on Education (1969–77), supposedly traditional and right wing in their views of education. I presume neither Mr Baker nor Mrs Rumbold was aware that for over ten years I had been conducting a campaign to make creative writing a central feature of the English curriculum, and that in October 1983 I helped to organise a manifesto on this subject which was published in the *Times Higher Education Supplement*.

## THE WORKING GROUP

When I first met my Working Group I was astonished to discover that they were far more progressive in outlook than the members of the Kingman Committee. The Kingman Committee included traditionalists of an older generation such as Peter Levi, Professor of Poetry at Oxford, and Patrick Kavanagh, a poet whose conservative views were well known from his regular column in the *Spectator*. They were with difficulty persuaded by the linguists on the Committee, particularly the

Secretary, Peter Gannon (an HMI), and Professor Gillian Brown, at that time Professor of Applied Linguistics at the University of Essex, to accept a model of language in tune with modern ideas and the needs of the contemporary school. The only linguist on my Working Group, Professor Michael Stubbs (Professor of Education at the University of London Institute of Education), proved more radical than Professor Brown in his ideas about the teaching of language, and was deeply concerned about the problems of British ethnic communities and of multi-cultural education. Mr Baker appointed him without interview because he had been impressed by Professor Stubbs's publications on the importance of knowledge about language.

My Working Group was small, only nine in number, including myself. Dr Charles Suckling, formerly General Manager (Research and Technology) at ICI, provided a sharp mind and clarity of thought invaluable both when we discussed our assumptions about values and in the final drafting stages. Professor David Skilton, Head of English at the New University of Wales College of Cardiff, took over respon-sibility for our chapter on the teaching of English language and literature in the schools of Wales, and proved usefully at home with structuralist and post-structuralist approaches to literature. Roald Dahl, the children's writer, attended the first meeting, admitted he hated committees, and never reappeared. Apparently Mr Baker had met him on a social occasion, and had been impressed by his traditionalist views. Our four teachers represented the best in modern ideas about teaching English, the new consensus between the traditional and the progressive which had become increasingly dominant in Britain during the 1980s. Mrs Di Billups was head of Broughton Junior School, South Humberside, which I visited with great pleasure and profit in the summer of 1988. Linda Cookson, short story writer and Senior Tutor at the London Central School of Speech and Drama, proved a strong advocate for drama in the curriculum. Brian Slough, Deputy Head of Kettering Boys' School, admitted to voting Conservative, but in his classroom practice adopted a wide range of progressive and non-traditional techniques. He brought to the Group a list of such activities which was published as an appendix to the Report. Roger Samways, Adviser for English and Drama in Dorset, was very progressive in outlook, holding views about children's learning which were anathema to most right-wing Conservatives. Roger recounted with delight what happened when he was interviewed by Mr Baker. They spent the first ten minutes talking about Thomas Hardy, because Roger came from Dorset, and then Mr Baker read passages from the Kingman Report, which was still unpublished, and asked if Roger agreed. Unsure about what Kingman really advocated, Roger could only mutter polite words of assent.

When the Working Group's names were announced the left-wing press accused Mr Baker and Mrs Rumbold of choosing political appointees to reflect the Prime Minister's Conservative ideology. My own view is that neither Mr Baker nor Mrs Rumbold knew very much about the complex debate that has been going on at least since Rousseau about progressive education, and that they did not realise that my Group would be strongly opposed to Mrs Thatcher's views about grammar and rote-learning. The politicians were amateurs, instinctively confident that common sense was sufficient to guide them in making judgments about the professional standing of the interviewees. I suspect they did not realise that words such as 'grammar' or 'progressive' reflect very different meanings according to context, or that the language of educational discussion had changed radically since they were at school.

My Working Group co-operated very well together, and we enjoyed our weekly meetings. On several occasions we spent weekends working furiously hard in small groups at drafts of attainment targets and programmes of study. I had been allocated an efficient back-up team from the Civil Service: Jane Benham (promoted near the end and replaced by Martin Howarth), Michael Phipps and Jenny Bacon, all of whom impressed me with their loyalty to me and their diplomatic skills. After the stories that circulate about Civil Service chicanery, I can attest to the professionalism of my team. They were joined by Graham Frater, the chief HMI for English, more progressive in inclination than I am, but invaluable for his intimate understanding of the teaching profession. It was essential that our recommendations should arouse enthusiasm among the best teachers; if they disliked our plans, the National Curriculum would never be properly implemented in the classroom.

Roald Dahl received our committee papers, and sent comments to me. Very soon I realised that he was not in tune with the rest of the Group. For example, he seemed to be advocating *no* advice from the teacher in a child's selection of books. I knew that, when we reported in September, if he expressed his adverse opinions to journalists he would dominate the headlines, and the Report might be irretrievably damaged. I wrote to Mr Baker to propose that he should tactfully suggest to Mr Dahl that, as he was not attending the Working Group's meeting, he should resign. I explained the danger of a September confrontation. A few days later Mr Baker was hosting a dinner to thank the members of the Kingman Committee for their work. After coffee he drew me aside, quietly admitted I was right, and agreed that Roald Dahl must withdraw. 'Would you handle it?' he asked. Amused by Mr Baker's diplomatic skills, I composed a letter to Roald Dahl, and luckily by the end of July he had sent us a sensible letter of resignation.

After this letter was received I managed, with some difficulty, to persuade Mrs Rumbold and Mr Baker to invite Mrs Katharine Perera, Senior Lecturer in Linguistics at Manchester University, to act as a replacement. They were worried that a new member might delay our work, and cause divisions. I had known Katharine for many years, and, in common with other members of the Kingman Committee, I had been impressed by her presentation when she appeared before us to answer questions. She combined considerable teaching experience with classroom research on the teaching of English. She provided exactly the kind of professional expertise we required, particularly as I had no training in linguistics.

The Working Group's terms of reference defined attainment targets as 'clear objectives for the knowledge, skills, understanding and aptitudes which pupils of different abilities and maturity should be expected to have acquired at or near certain ages'. Programmes of study were defined as 'describing the essential content which needs to be covered to enable pupils to reach or surpass the attainment targets'. We were asked to submit recommendations on the primary school stages with attainment targets for ages 7 and 11 by 30 September 1988, and to extend our work to cover the secondary stages with attainment targets for ages 14 and 16 by 30 April 1989. This meant we had to complete our first Report in five months and our second only seven months later. I am proud that we succeeded in submitting our Reports on time. In the first few months we received a considerable amount of written advice from individuals and professional organisations, and so in making our decisions we could draw on a range of expertise.

## THE REPORT ON THE PRIMARY STAGES

When our first Report on the primary stages was submitted to Mr Baker at the end of September 1988, he felt that we had given insufficient emphasis to the teaching of grammar. In his proposals, printed at the front of the Report, he asked that 'the programmes of study for writing should be strengthened to give greater emphasis to the place of grammatical structure and terminology within the matters, skills and processes otherwise covered.' This was seized upon by the press, who in headlines proclaimed that the Report was weak on grammar. The misunderstandings were legion. The leader in the *Daily Mail* (16 November 1988) read 'Baker in row over basic English', and the article began: 'Bad grammar is acceptable for schoolchildren, an official report recommended yesterday.' The London *Standard*'s headline read 'Baker's hard man "soft" on grammar.' The *Mail on Sunday*'s headlines (13 November 1988) were: 'Thatcher furious with "trendy" Experts' and 'English report fails the test.' The article began: 'A Report telling schools to ignore English teaching in favour of trendy methods has infuriated Mrs Thatcher', and continued by saying that the lengthy report 'dismisses grammar in a few paragraphs'. It is difficult to believe these comments refer to the same Report as that evaluated in a balanced leader in the *Independent* (16 November 1988) under the headline 'A blow for literacy'. After describing the controversies about the teaching of grammar in the past, the article continues: 'Common sense has since begun to prevail. Professor Cox and his team compromise by stressing the value of knowledge and grammatical discipline, while recommending that these should be achieved through experience with words rather than through the study of grammatical terms in isolation.'

Since my appointment to chair the Working Group I had seen Mr Baker only on one occasion. I had never been given the opportunity to explain to him the difficulties in making recommendations about the teaching of language. Firm statements about the importance of grammar would be taken by many teachers and members of the general public to mean a return to Latinate grammar, and we did not wish to give this false impression. Many people did not realise that there are different kinds of grammar, and that conventions in the use of language keep changing. We explained all this in detail in the Report (see chapters 2 to 5 this book), and in fact our Report demanded far more teaching about language than had been customary in most classrooms during previous decades. Mr Baker's demands for more emphasis on grammar began a ridiculous debate in the newspapers, during which most participants revealed their misunderstanding of language by taking for granted that the rules of grammar are fixed and permanent throughout time.

I was not invited to the press conference at which our Report was presented to the media. Throughout my time as Chairman I was very anxious to co-operate with Mr Baker as far as possible, for I feared I might be asked to resign. I might be replaced by an old-fashioned advocate of Latinate grammar, and that would be a disaster for the schools. Mr Baker was determined to control the presentation of the Report so that he and the Prime Minister would be rewarded with good publicity. Unfortunately at the press conference our careful recommendations about the importance of Standard English were presented in such a way that many journalists came away with the false impression that we did not mind if children spoke dialect rather than Standard English. The headline in the London *Standard* read 'The professor what don't know nothing', and the subheading expressed the exact opposite of the truth: 'Is correct English just a dialect or could it possibly be a useful tool for a youngster in search of a job? An education report that appears to support the former theory is a pussyfooting piece of dangerous nonsense, says John Rae.' (17 November 1988) During subsequent weeks I gave many interviews to journalists to correct their inaccurate accounts. Most of the discussion in the media was trivial, with much attention given to the list of authors for children's reading, which excluded Enid Blyton and Captain W. E. Johns (see chapter 6 on literature).

# FRAMEWORK FOR THE REPORT

Throughout our discussions my Working Group was very anxious to compose chapters which would make clear our rationale to teachers and politicians of good will. We worked at a hectic pace. In formulating attainment targets we were required to follow the recommendations of the National Curriculum Task Group on Assessment and Testing (TGAT 1987). This assessment framework, adopted by the government, required that:

a) attainment targets are set for the knowledge, skills and understanding normally expected at the ages of 7, 11, 14 and 16;

b) the pupils' performance in relation to attainment targets should be assessed and reported on at ages 7, 11, 14 and 16. Attainment targets should be grouped for this purpose into *profile components* to make assessment and reporting manageable;

c) ten different levels of attainment should be identified within each target covering all the years of compulsory schooling. Pupils' progress should be registered against these levels: level 2 should be assumed to represent the performance of the median 7 year old; level 4 that of the median 11 year old; the boundary between levels 5 and 6 that of the median 14 year old; and the boundary between levels 6 and 7 that of the median 16 year old;

d) assessment should be by a combination of national externally set Standard Assessment Tasks (SATs) and assessment by teachers. In order to safeguard standards, the latter should be compared with the results of the SATs and with the judgement of other teachers. At age 16 the General Certificate of Secondary Education (GCSE) should be the main form of assessment, especially in the core subjects;

e) the results of assessment should be used both formatively to help better teaching and to inform decisions about next steps for a pupil, and summatively at ages 7, 11, 14 and 16 to inform parents in simple and clear terms about their child's progress. Aggregated results should be published to enable informed judgements about attainment in a school or local education authority (LEA) to be made.

When my Group first met in the summer of 1988 we soon decided to divide the English curriculum into three profile components:

a) *speaking and listening* – with one attainment target; the development of pupils' understanding of the spoken word and the capacity to express themselves effectively in a variety of speaking and listening activities, matching style and response to audience and purpose;

     b) *reading* – with one attainment target: the development of the
     ability to read, understand and respond to all types of writing,
     as well as the development of information-retrieval strategies
     for the purposes of study;
     c) *writing* – with three attainment targets in the primary stages:
     a growing ability to construct and convey meaning in written
     language, matching style to audience and purpose; spelling;
     and handwriting; but two in the secondary stages, with
     spelling and handwriting merged into an attainment target
     called presentation.

We chose these three profile components because this division of the
English curriculum would be familiar to English teachers and in accord
with good practice.

## THE REPORT ON THE SECONDARY STAGES

When we began our work on the secondary stages we considered
whether to add a fourth profile component, knowledge about language,
but we rejected this plan for two reasons. Many teachers were ill
prepared to teach language, and so might present the subject in an
unenthusiastic manner, so repressing the pupils' natural interest in
language. And secondly, language should be mainly studied in use, as it
appears in texts, not in isolation.

    During our last seven months, as we prepared our recommenda-
tions for the secondary stages, the officials of the National Curriculum
Council under their Chairman, Duncan Graham, were rewriting the
attainment targets for the primary stages, supposedly in accord with the
consultation exercise and Mr Baker's own proposals about grammar.
In February we were shown their drafts, and we did not like what we
saw. The word 'grammar', for example, had been inserted seven times
without any indication of exactly what it implied. Some weeks later
there were headlines in the newspapers saying that I threatened to
resign. What actually happened is that my Group said simply that our
proposals for 11 to 16 year olds were built on our work for the primary
stages, and that it would be absurd for us to bring out our second
Report if its proposals were out of tune with the earlier attainment
targets. Unless there were radical changes in the NCC drafts, we could
not proceed with our work. Informed of this impasse, Mr Baker
instructed the civil servants to go away and sort it out, which they did
with admirable diplomacy. On Friday 24 February 1989, my Group
was meeting for the weekend at Oxford. We spent all our time rewriting
the NCC drafts, keeping their improvements, which we accepted were
valuable, but mainly restoring our original wording. The civil servants
ensured that our drafts were the ones that eventually went into the
Statutes, so we were able to return to our second Report.

    This hiccup was time-consuming, and put us behind schedule.

We were forced to arrange an extra weekend in Birmingham from 12 to 14 May. On this occasion, so late in the proceedings, we continued to make major alterations. We decided that our programmes of study for knowledge about language were too difficult, too close to a first-year undergraduate course, and so we cut these drastically. We also realised that there was insufficient classroom time for the testing of children individually in dramatic performance. At least thirty minutes would have to be allocated to each child, if they were to do justice to their abilities, and this meant about fifteen hours for a class of thirty. This was out of the question. We were in danger of creating a system which would involve testing over far too long a period of time. Until the last minute I was revising our document, often making significant alterations, and ringing up members of the Group for their assent. I finished the final draft with Mrs Perera in an intensive session of eight hours one hot June Sunday, starting in her garden in Cheshire and ending towards midnight with the dispatch of the document by express courier for delivery to Mr Baker in London on the Monday.

## REACTIONS TO THE REPORT

Mr Baker very much disliked the Report. He had wanted a short Report, with strong emphasis on grammar, spelling and punctuation, which would have been easy for parents to read. In contrast, as I have already said, I was most anxious to persuade the teaching profession to implement our recommendations with good will, and so I felt it essential to explain our assumptions in detail. I understand that Mrs Rumbold also found our Report distasteful. I was never asked to discuss the final Report with her or with Mr Baker, so I cannot be sure about her reasons, but from her radio and television appearances it seemed she found repugnant our insistence that a child's dialect is not inaccurate in its use of grammar and should be respected.

The Report was submitted to Mr Baker and Mrs Rumbold by the civil servants, and again I was not invited. There was some question about whether the Report should be published in its entirety, for Mr Baker and Mrs Rumbold were worried that there were sections which the Prime Minister would not like. On the other hand, if they refused to publish the whole Report this would anger the teaching profession and provide the journalists with a sensational story. A compromise was agreed. They were reasonably satisfied with chapters 15 to 17, which included the attainment targets and programmes of study, and so, as I have already explained, it was decided to print these first. I decided not to protest, because at least the whole Report would be published, and teachers would be able to read the total rationale. It was agreed that chapters 15 to 17 should be printed on yellow-tinted paper, with the following explanation at the top of the contents page: 'For ease of reference, chapters 15 to 17 have been placed at the front of the report, adjacent to the proposals, and are printed on tinted paper.' At least I was able at future lectures to raise a laugh by pointing out that by printing chapter 15 first the Report provided an example of the pervasive influence of post-structuralism.

When the Report was sent to Mrs Thatcher's office with summaries and references prepared by the civil servants at the DES, they naturally drew attention to our firm proposals for the teaching of spelling, punctuation, grammar and written and spoken Standard English. Mrs Thatcher agreed to allow the Report to be sent out for consultation, but asked for one alteration. In the attainment targets for Writing we had put: 'Use Standard English, where appropriate.' The Prime Minister asked for 'where appropriate' to be deleted. I presume she feared – rightly, I suspect – that in some schools where children spoke in dialect the teachers might decide it was never appropriate. I rewrote the sentence as follows: 'Use Standard English (except in contexts where non-standard forms are needed for literary purposes, e.g. in dialogue, in a story or a play-script.)' This was accepted, and printed in the final version.

The programmes of study were introduced in the classroom for 5 year olds in the autumn of 1989 and for 11 year olds in 1990. Some changes were made by NCC as a result of the consultation process, but these were never substantial. When we submitted our first Report on the primary stages we recommended that the three profile components, speaking and listening, reading and writing, should be weighted equally in the assessment process. In his comments (published with the Report) Mr Baker agreed that this was appropriate for 7 year olds, but proposed that for 11 year olds greater emphasis should be given to the key skills of reading and writing. When the document was sent out for consultation, teachers, advisers and inspectors came down almost unanimously on our side. As the Working Group continued its deliberations on the secondary school curriculum, I was informed privately that Mr Baker would give way on this issue as long as the weighting for 16 year olds gave more emphasis to reading and writing. I was happy to agree with this because it seemed to me that teachers were not ready for all the problems of assessment of speaking and listening for pupils aged 14 to 16, and for the profile component to be given a 20 per cent weighting would be a considerable step forward. To my surprise my Working Group insisted after a lively debate that we kept the weighting at 33⅓ per cent for 14 year olds. After the Report was sent off for consultation, there was large support, particularly from the business community, for one-third weighting for assessment of speaking and listening throughout the curriculum, even for 16 year olds, and this was the final decision.

## CONTROLLING THE CURRICULUM

During the period when I was preparing my Report, three groups of people were involved in manoeuvres to control the National Curriculum in English: journalists, politicians and professional teachers. The journalists were mainly concerned to please their readers, and although there were good factual accounts in the *Independent* and the *Times Educational Supplement* there was little serious discussion of ways in which a curriculum in English affects our ideas of national identity. Even *The Times* gave the kind of distorted account of our treatment of grammar which would please retired head teachers of an old-fashioned cast of mind. Such falsities are quickly forgotten, and I was not too worried by the press response as long as the actual details of the National Curriculum remained in my control.

Conservative politicians were over-confident that they knew the right policies, and to a large extent they were contemptuous towards the professional teacher. This contempt derives from the 1950s and 1960s, when some senior educationalists committed themselves to fashionable ideas about teaching English: that children would learn to read naturally without the help of formal instruction, or that their writing should be the product not of craft but of free expression. By the late 1980s such excesses had been banished from the best classrooms; the teachers in my Group all acknowledged the need for a sensible balance in the classroom between the formal and the informal. An urgent need in the 1990s is for this professionalism to gain control of all classrooms, in order for the National Curriculum in English to be properly implemented.

# *Assumptions*

The Kingman Report proved to be of great value to my Working Group. On 29 April 1988, when both the Kingman Report was published and the membership of my Working Group announced, the press presumed that I was to lead a Group which would make firm recommendations on grammar, in contrast to the equivocations of Kingman. They conveniently forgot that I was a member of the Kingman Committee. I fully endorsed the Kingman approaches to the teaching of grammar, which were not 'equivocations', but carefully balanced descriptions of the place of English language in the curriculum. During the time he was chairing his Committee, Sir John and I got on well together. The only time we sharply disagreed occurred when near the end of our deliberations I argued that we should say far more about classroom practice. Our 'model' of the English language was prepared for teachers; in what ways would it be implemented in the classroom? Sir John, perhaps rightly, thought that this was not our brief, and that the complexities of this problem would prevent us from submitting our Report on time. As Chairman of the National Curriculum English Working Group I was given the responsibility of deciding on programmes of study for all children from 5 to 16, of putting right what I regarded as a major omission in the Kingman Report. It was to prove a daunting task.

## APPROACHES TO TEACHING ENGLISH

The problems we faced had been at the centre of passionate argument for many decades. In the 1950s many teachers found that exercises in grammatical analysis did not help children to raise their standards in the use of English. At primary school, children would learn definitions off by heart ('a verb is a doing word'), without regular practice in using verbs in real communications to real audiences. Similarly at secondary school level lessons in English language were often nothing more than pedantic exercises. In many schools in the 1960s a revulsion against decontextualised exercises brought about a complete abandonment of the teaching of grammar. Also many teachers of English succumbed to a kind of vitalism, a muddled belief that children's acquisition of language skills depends not on craft and knowledge, but upon a living, spontaneous response to their reading and to their own experiences. Self-expression, of course, is a most important element in child development, but often in the 1960s it was espoused with pseudo-religious fervour. The Kingman Report said this about these extremes:

> *Widely divergent views are now held on the value of the formal elements of knowledge about language. Many people believe that standards in our use of English would rise dramatically if we returned to the formal teaching of grammar which was normal practice in most classrooms before 1960. Others believe that explicit teaching or learning of language structure is unnecessary. We believe that both these extreme viewpoints are misguided. Research evidence suggests that old-fashioned formal teaching of grammar had a negligible, or, because it replaced some instruction and practice in composition, even a harmful, effect on the development of original writing. We do not recommend a return to that kind of grammar teaching. It was based on a model of language derived from Latin rather than English. However, we believe that for children not to be taught anything about language is seriously to their disadvantage. (paragraph 2.27)*

My problem was to persuade the teaching profession that this approach could generate lively teaching in the classroom.

The difficulties were described at length in the Bullock Report of 1975. In its 609 pages, which included 333 recommendations, one of the most important concerns was the competence of both teachers and pupils in respect of their knowledge of the English language. This Report had great influence, but many of its recommendations were never implemented. In the words of the Kingman Report, 'their implications have not been followed through with sufficient rigour or in detail.'

In the late 1970s, notably after the Ruskin College lecture given by Mr James Callaghan, the Prime Minister, there was growing concern about standards of pupils in their use of English. As a result HMIs published *English from 5 to 16* (1984), which proposed four aims for English teachers. After describing the first three, involving speech, reading and writing, the fourth aim was described as being: 'to teach pupils *about* language, so that they achieve a working knowledge of its structure and of the variety of ways in which meaning is made, so that they have a vocabulary for discussing it, so that they can use it with greater awareness, and because it is interesting.' (p. 3) This aim, which seems to me an obvious piece of common sense, caused uproar among many teachers of English, who feared a return to the rote-learning of the 1950s. Because they had been told that research shows that the teaching of grammar restricts the imagination, imposing a strait-jacket of conventions, they did not realise that it all depends on what kind of grammar is taught and in what contexts.

The Kingman model of language was greeted with anger by some teachers who looked back nostalgically to the 1960s, but it paved the way for a more judicious approach to the teaching of English. After Kingman there was a growing consensus that some kind of explicit knowledge about language was necessary for both teachers and pupils. This helped my Group when we set about persuading the teaching profession, represented mainly by the National Association of Teachers of English, to accept our recommendations. Teachers had begun to realise there was a strong case for the teaching of knowledge about language in ways very different from those that had been fashionable thirty years earlier. Our task was to devise classroom practices which would maintain the imaginative developments of the 1960s while introducing more emphasis on craft and on the structures of language. If we failed to get the balance right, teachers would lack the necessary motivation to implement our programmes of study. The kind of balance we had to achieve is well summarised in the first chapter of the Kingman Report:

> Nor do we see it as part of our task to plead for a return to old-fashioned grammar teaching and learning by rote. We have been impressed by the evidence we have received that this gave an inadequate account of the English language by treating it virtually as a branch of Latin, and constructing a rigid prescriptive code rather than a dynamic description of language in use. It was also ineffective as a means of developing a command of English in all its manifestations. Equally, at the other extreme, we reject the belief that any notion of correct or incorrect use of language is an affront to personal liberty. We also reject the belief that knowing how to use terminology in which to speak of language is undesirable. Language is, as a matter of observable fact, plainly governed by a series of conventions related to the varying audiences, contexts and purposes of its use. Successful communication depends upon a recognition and accurate use of the rules and conventions. Command of these rules and conventions is more likely to increase the freedom of the individual than diminish it. (paragraph 1.11)

These points are taken up again in the second chapter of Kingman, where it is argued that language 'expresses identity, enables co-operation, and confers freedom', and that an understanding of language is vital to children's intellectual, social, personal and aesthetic development.

# OUR RATIONALE

After the fierce arguments of the previous decade it was necessary for my Group to explain its own rationale, and we did this in the second chapter of our Report. We needed to be clear about the nature and purpose of English as a school subject. These explanations are crucial for parents and teachers who are trying to understand the thinking which underlies the attainment targets and programmes of study; a main reason why I have written this book is to give our rationale a wider audience. The arguments in chapter 2 of the Report have brought teachers together in a common purpose, and many old divisions have been overcome.

If we look at the range of statements about English teaching in books written before our Report we see how broad the subject is. It includes, for example, language use, language study, literature, drama and media education; it ranges from the teaching of a skill like handwriting, through the development of the imagination and of competence in reading, writing, speaking and listening, to the academic study of the greatest literature in English. Such broadness poses problems, both for the identity of English as a distinctive school subject, and for its relations with other subjects on the school curriculum. Another consideration is that English can seem at first glance rather different in primary and in secondary schools. Primary teachers normally teach English as part of an integrated curriculum, whereas in secondary schools it is more usually taught in timetabled slots by subject specialists. This makes it doubly important to identify clear aims in order to secure continuity and progression within the English curriculum from 5 to 16.

In his Introduction to *Modern Criticism and Theory* (1988), a collection of major critical essays of recent years, David Lodge writes: 'Literary criticism can no longer be taught and practised as if its methods, aims and institutional forms were innocent of theoretical assumptions and ideological implications.' The revolution of thought which took place in France in the 1960s, with the work of Barthes, Foucault, Kristeva, Derrida and Lacan, has transformed our perception of the subject, the teaching of both language and literature, and we realise that the varieties of English teaching reflect a variety of ideological assumptions. The Kingman Report explained:

> *The recent structuralist and post-structuralist revolutions in literary theory have caused people to think very energetically and critically about the relationship between the structures of language and the structures of culture. Today many graduates in English are excited by and well-informed about these ideas. Some of them may become teachers in schools, and may, as a result of those interests, welcome a greater emphasis on the*

*teaching of knowledge about language. For the central ideas of*
*structuralism and post-structuralism do indeed spring from the*
*study of language as the human way of ordering experience.*
*(paragraph 2.25)*

Kingman concluded: 'It is not necessary to specialise in such studies to
be aware that our ways of structuring sentences and thoughts, and, by
extension, our ways of structuring our cultural values and beliefs, affect
the whole of our individual and social lives.' So a national curriculum in
English must reflect our values and beliefs, and we need to be as explicit
about these as possible.

My Group was anxious that all teachers should understand and
think about the ideological assumptions implied by their approach to
the teaching of English, for this is one way to overcome dogmatism. We
hoped our approach to the curriculum would be seen as enabling rather
than restricting, a starting point for teachers in their discussions with
their colleagues, not a strait-jacket. From the 1950s to the 1990s radical
changes in teaching styles reflect major changes in social and cultural
values. We can only protect a national curriculum from the political
dogmas of either the right or the left if we understand the reasons for
these changes.

We were also conscious that many English teachers are non-
specialists: the Kingman Report points out that 28 per cent of teachers
in secondary schools have no formal qualifications in English beyond
O-level and that they are responsible for 15 per cent of English teaching
(paragraph 6.4). Many primary teachers too are not English specialists.
Such teachers are easily swayed by forceful expression of dogmas about
English teaching, and need to be aware of the false polarisation of views
typical of debate in the 1960s and 1970s. For example, people set in
opposition individual and social aims, or utilitarian and imaginative
aims, or language and literature, or reading for meaning and decoding,
or craft and creativity in writing, and so on. We believed that the best
practice reflects a consensus rather than such extreme positions, and we
did not see this as some timid compromise. Our task would be to
explain the relations between these different views within the large
framework of the National Curriculum.

## ENGLISH AND OTHER LANGUAGES

Passionate debate is provoked by the problems of children whose first
language is not English. We decided that all children must be able to
speak and write Standard English, when appropriate (see next chapter).
But we wanted from the start to dissociate ourselves from the arrogant
and ignorant belief that in some mysterious way English is superior to
other languages, and that children who speak Bengali or Hindi at home
should abandon these languages as soon as possible. The Bullock

Report clearly stated in 1975: 'No child should be expected to cast off the language and culture of the home as he (or she) crosses the school threshold . . . The curriculum should reflect many elements of that part of his (or her) life which a child lives outside school' (paragraph 20.5). A major assumption of the Cox Report is that the curriculum for all pupils should include informed discussion of the multi-cultural nature of British society, whether or not the school is culturally mixed. It is essential that the development of competence in spoken and written Standard English is sensitive to the knowledge of other languages which many children have. The resolution of difficult issues of language in an increasingly multi-cultural society requires informed citizens, and this may be the strongest rationale for knowledge about language in schools.

The presence of large numbers of bilingual and biliterate children in the community should be seen as an enormous resource which ought to become more, not less, important to the British economy in the next few years. The curriculum should also have in mind education in a European context, with reference both to the position of English as an international language, and to increasing labour mobility and inter-cultural contact within the European community, especially after 1992. It is not possible to predict what new language demands will arise. But, whatever form they make take, language demands will almost certainly be greater than in the past; more pupils will be studying foreign languages for longer periods of time, and children's perceptions of foreign languages are likely to change. This will affect English teaching, since English will exist in a still richer linguistic and cultural context. All this is likely to have implications for children's knowledge about language.

Teachers should accordingly be encouraged to develop whole-school policies on language, which are sensitive to their local circumstances. These policies should bear in mind principles such as that when children leave school they should have acquired as far as possible:

a) a firmly based, but flexible and developing, linguistic and cultural identity;
b) an awareness of some of the basic properties of human languages and their role in societies;
c) a respect for other languages and cultures, and an understanding of the increasing interaction of cultures in society;
d) a willingness and capability to overcome communication barriers.

These principles are just as important for children in schools in country areas which are not culturally mixed as for children in the inner cities. We are advocating a new cultural awareness for pupils in all schools from all neighbourhoods. It is to be hoped that schools in the independent sector will recognise how vital these principles are if we are to promote true peace and co-operation in British society.

# THE AIMS OF THE ENGLISH CURRICULUM

But all children, whatever their background, must be able to speak and write Standard English, when appropriate. What are the main principles teachers and parents should hold in mind as they try to help children to develop to the full their ability to use and understand English?

First, English contributes to the personal development of the individual child because of the cognitive functions of both spoken and written language in exploratory learning and in organising and making sense of experiences. Secondly, English contributes to preparation for the adult world: people need to be able to communicate effectively and appropriately in all the widely different social situations in which they find themselves.

In pursuit of these two complementary purposes, teachers should aim to extend the range of varieties of English in which children are competent. From a developmental point of view this will mean adding to the local varieties used within the family and peer group those varieties used for wider communication (in school and higher education, in adult work and society); it means adding written language to spoken language, Standard English to non-Standard English, literary language to non-literary language and, for children who have a different mother tongue, it means adding English to their first language. For example, they can do more when they can produce written language because they can write to people who are far away, or to institutions, government departments, newspapers etc.; they can keep written records; they can write down ideas in order to reflect on them and reformulate them; they can elaborate complex arguments which require written support; they can create and keep artistic artefacts — poems, plays, stories; and so on. They can do more when they have a mastery of Standard English because they can communicate in a wider circle both socially and geographically.

A closely related objective is to develop children's understanding of the different ways in which meanings are conveyed. A traditional concern of the English teacher has always been to develop the ways in which children interpret texts, spoken or written, literary or non-literary, and to increase children's understanding of how texts convey multiple layers of meaning and meanings expressed from different points of view. How texts achieve their effects has been of particular significance in the teaching of literature, including drama.

Children should be able to make sense of how messages are conveyed in a variety of forms and contexts: in the heritage of literature written in English, but also in the mass media, in film and television, and in the newer technologies. Children should be enabled to understand the codes and conventions by which meanings are represented in documentary and fictional accounts, narrative and argumentative texts, and so on. The Kingman Report emphasised the need for such abilities when it stated: 'A democratic society needs people who have the linguistic abilities which will enable them to discuss, evaluate and make sense of what they are told, as well as to take effective action on the basis of their understanding . . . Otherwise there can be no genuine participation, but only the imposition of the ideas of those who are linguistically capable' (chapter 2, paragraph 2). The understanding of the different ways in which meanings are conveyed is one area in which a vocabulary for the description and analysis of language is essential.

Our attainment targets and programmes of study reflect our conviction that the personal and social development of the child are inextricably linked. Interactive spoken language is widely recognised as a powerful means of learning; it is also obviously essential in the world outside school. Reading has essentially personal value as a source of enjoyment, as a stimulus to the imagination, as a means of gaining vicarious experience, and as an agent in language development; but it also allows warnings, instructions, information and so on to be absorbed. Writing serves cognitive functions in enabling the child to redraft and refine thoughts and ideas, but it also serves social functions in transmitting messages in the wider world. Both aspects of language development, the personal and the social, contribute to giving pupils power over their own lives.

In our Report we listed five different views of the purpose of teaching English. They were not to be seen as sharply distinguishable, and certainly not mutually exclusive. This list is of vital importance, for it gives a broad approach to the curriculum which can unite the profession. The five views are as follows:

a) a 'personal growth' view focuses on the child: it emphasises the relationship between language and learning in the individual child, and the role of literature in developing children's imaginative and aesthetic lives;

b) a 'cross-curricular' view focuses on the school: it emphasises that all teachers (of English and of other subjects) have a responsibility to help children with the language demands of different subjects on the school curriculum: otherwise areas of the curriculum may be closed to them. In England, English is different from other school subjects, in that it is both a subject and a medium of instruction for other subjects;

c) an 'adult needs' view focuses on communication outside the school: it emphasises the responsibility of English teachers to prepare children for the language demands of adult life, including the workplace, in a fast-changing world. Children need to learn to deal with the day-to-day demands of spoken language and of print; they also need to be able to write clearly, appropriately and effectively;

    d) a 'cultural heritage' view emphasises the responsibility of schools to lead children to an appreciation of those works of literature that have been widely regarded as amongst the finest in the language;

    e) a 'cultural analysis' view emphasises the role of English in helping children towards a critical understanding of the world and cultural environment in which they live. Children should know about the processes by which meanings are conveyed, and about the ways in which print and other media carry values.

Some of these views look inwards: either in the sense of developing the individual child or in the sense of developing English as a separate school subject. Other views look outwards: they are concerned with helping the child with the needs of language elsewhere in the curriculum, or in the outside world of work. Alternatively, they are concerned with passing on the culture from one generation to the next, and with critically understanding what that culture consists of. Another distinction is that some of the approaches concern essentially the children's developing use of language, whereas others concern the knowledge about language and literature required of an informed and educated citizen in a democratic society.

    Teachers of English will differ in the weight they give to each of these views of the subject. Indeed, some differentation will derive directly from the stage children have reached at school: for example, the 'adult needs' view is more relevant to the later years of compulsory schooling than to the primary years. Some aspects of 'cultural analysis' are also more relevant to older children. However, aspects of media education are important for children in the primary phase too, because these children can be influenced by the conventions and assumptions of mass media, and should learn to recognise this.

    In my talks to teachers I often repeat these five views. They acknowledge the utilitarian functions of English teaching, and yet place these in a wider cultural and imaginative framework. When we were discussing these issues in our Working Group the teachers often reminded me that we were not preparing a thesis for university dons. Mr Baker was not entirely wrong in wanting a simple, forceful document for parents, though he failed to understand that some difficult issues – the teaching of grammar or Standard English, for example – need careful and detailed explanation. In our first Report on the primary stages we included an early chapter which tried to summarise our views with simple eloquence. As an epigraph to this chapter we included a quotation from the Plowden Report of 1967 (*Children and their Primary Schools – the Report of the Central Advisory Council for England*): 'At the heart of the educational process lies the child. No advances in policy, no acquisitions of new equipment have their desired effect unless they are in harmony with the nature of the child.' The inclusion of this quotation attracted considerable good will. Before the Report was published teachers were prey to the wildest fantasies about its contents – we would insist on rote-learning, daily exercises in grammar, no more creative writing. When they discovered this famous Plowden sentence about the importance of the child at the top of this chapter, they welcomed it with a great sigh of relief.

## GOOD TEACHING PRACTICE

We also included a statement from a 1988 publication of the National Association of Advisers in English, *English, Whose English?*, by David Allen. This repeated general principles well known to all good teachers, but I wanted them in the Report so there could be no doubt about the kind of teaching we admired. I feared that many readers, prejudiced by the supposed right-wing commitment of the Group, would misread the Report, and take for granted that we were opposed to all the innovations of recent years. Our recommendations on the teaching of knowledge about language had to be accompanied by an insistence that our policies did not necessitate any change in good teaching practice.

David Allen lists the following characteristics of successful teaching and learning in language:

a) a very high expectation of success for the learner;
b) an 'apprenticeship' approach to acquiring written and oral language, in which the adult represents the 'success' the child seeks and yet offers endless help;
c) maximum encouragement and support whilst errors are mastered;
d) motivation for the learner to make sense of and acquire control over language and the power it can have;
e) a constant respect for the child's language.

Allen continues by defining the needs of learner and teacher:

*the learner needs,*
◇ expectation of success,
◇ the confidence to take risks and make mistakes,
◇ the willingness to share and to engage,
◇ the confidence to ask for help,
◇ an acceptance of the need to readjust,
*and the teacher needs,*
◇ respect for and interest in the learner's language, thought and intentions,
◇ the ability to recognise growth points, strengths and potential,
◇ the appreciation that mistakes are necessary to learning,

◇ the confidence to maintain breadth, richness and variety,
  and to match these to the learner's interests and direction
  (i.e. to stimulate and challenge),
◇ a sensitive awareness of when to intervene and when to
  leave alone.

We argued that such statements reflect the growing consensus
nationally about what constitutes good practice in the teaching of
English. Recent initiatives such as the National Writing Project and the
National Oracy Project have done much to foster such developments
and to disseminate good practice. At the same time the emergence of
GCSE English has come to mean more than mere changes of emphasis
at the upper end of secondary schools. Increasingly we are seeing the
influence of the positive developments and changes brought about by
GCSE on work done in the earlier secondary years.

We tried to identify the main features of current best practice in
English by describing classrooms where, individually and collaboratively, pupils are seen:

a) using language to make, receive and communicate meaning,
   in purposeful contexts;
b) employing a variety of forms with a clear awareness of
   audience;
c) working on tasks which they have chosen and which they
   direct for themselves;
d) working with teachers who are themselves involved in the
   processes – albeit with special expertise – as talkers, listeners,
   readers and writers;
e) reading literature for enjoyment, responding to it critically
   and using that reading for learning.

We concluded this short chapter (chapter 3 in the final Report) by
summarising the best teaching practice for our three profile components: speaking and listening, reading and writing. Primary schools
must respect children's talk, as pupils put into words their thoughts and
feelings, explore new ideas and deepen understanding. This process
continues in secondary school, where oral communication remains an
essential part in the learning process across the whole curriculum.
Reading for pleasure is an essential part of a child's development of
language skills. Children should be encouraged to behave like real
writers, suiting their written work to audience and purpose. These
ideas, familiar to all good teachers of English, are so important they
bear constant repetition.

# Teaching Standard English

Many highly educated people, including a substantial number of teachers, do not understand the difference between Received Pronunciation (RP) and Standard English. This ignorance among the general public is one good reason for including knowledge about language in the English curriculum. It is also true that many older people, who were trained rigorously in the disciplines of study fashionable before 1960, think that they know a great deal about language, but in fact imbibed many false notions from their schooling. I provide a notable example in my next chapter on grammar and linguistic terminology. I was told that one reason why many Conservative politicians were sympathetic towards our Report was because they did not at first realise that our insistence that all children should speak and write Standard English did not involve any recommendation about RP.

## RECEIVED PRONUNCIATION

Received Pronunciation is the accent, used by a minority of speakers in Britain, that developed in the nineteenth century in the public schools and universities, and was associated in the 1930s and 1940s with BBC newsreaders. The Kingman Report explained that although this accent must be the standard for foreign students of English in Britain, it is not used as the model of English pronunciation in British schools, since speakers may be rightly proud of their regional pronunciation, which identifies where they come from. The Kingman Report recommended that all children at the age of 16 should speak in Standard English, 'using their own accents (provided that these accents do not impair comprehension by other speakers of English)' (chapter 5, p. 52). As we all know, there is still great prejudice among speakers of RP against other accents such as Cockney, and in England the correct accent is a mark of social acceptability. The English curriculum ought to help to overcome such snobbery by encouraging children to discuss their accents and to be proud of regional differences, but the task of overcoming arrogance about accents is formidable.

As John Honey shows in his *Does Accent Matter?* (1989), Received Pronunciation itself is gradually changing, and there are marked differences between what is socially acceptable in 1991 and the fashionable accents of the 1930s. All these considerations persuaded my Group to follow Kingman, and to argue forcibly, in a passage we underlined, that although children should speak Standard English, we 'do not, however, see it as the school's place to enforce the accent known as Received Pronunciation'.

## STANDARD ENGLISH AND DIALECT

Standard English caused us enormous problems. When I submitted our first Report to Mr Baker he asked me how he should explain what was meant by Standard English to the education journalists. It was not an easy question to answer.

This first Report was read by Professor Brian Griffiths, whose duty as Prime Minister's adviser was to present it to Mrs Thatcher with his comments. He protested that we had made no recommendation that children should use Standard English. I read to him sentences from the Report such as: 'Schools have the clear responsibility to ensure that all children have full access to Standard English, given its role as an international language used throughout the world and essential for many purposes.' He reread the appropriate chapter, and acknowledged that I was right. This incident made me realise that our careful descriptions of the relationship between dialect and Standard English might be misread, and so in the final Report I insisted that we should reiterate many times that all pupils should learn, and if necessary be explicitly taught, Standard English. Unfortunately I had shut the stable door after the horse had fled.

After our first Report the tabloid journalists enjoyed themselves by writing provocative articles about how I was the professor for whom correct English did not matter. The journalists found especially useful a passage about Standard English where we explained that dialects obey their own grammatical rules. We said that non-standard forms are rarely more than a social irritant to some people, and that there are few situations where such forms could cause real communication problems. They include a small set such as: 'we was; he ain't done it; she come here yesterday; they never saw nobody; he writes really quick; theirselves etc.' These examples gave the journalists the story for which they were looking, and they used them in headlines to show that our Report was against the teaching of grammar and 'correct' English, and that we favoured a policy of 'anything goes'. At a conference at Oxford in December 1989, Professor Randolph Quirk, the famous linguist, attacked me fiercely for including material like this, which could be easily misrepresented by the press. After the furore which greeted our first Report I felt – perhaps pusillanimously – that we should excise this explanatory passage. Professor Michael Stubbs felt strongly that it should be retained, partly because journalists would draw attention to its omission, and partly because our readers needed to understand the truth about dialects. A majority of the Group agreed with Professor Stubbs, and so we retained the examples, though with additional explanatory material. On Professor Stubbs's behalf it can be said that the Report reflects a total view of society, of co-operation and tolerance between cultural and social groups, and that to achieve this aim all teachers and pupils need to understand clearly why contempt for other people's dialects is wrong.

After our Report was published we were criticised by both left-wing and right-wing educationalists. The left argued that children who speak dialect at home could not be expected to speak Standard English, which they regarded as middle class, and that it was improper to make this an essential attainment target in a national curriculum. The right thought we were too soft on primary school children, who should be expected to speak and write Standard English as soon as they arrive in the classroom. In the rest of this chapter I will explain our thinking as clearly as I can, for there has been much misunderstanding.

## THE DEVELOPMENT OF STANDARD ENGLISH

The Kingman Report explains that Standard English

> developed from one of the Middle English dialects (East Midlands – the dialect first printed by Caxton) to become the written form used by all writers of English, no matter which dialect area they came from. It is the fact of being the written form which establishes it as the standard. And it is the fact of being the written form which means that it is used not only in Britain but by all writers of English throughout the world, with remarkably little variation. Since it holds this important role in the written form, it is also used to communicate across local areas and between regions in a spoken form. (paragraphs 2.32 and 2.34)

As we have seen, this spoken form may be in a variety of accents, from Devon to East Anglia, from the United States to Australia. Speakers of Standard English in different parts of the British Isles and elsewhere in the world may use the same grammar and vocabulary, but different pronunciation. For example, many speakers from the United States, Scotland or south-west England pronounce the r sound after the vowel in words such as car and farm; most speakers in south-east England do not. Accent refers to pronunciation. Dialect refers to vocabulary and grammar. Most people know some dialect words: for example, bairn for child in Scottish English. And dialects differ in their grammar: for example, Standard English has *I was, you were, he was, we were, they were*. Many non-standard dialects have (more regularly, as it happens) *I was, you was, he was, we was, they was*.

Standard English itself is usually analysed by linguists as a dialect of English which clearly has social prestige. This is partly because of the purposes which it now serves; it is the expected language in the education system, in other social institutions (such as the courts and business) and in almost all published writing, and it has also spread far beyond its historical base in Britain and is used as an international language in many parts of the world. Non-standard dialects of English are regional dialects: that is, they are relatively restricted in their geographical spread. Standard English used to be restricted in this way: if we look at Standard English as an historical dialect, then we find that 200 years ago it had a much smaller number of speakers in England, and had nothing like the geographical spread it has nowadays. Standard English is also a social dialect: its use is a marker of social group membership, and the relationship between standard and non-standard dialects and social class in Britain is particularly strong.

Because of its long use, especially in writing for academic and administrative purposes, the vocabulary and to some extent the sentence syntax of Standard English have been greatly elaborated. Non-standard dialects have the potential to be so developed, but for social and historical reasons they have not been. The words 'greatly elaborated' are of considerable significance. Linguists do not like to say that Standard English is 'superior' to other dialects, because all dialects have their own richness, their own specific identity. And left-wing educationalists do not like to say that the Standard English spoken by the middle classes is superior to working-class speech. But Standard English serves particular functions: for example, in the education system and in professional life, in public and formal uses, in writing and particularly in print. It is precisely because Standard English serves as a wider language of wider communication for such an extensive and important range of purposes that children must learn to use it competently. In an article on the Cox Report published in *Critical Quarterly* (Winter 1990), Gillian Brown writes:

> *Standard English today differs from local dialects not only in permitting the expression of complex relationships in familiar written forms, but also in the astonishing wealth of vocabulary which has accrued to it through its intellectual and imperial history. Dialects, we should remember, are essentially local to particular parts of a particular country, and specialized for talking about local and domestic life. . . . Many would argue that learning a school subject – geography, chemistry or English literature – entails learning the language in which that subject is expressed. Since subjects learnt at school have been*

> *codified and developed through written texts, and written*
> *texts are written in Standard English, it follows that children,*
> *to have any hope of mastering these subjects, must learn to*
> *read and write Standard English. (pp. 35–36)*

If pupils do not have access to Standard English then many important opportunities are closed to them, in cultural activities, in further and higher education, and in industry, commerce and the professions. Those educationalists who deny children these opportunities are confining them to the ghetto, to a restricted discourse which will close to them access not only to the professions but also to leadership in national politics. In our democracy, Standard English confers power on its users, power to explain political issues and to persuade on a national and international stage. This right should not be denied to any child.

Standard English should not be regarded as fixed. It changes over time, just as any language does: no one nowadays speaks in the same way as the contemporaries of Chaucer or Shakespeare or even Dickens. Moreover, it varies according to style, purpose and audience: no one speaks or writes in the same way on all occasions. Nor should Standard English be confused with 'good' English. Speakers of Standard English can use English just as 'badly' as anyone else: they can write unclear prose, use words ambiguously, and so on. Standard English and non-standard dialects have much in common. Where there are differences, it is important to understand that dialect forms are grammatical and rule-governed in non-standard dialects, but the rules are different from those of Standard English. For example, Standard English does not distinguish between *do* as a main verb and as an auxiliary verb: *He did it, did he?* Many non-standard dialects do make this distinction, which is not available in Standard English: *He done it, did he?* The non-standard dialect is not a haphazard variant, since no speakers of non-standard dialects would say *He done it, done he?* Or *He did it, done he?*

Much more difficult problems of definition arise with creole varieties of English, including creoles of Caribbean origin. These language varieties are known by various names, such as West Indian Creole, Black British English and Patois. The main points are:

⋄ such language varieties are not random and simplified deviations from Standard English: they are highly complex and rule-governed varieties of English;

⋄ their linguistic variation is typically greater than with other dialects of English. Speakers' use of creole varieties lie along a continuum, from varieties of creole which may well be incomprehensible to a speaker of Standard English, to varieties much closer to Standard English;

⋄ the term 'dialects of English' is itself problematic. Whether

creole varieties are termed 'dialects of' English or are regarded
as languages in their own right is a political and ideological
question, which concerns the social identity of groups of
speakers. It is not a matter which has a simple linguistic
definition.

Given this variation in language forms and use, the danger may be that
teachers do not realise the extent of the variation, or that they regard the
creole language forms as haphazard. They may therefore not realise
those cases where there is genuine dialect interference between the
pupil's home language and the language expected in the school.

## OUR RATIONALE

All pupils, therefore, must be able by the age of 16 to use spoken and
written Standard English; but schools have the responsibility to develop
their own policies on the detail of how this should be done. Across
England and Wales, schools differ greatly in their linguistic profiles. In
some schools, most pupils use spoken Standard English as their native
dialect; in others, most have to learn it as an additional language.
Therefore it was not possible for my Working Group to prescribe a
single policy which would suit all circumstances. We did, however,
attempt to outline the principles which should inform school policies on
the teaching of Standard English.

A coherent school policy on Standard English can be based on the
different views of the main aims of English teaching which I listed in the
previous chapter:

    a)  a personal growth view;
    b)  a cross-curricular view;
    c)  an adult needs view;
    d)  a cultural heritage view;
    e)  a cultural analysis view.

The first view is related to the need for the pupil's own native language
or dialect to be respected: Standard English has to be treated very
sensitively in schools, since dialect is so closely related to pupils'
individual identity. The second and third views emphasise the importance of using Standard English for wider communication, inside
and outside school. The fourth and fifth views relate to the fact that
Standard English is a topic which pupils should reflect on, understand
and analyse. A coherent school policy on Standard English is possible if
it is recognised that all these views are legitimate.

To be effective in their teaching of Standard English, schools
should teach it in ways which do not denigrate the non-standard
dialects spoken by many pupils. It should not be introduced at too early
a stage; teaching pupils a new dialect may be confusing when they are
learning many other aspects of language use. The profound implica-

tions for pupils' relationships with their families and communities should be recognised.

There is considerable debate over when to expect pupils to use Standard English in writing. Schools should develop their own coherent policies, which are sensitive to their local circumstances, on exactly how and when Standard English should be taught. In general terms, we advocated that there should be explicit teaching about the nature and functions of Standard English in the top years of the primary school; that there should be the beginnings of the expectation of Standard English in written work when appropriate by the age of 11; that there should be the provision of opportunities for oral work where spoken Standard English would be a realistic expectation in the secondary school; and that all pupils should be in a position to choose to use Standard English in speech when appropriate by the age of 16. The teaching of Standard English should be related to the teaching of public, formal, written varieties of English. A main focus should be on the differences between written and spoken English. For example, written language typically has to express things more explicitly, because it has to stand on its own. If the teaching concentrates on the relationship between language forms and use, then it need not reject the language of the home. These written forms must, in any case, be taught even to those children whose native dialect is Standard English, since spoken and written Standard English differ considerably in some respects. No one uses written Standard English as his or her native dialect.

This is consistent with a general policy of widening the linguistic repertoire of pupils. It does assume, however, that teachers themselves have an accurate understanding of the differences between written Standard English, spoken Standard English and spoken local varieties of English.

The uses of Standard English should be discussed explicitly with pupils. This has considerable implications for knowledge about language. Pupils need to be able to discuss the contexts in which Standard English is obligatory and those where its use is preferable for social reasons. By and large, the pressures in favour of Standard English will be greater when the language is written, formal and public. Non-standard forms may be much more widely tolerated – and, in some cases, preferred – when the language is spoken, informal and private.

Standard English should form an important part of the teaching of knowledge about language: its historical, geographical and social distribution and the uses to which it is put (in different countries, in different areas of society, in print and in the mass media, etc.). Teachers should encourage an interest in both rural (traditional) and urban dialects of English, by contrasting local non-standard dialects with Standard English, often using pupils as the linguistic experts on the former. The grammar of both should be discussed and contrasted. Non-standard usages should be treated as objects of interest and value, and not ridiculed. Sometimes, with older pupils, it will be possible to discover the antecedents of a regional form in historical usage.

For pupils who do not have Standard English as their native dialect, teaching Standard English should draw on their knowledge of other dialects or languages. The aim is to add Standard English to the repertoire, not to replace other dialects or languages. It should also be recognised that non-standard forms are systematic and not haphazard.

Teachers should differentiate clearly between different kinds of correction, and avoid indiscriminate correction. It can only be confusing to a pupil if features of dialect are 'corrected' at the same time and in the same way as, for example, spelling errors. The latter may be due to carelessness, or to a principle which has not been grasped. But dialect features are not errors in this sense at all, but are characteristics of a pupil's native language. It is advisable to concentrate on (a) frequently occurring non-standard forms and (b) highly stigmatised forms. These will include forms of the verb *to be*, past tenses of a few highly frequent irregular verbs (e.g. *do, see*), personal pronouns and negatives.

## CONCLUSION

To sum up, teachers need to remember that:

◇ all languages and dialects change over time;
◇ spoken and written language differ significantly.

Standard English varies stylistically according to audience, purpose and situation. The aim is the competent use of Standard English. This aim is best attained by helping pupils to understand fully the linguistic and social nature of Standard English. Pupils need to be able to produce spoken Standard English if they are to have access to many public areas of life. However, although correcting written English is relatively unproblematic, the alteration of spoken English is more difficult. Several of the principles which apply to written Standard English, such as the clear expression of meaning, apply equally to spoken English. But the main problem is that it is far more difficult to teach a new spoken dialect because so many aspects of spoken production are automatic and below the level of conscious control.

It is therefore important to set out some principles for the learning process:

◇ there is little point in correcting the spoken language of pupils in any general way and as part of their routine language use because it is unlikely to have a beneficial effect: against the pressure of home and the peer group, teachers can have little hope of changing how pupils speak. Moreover, criticism of pupils' spoken language will be interpreted as criticism of their families and friends;
◇ if teachers concentrate on pupils' competence in written

Standard English, pupils will gain sufficient knowledge of Standard English to be able to convert this into competence in spoken Standard English when appropriate. Research shows that secondary pupils do use fewer non-standard forms in talk with the teacher than they do in the playground;

◇ it is helpful to set up situations in which it is natural to use Standard English. Role-play may often be appropriate: in drama, or in media work (for example in producing news programmes), but also in class panel discussions, debates, etc. Standard English is the language of wider communications. It is therefore desirable to enable pupils to widen the circle of their audience: small groups within the classroom, larger groups in the class or in the school, and, for more public presentation of ideas, with pupils from other schools or with adult strangers. Pupils should be able to take the roles in which spoken Standard English is conventional: radio pre- senter, interviewer, expert in front of lay audience, etc.;

◇ if people need to learn a language for some real purpose, then they learn it. Furthermore, the desire to join a group is often very strong indeed. If pupils are motivated to learn to use spoken Standard English because they wish to adopt a social role, they will learn it if they are given the appropriate educational experiences and opportunities.

As we have seen, teaching Standard English demands great sensitivity from the teacher. It is dangerous to tell a 5 year old boy or girl that his or her mother uses language incorrectly. Adolescents are going to be embarrassed and ashamed if a teacher suggests that their dialect, which is part of their identity, must be radically changed. How to teach spoken Standard English needs continual discussion among teachers. I would not want anyone to think we had provided the final word.

# Grammar in the Classroom

*Grammar, perfectly understood, enables us, not only to express our meaning fully and clearly, but so to express it as to defy the ingenuity of man to give to our words any other meaning than that which we ourselves intend them to express.*
*(William Cobbett,* A Grammar of the English Language, *1818)*

My Group faced great difficulties when we tried to formulate our recommendations for the teaching of grammar. As I have already explained, the word attracts conflicting prejudices. If we said we were in favour of the teaching of grammar, some teachers would think we were advocating a return to old-fashioned exercises in parsing and clause analysis. On the other hand, for right-wing pressure groups the word had become a shibboleth: if only 'grammar' was taught in a formal manner, standards in the writing of English would improve dramatically. Speaking on Radio 4 in November 1985, Norman Tebbit, later to become Chairman of the Conservative Party, claimed that the decline in the teaching of grammar had led directly to the rise in football hooliganism. Correct grammar was seen by him as part of the structures of authority (such as respect for elders, for standards of cleanliness, for discipline in schools) which in recent decades had fallen into decline. In our first Report we tried as far as possible to avoid the word 'grammar', and to explain how important it was for children to use linguistic terminology. But this ruse failed, for the education journalists were not interested in the nice distinctions I offered them when they interviewed me on the phone. We ended up with a rash of headlines, some announcing that we were in favour of the teaching of grammar, some that we were against. The journalists who worked for the popular newspapers were only concerned to please their readers, and the truth was irrelevant.

## THE MEANING OF 'GRAMMAR'

In our final Report we defined carefully and at length what we meant by 'grammar' and by knowledge about language, and what kinds of programmes of study we thought appropriate. We said that secondary school pupils might themselves begin to discuss explicitly the different meanings of 'grammar', and become conversant with the controversies aroused by this word. In everyday usage, for example, in the conversation of people such as Mr Baker, Mr Tebbit and the journalists, 'grammar' is associated with the correct use of the standard language. But linguists use the term very differently. They use it, first, to refer to ways in which words are combined to make sentences (in any dialect), and second, to label the body of statements they write about the language as they attempt to make explicit the implicit knowledge possessed by all native speakers of English.

Linguists distinguish between prescriptive and descriptive views of language, and teachers need to understand when they need to insist on rules, to prescribe, and when it is more appropriate to describe the differences between dialects and Standard English, or between spoken and written usage. Prescriptivism is, in essence, the view that it is possible to lay down rules for the correct use of language. There are two problems with the way this view can be implemented. The first is that sometimes the rules do not relate to the actual language use of native speakers. (An example is the suggestion that *It is I* is the only correct form whereas, in fact, most educated speakers of English generally say *It's me*.) The second is that the rules may be those that apply to formal, written language but they may then be prescribed for all circumstances.

Descriptivism is the name given to the view that the way people actually use language should be accurately described, without prescription of how they ought to use it. Careful descriptions of speech are necessary because people's beliefs about their actual linguistic behaviour are often very inaccurate; many people think they speak in the same way as they write but, in fact, no one does. Soon after our Report was published, Mr Baker took part in a radio discussion. A letter appeared in the *Independent* pointing out that he made a number of grammatical errors. But the conventions of speech are very different from those appropriate for writing. In a conversation we can explore meanings, often changing tense as our thought jumps from idea to idea, and we can enforce our reasoning with gesture and facial expression. In lively talk with friends we all continually break the rules appropriate for the written form, and Mr Baker on the radio was no exception.

Both prescriptive and descriptive linguisticians are sometimes parodied. Prescriptivists are seen as blind adherents to outdated norms of formal usage. Descriptivists are seen as advocating 'anything goes', and as condemning all forms of linguistic correction. We must recognise that we need both accurate descriptions of language that are related to situation, purpose and mode (i.e. whether the language is spoken or written), and prescriptions that take account of context, appropriateness and the expression of meaning. Because we know that the rules keep changing slightly during the course of time, it does not follow that there should be no rules. If we are to communicate clearly and precisely with each other over a wide geographical and social range, we must obey the rules of Standard English as they are current at the time we are speaking or writing.

Many people still believe that English grammar is a fixed form, stable and unchanging, which obeys logical rules. An example of such mistaken ideas appeared in the *Evening Standard* in a scathing review of our Report written by John Rae, ex-head of Westminster School. That a man so well known in educational circles should be so ill-informed demonstrates the problems we had in helping our readers to understand our proposals. He wrote:

> *I thought it was correct to write we were and incorrect to write we was. I did not realise it was just a question of dialect; I thought it was a question of grammar or, if you do not like that word, of logic. You cannot use a singular form of the verb with a plural pronoun. (17 November 1988)*

His appeal to logic is mistaken: *you were* is both singular and plural in Standard English. Logic, however, is a feature not of the grammar of a language or dialect, but of arguments in sentences and in texts. It is people in their use of language who are logical or illogical, not languages or dialects themselves.

Similarly, references to accuracy, precision, clarity or lack of ambiguity cannot be conflated with *grammar*. There is no ambiguity about the meaning of *we was*. There are, however, other features of grammar (ways of relating clauses in complex sentences, for example) which pupils do have difficulty with and which affect the logic and clarity of written and spoken language. Accuracy, clarity and precision are obviously important, and we need to identify correctly those parts of the grammar of English which are relevant to constructing accurate, clear and precise arguments.

When grammar teaching fell into decline much of value was lost: a certain analytic competence, and with it the valuable ability to talk and write explicitly about linguistic patterns, relations and organisation. The reintroduction of the teaching of grammar does not mean that teachers need to neglect the subjective, creative, personal and expressive, for our ability to express ourselves depends on craft, and craft involves understanding of the forms of language. Most successful creative writers take this for granted. Some form of analysis (which may be more or less explicit) is necessarily a part of the interpretation of texts, of understanding how a poet or novelist achieves his or her effects, and consequently must figure in the production of accurate writing.

For grammar to be of relevance to English teaching, it should be:

a) a form which can describe language in use;

b) relevant to all levels from the syntax of sentences through to the organisation of substantial texts;
c) able to describe the considerable differences between written and spoken English;
d) part of a wider syllabus of language study (this is outlined in chapter 5).

The ways in which meaning is expressed must always be central to any language study; how language uses grammatical patterns to create both predictable and new meanings. Everyone has an implicit knowledge of the grammar of his or her native language(s). The problem for the teacher is how and in what contexts it should be made explicit to pupils.

## HOW TO TEACH GRAMMAR

On my visits to schools as a member of the Kingman Committee, I discovered that often the English department's description of its syllabus would explicitly state that children should not be taught the definition of grammatical terms. But in the classroom teachers constantly used technical terms such as noun, verb, adjective, metaphor, simile, paragraph and sentence, and took for granted that children would know what they meant. I also saw many examples of good practice where a teacher introduced children to terminology to discuss their own writings. At a primary school a class of 5 and 6 year olds was making entries in a folder entitled 'My own sentences'. The teacher had discussed a topic with the children, and then encouraged them to write down sentences constructed from words used in their own speech. The teacher had helped them with the capital letter to begin the sentence and the full stop at the end. She had not made them learn a definition of a sentence, which would be entirely inappropriate for this age group, nor did she ask them to complete meaningless exercises. The children were being encouraged to learn about sentences by using them in real contexts.

Professor Stubbs provided a much lengthier example of classroom discussion to illustrate good practice in the teaching of linguistic terminology. The civil servants (not often wrong, but this time they gave bad advice) wanted to remove this long example from the body of the Report, and relegate it to an appendix, or, better still, cut it out completely. I was determined to give it maximum prominence. Our task was to persuade teachers that classroom discussion of linguistic terms could be stimulating and creative, even if a long account of children's talk looked a little strange in an official Report directed to the Secretary of State.

The extracts are from transcripts of an audio-recorded classroom discussion with five first-year juniors, in a north London primary school. K is the teacher; L is another teacher, but not the regular class teacher; A, B, H, N and P are the children. The comments after each extract are the teacher's own. The extracts illustrate several things:

◇ children's natural instinct to play with language and their metalinguistic awareness;
◇ the teacher's role in developing such awareness;
◇ the large number of terms which can arise in such discussions: *palindrome, word, spell, sentence, name, alphabetical order, story, rule, vowel, letter, rhyme, dot/full stop.*

**Extract 1**
*N: Palindromes are a word where you can spell them the other way like* dad . . . *and* toot.
*P: And you can do it in numbers.*
*A: And it goes back the same way.*
5    *L: And* toot?
*A: And* Panama.
*N: Yeh 'cos you just turn it round and it goes* toot.
*L: Like this? (writes the word* toot) *then if I turn it around . . .*
*N: It's just the same.*
10   *H: It's exactly the same.*
*A:* Toot!
*N: Yeh and if you do another one underneath it's just the same.*
*L: What's another one?*
15   *H: (as she re-writes* toot): *T . . O . . O . . T*
*A: Like* Panama.
*K:* Panama *isn't a sentence on its own. What's the whole sentence?*
*H: Was it a cat I saw. That's another one.*
20   *K: Was it a cat I saw?! Can you write that one down?*
*(Hedda writes the sentence.)*
*N: Was it a . . . elephant I saw?*
*K: That wouldn't work would it?*
*H: . . . cat . . . I . . . saw . . .*

**Teacher's comments**
*I had recently talked about palindromes and palindromic numbers with the class. This had caused great excitement, and many of the children attempted to make up their own.*
*        Whenever I talk about language with a group of children, be it this style of informal discussion or a more structured shared writing session, I always have a large sheet of paper handy so that ideas can be shared by all. The children feel free to take hold of the pen and write (see lines 15, 21).*
*        Here is an instance where I am able to extend the discussion.*

**Extract 2**
H: *My name backwards is in alphabetical order.*
L: *Is it?*
A: *Is it? . . . Hedda? . . . Yes it is.*
All: *A . . . D . . . D . . . E . . . H.*
5      K: *Gosh that's wonderful. And Paul, yours is LUAP. Yours is*
*NEB.*
B: *Neb.*
P: *Hello Neb. I'm Luap.*
K: *What's her name backwards?*
10     A: *Mine's Noraa, isn't it?*

**Teacher's comments**
*Hedda is a fluent reader and was well aware of alphabetical*
*order at the start of her top infant year. Her reference here is*
*totally spontaneous but may have been influenced by some of*
*the class activities. We had spent time earlier this year working*
*on alphabetical order and had had fun re-writing various*
*words alphabetically. Similarly, we had a register of names*
*backwards (in addition to one in alphabetical order, one in*
*descending age and one by surname). Her comment stimulates*
*an examination of everyone's name.*

**Extract 3**
K: *Do you think there might be something . . . But do you*
*think that when the person who invented words invented*
*palindromes, they did it specially . . .*
A: *But there's no-one who invented words.*
5      N: *Captain Caveman did.*
K: *Who did?*
N: *Captain Caveman.*
K: *Invented words?*
N: *CAPTAIN CAVEMAN!*
10     K: *Aaron, how do you know . . . How do you know no-one*
*invented them?*
A: *Well because it's not really possible that one person found*
*out all these words like . . . dinosaur . . . tyrannosaurus*
*rex . . .*
15     P: *Dinosaur . . . um . . . isn't English.*
K: *Isn't it? Where's that from?*
P: *Um . . . it's . . . I'm not sure what country.*
A: *Probably and as well.*
P: *No, it means . . . um . . . 'big lizard'.*
20     K: *That makes sense, doesn't it. It fits in.*

**Teacher's comments**
*1. This extract begins with an outrageous statement by me!!*
*Luckily, Aaron jumps on this and challenges me.*

5. *Captain Caveman is a cartoon character.*
15. *Paul volunteers some information which is then accepted and built on. The children's expertise and knowledge are valued.*
18. *Aaron's brief interjection could become the basis for further discussion. In this instance, however, I was more concerned to draw Paul into the discussion.*
19. *Paul concludes his contribution with a definition that is accurate and presumably drawn from his personal interest in prehistoric life.*

**Extract 4**
*K: Have you invented any words in your time?*
*A: Yes, in my stories I just make them up. I just do any words . . .*
*K: What rules then do you make to make them up?*
5  *A: I just come up with the words.*
*K: What, you must have some –*
*P: What, like* rzthzn?
*K: Aaron, you wouldn't make this a word, would you? (As she writes* zyghpzgh. *They all try to read it.) Why couldn't that be*
10  *a word?*
*A: 'Cos I don't just write it down. What I do is to find out the word and then I just write it down.*
*K: But you must have something –*
*N: I know . . . ain't go no . . . wait . . . what's it called? . . .*
15  *vowels. Ain't got any vowels!*
*K: Very good Niki! He's right you know, and you missed that one Aaron. It couldn't possibly be a word, could it? Actually, unfortunately Niki, why is sometimes y a sort of a –*
*H: Because* i *and* y *are sort of the same letters together.*

**Teacher's comments**
2. *Aaron is a talented and prolific story writer. His writing is very strongly influenced by that of C. S. Lewis and his stories are full of imaginary characters with fantasy names.*
3. *Rules is a word that the children are used to. When we talk about spelling they are made aware that there are conventions of written language. However, we also kept a note of 'silly spellings', i.e. those that broke the rules e.g. ocean, and instances where words that looked the same sounded different e.g. tough, cough, bough. They quickly realised that simply learning sound/symbol rules was not enough.*
9. *I deliberately chose a nonsense word that excluded vowels.*
14. *It is Niki who sees the 'deliberate mistake'! I was thrilled at this because he is unable to read as yet and I wrongly assumed that he therefore had little metalinguistic awareness.*

19. *Vowels was a term that the class met last year in top infants. I mentioned y at the time, but I would imagine that this is something Hedda has realised for herself. However, I am able to give her the cue to articulate this knowledge.*

## Extract 5

*L: Could you just make up a word Paul?*
*A: It just comes up.*
*H: I couldn't.*
*N:* Henya.
5 *K: You could be sneaky –*
*L: What was your word Niki?*
*N:* Kinder!
*K: Kinder's the chocolate eggs though.*
*N: No, 'cos it's a German word . . . children . . .*
10 *K: That's right.*
*N: I was tryin' to get away with it.*
*K: Niki,* henya, *how do you think you spell* henya?
*B: Henya,* hey that's odd! My mum wasn't born in henya, *but she was born in* Kenya!
15 *K: Kenya. That rhymes with* henya. *So let's think, if you know how to spell* Kenya, *we can probably guess how to spell* henya.
*A: That's really funny –*
*H: The* c, *the* c . . . *the* c *is not a* c *it's an* h . . .
*K: How do you spell* Kenya?
20 *B: I don't know.*
*A: K . . . E . . . N . . .*
*K: You should know 'cos Hettie lives there.*
*A: . . . Y . . . A*

## Teacher's comments

7. *When I ask Niki to repeat his word, he actually changes it.*
8. *Kinder eggs are the small chocolate eggs, that contain simple toy construction kits.*
9. *Niki is quite right! Presumably this is something he has learnt as a result of liking these eggs! This is another instance where the children's own knowledge is built on.*
12. *I wanted to draw the discussion back to Niki's original word.*
13. *Ben's interjection illustrates how young children's minds are able to work. Word play and nonsense rhymes are a significant way in to developing a metalinguistic awareness.*
15. *I then crystallise and extend Ben's contribution.*
18. *Hedda is busy trying to work out the spelling; she is using her knowledge of initial sounds.*

**Extract 6**

K: *The* dots *aren't just something that we think Hah! let's make their life miserable. There's a very good reason why we put* dots, *isn't there?*

H: *Yeah, so you know . . .*

5   A: *So you know.*

B: *It's 'cos you need* full stops, *'cos if you didn't have* full stops *in books, books would be enormous, they would reach Pluto!*

K: *No, they'd just be one sentence long, wouldn't they?*

10  *(indecipherable chatter)*

A: *No, because you'd have the 'there-he-is-the-thief-and-the-bone . . .' You wouldn't know what's happening.*

H: *You wouldn't have a rest, you wouldn't have the time for a rest.*

15  A: *You wouldn't know what's happening.*

L: *So . . . what do* full stops *do?*

H: *They give you a rest, they kind of breathe.*

L: *Here's a tricky question for you then. Do you think people use* full stops *when they talk?*

20  A: *No, of course they don't.*

H: *Yes, yes they do . . . [if] they breathe in the middle of it somehow . . .*

N: *When they . . . Hello, then they have a little blow.*

A: *You have a little rest.*

**Teacher's comments**

1. *I introduced the discussion about* full stops *after one of the children made a reference to finding it hard to remember about them.*

6. *Although I used the word* dot, *the children quickly switch to* full stop.

6 to 17. *The children have a brief discussion about the function of* full stops. *Interestingly, it is the three fluent readers who contribute. They all use* full stops *accurately in their writing but seem unable to give a precise definition. Does this conversation reflect explicit knowledge about 'sentence boundaries'? (Kingman attainment target at 7 – no. 3.)*

21. *Hedda's definition of sentence boundaries is linked to reading aloud. I would argue that this is a crucial part of developing awareness of sentence structure.*

22. *Niki quietly interjects one of his rhymes, which in this instance makes good sense!*

23. *Aaron corrects Niki's meaning.*

# OUR RATIONALE

Teachers of all subjects require technical terms for important concepts. English teachers require technical terms to be able to make conceptual distinctions which are important to their subject. It would be inefficient and uneconomical to avoid such terminology when it can be used to crystallise a concept. Words are aids to thinking, tools for learning: they can consolidate implicit awareness. This is a cognitive rationale for using linguistic terms.

In addition, our use of our mother tongue is often so automatic and habitual, and so much a part of our individual and social identity, that help is needed to stand back and reflect on aspects of language with some degree of objectivity. It also points to a social rationale: this reflective stance, helped by the use of appropriate terms, can encourage a tolerance of linguistic diversity through the recognition that all languages are rule-governed and systematic. Linguistic terms are required in order to allow teachers and pupils to discuss children's own written and spoken work, language diversity and aspects of literature. Many terms have traditionally been used in literary criticism.

To illustrate good practice we also included a passage from Jerome Bruner's *The Relevance of Education* (1974). We quoted this to show that Bruner, the doyen of discovery learning, thought the teaching of grammar an essential part of the learning process. Bruner starts by leading children to discover what is in their own heads, and describes a lesson on sentence structure. This involved writing a sentence on the board, and getting the children to form similar sentences.

| | | | | |
|---|---|---|---|---|
| *The* | *man* | *ate* | *his* | *lunch.* |
| *A* | *boy* | *stole* | *a* | *bike.* |
| *The* | *dog* | *chased* | *my* | *cat.* |
| *My* | *father* | *skidded* | *the* | *car.* |
| *A* | *wind* | *blew* | *his* | *hat.* |

Usually, he says, the children use their intuitive knowledge of the language to form sentences with the same structure. It is then possible to ask how different combinations of the words are possible, such as:

| | | | | |
|---|---|---|---|---|
| *A* | *man* | *stole* | *my* | *cat.* |
| *My* | *father* | *chased* | *his* | *hat.* |

Other questions can also be introduced: how is it possible to go on forming such sentences for ever? What columns are emerging in the sentences? Can other columns be added? Bruner writes:

> *[The children] talked about the family of words which would fit [in the various columns] . . . Only then did we introduce*

*some terminology. We talked about type and order . . . We*
*were soon building up the idea of productivity . . . Once the*
*children break into an idea in language, once they get a sense*
*of a distinction, they quickly 'turn around' on their own usage*
*and make remarkable strides towards linguistic understanding.*
*The only point I would make is that you must wait until they*
*are willing reflectively to turn around before you start*
*operating with the abstractions.*

Terms are needed to allow teachers and pupils to discuss many
aspects of language. But it is important that the terms are introduced as
they are needed, in order to focus attention on important distinctions or
similarities. Their meaning will be apparent because they relate to an
immediate context. They should be introduced to initiate linguistic
understanding, serving as a focus for wider discussion, when the teacher
judges that an intervention to make something explicit will help the
pupil. Indeed they must be introduced on occasions, if discussion is not
to remain unformed, vague and inexplicit. However, terms should not
be introduced through drills. In a typical situation, a teacher might
introduce terms such as *paragraph, sentence, topic sentence, phrase,
cohesion* or *reference*, if a pupil is having difficulty with some aspects of
the textual organisation of his or her writing. Terms such as *accent,
Received Pronunciation, dialect, slang* or *style* might be introduced to
make more precise distinctions which are required for an understanding
of linguistic diversity.

Although the old grammatical drills and exercises do not seem to
have raised standards of composition, it appears that new ways of
teaching language can be of help. Performance does seem to be helped
by the systematic discussion of language in use: e.g. the match between
language, situation and purpose; and elements larger than individual
sentences. These aspects of language performance are more under
conscious control than are aspects of sentence structure and morphology. The same arguments apply to children's spoken language. Again,
it seems to help performance to reflect consciously about the higher
levels of linguistic organisation – how spoken language can be organised to suit audience, topic and purpose.

In addition, quite apart from the debate over the relation between grammar teaching and writing development, there are several
other valid justifications for teaching explicitly about language. The
simplest one is that the world would be a better place if people were
better able to talk coherently about the many language problems which
arise in contemporary society. Language is an essential part of our
cultural environment, and the diffusion of coherent knowledge about
language is an important aim of the English curriculum.

# CURRICULUM CONTENT AND TEACHING SEQUENCE

The Kingman Report (chapter 3 and appendix 8) presents a model of language in four parts:

*forms;*
*communication; comprehension;*
*acquisition;*
*variation.*

These are logical components of the model. There is no priority amongst them: all four parts are necessary. And there is no implication that children start by learning about language forms, and then eventually progress to learning about, say, dialects. Nevertheless, these implications have been taken by many readers, who feared a return to learning definitions off by heart.

For the purpose of formulating a curriculum, it is more helpful to present things in the following order:

a) starting from statements about what it is important for children to know about language: e.g. its uses in literature, language variation, bilingualism, language change, ambiguities and problems in communication, the writing system, etc.;

b) then showing that some terminology is required to discuss such things: terms are taught in context for a purpose. Two problems are thus solved at once: it becomes clear that terminology does not refer only to grammar, and the reasons for the terminology come before the terminology itself. Terms are used as a way of encouraging active thinking about language and its uses. When talking about grammar, many people tend to limit discussion to parts of speech and to simple structures at sentence level. When talking about terminology there is a tendency to focus on terms such as *noun*, *verb*, etc., and on isolated features of surface structure (punctuation, the apostrophe, spelling of individual words, etc.).

Terms for grammatical surface structure are certainly necessary. However, as the Kingman Report makes clear, the structure of language means not only grammar (in the sense of sentence syntax) but also phonology, graphology, vocabulary and discourse organisation, and terms are needed for:

◇ the sounds of English (pronunciation or accent);
◇ the spelling and writing system of English;
◇ the grammar of English (i.e. sentence syntax);

◇ the semantic relations between words in English vocabulary as a whole and in texts;
◇ the textual or discourse structure of English.

In addition to all this, terms are also needed to discuss the functions and varieties of language.

The above points refer to English; but the grammar of different languages requires different terms. This is precisely why a Latinate grammar cannot simply be transferred to English. This is not necessarily a central problem, but the Kingman Report does recommend that pupils should understand something of the systematic nature of languages other than English. It is essential to avoid discussing one language variety in terms appropriate only to another. It is, however, unfortunately very common for people to discuss spoken language as though it was a deviation from written English, and to discuss non-standard varieties of English as deviations from Standard English.

We did not specify lists of terms and concepts which should be taught. This could have a very restricting effect on teaching and assessment. It is the responsibility of teachers themselves to decide on and introduce terms as they become necessary at different stages in teaching. However, we stressed that the set of terms should not be restricted to those for parts of speech. Terms should be introduced, as appropriate, to allow teachers and pupils to discuss the topics set out below. Some will be needed from the early years of the primary school (e.g. *letter, full stop, sentence*, etc.); others are not likely to be introduced before the secondary school (e.g. *presupposition, genre, creole*, etc.). Topics which should be discussed, and examples of terms likely to be necessary, are as follows:

◇ the sounds of English: *pronunciation, accent, consonant, vowel, syllable, elision, ˙assimilation, intonation, stress, rhythm*, etc.;
◇ the spelling and writing system of English: *letter, capital letter, alphabet, punctuation, full stop, question mark, exclamation mark, quotation (speech) marks, apostrophe*, etc.;
◇ words: *loan word, prefix, word ending, word structure, Latinate word, pun, lexical and grammatical words*, etc.;
◇ the sentence grammar of English: *adjective, adverb, noun, proper noun, verb, main verb, auxiliary verb, preposition, conjunction*, etc., *singular, plural, possessive, tense*, etc., *negative, comparative, superlative*, etc., *subject, object*, etc.;
◇ the semantic relations in the vocabulary of English: *ambiguity, appropriateness, collocation, synonymy, antonymy, paraphrase, dictionary, thesaurus*, etc.;
◇ the structure of (written) texts: *paragraph, sentence, phrase, topic sentence, cohesion, reference, heading, sub-heading*, etc.

A range of terms is also likely to be needed to help teachers and pupils to discuss aspects of spoken and written language, in which pupils are required to do a range of things with their language: engage in small group collaborative discussions, present mini-lectures, explain and persuade, write narratives, descriptions and arguments, etc. Terms of the following kinds are likely to be needed:

◇ for speech acts: e.g. *describe, report, summarise, explain, request, instruct, argue,* etc. (There may be a difference between such terms in everyday and descriptive use: to argue for a point of view is not at all the same as having an argument, though this is a common confusion.)

◇ for different speech events: e.g. *conversation, lecture, discussion, narrative, report,* etc.

One fear of many English teachers is that a terminology for language forms takes attention away from the meaning of language. This is not necessarily true at all. On the contrary, it is essential sometimes to focus on language forms, in order to discuss cases where there is a difference between form and meaning, between what is said and what is meant. Terms of the following kinds are likely to be needed:

◇ for different kinds of meaning, direct or indirect: *inference, presupposition, connotation, referential v. emotive meaning, irony,* etc.

Knowledge about the way children acquire language is obviously important to teachers. It can also be very interesting to pupils, and important, for example, in preparation for parenthood. For these reasons, it is a common topic on many language awareness courses. It may not, however, require any particular terminology that is not dealt with elsewhere.

Variety in language arises because language changes according to topic, addressee, the formality of the setting, the nature of the task. It also changes over historical time, in different geographical regions, and in different social groups, defined by ethnicity, class, gender, occupation and so on. The main concept, which goes against much traditional thinking about language, is that such change is a natural and inevitable process. One of the most important topics for pupils to be able to discuss explicitly is the difference between spoken and written English. Terminology is required in particular here to allow distinctions to be made between prescriptive and descriptive approaches to language, and to show that the grammar of spoken English is different from that of written English, and not just a haphazard deviation from it. Terms of the following kinds are likely to be needed:

◇ for aspects of language variation: e.g. *formal language, casual or colloquial language, slang; first language, second language, foreign language; accent, dialect, creole, international language, lingua franca; historical, geographical and social dialects.*

The terminology used in discussing literary texts has been left till last because it is the one which has traditionally been most familiar to English teachers. Many of the terms proposed above are relevant to discussing the features of poems and prose from a literary point of view, and English teachers have many other terms at their disposal for discussing genre, stylistic effects, etc. Terms of the following kinds are likely to be needed, but English teachers will be able to add many other examples:

◇ for aspects of literary texts: *genre, point of view, irony, metaphor, simile*, etc.; *plot, character, setting, denouement,* etc.; *alliteration, rhyme, stress, rhythm, metre,* etc.

Some readers expected us to specify sets of standard terminology about language. We made the following comments on such expectations.

## USING TERMINOLOGY ABOUT LANGUAGE

There is no problem with many traditional terms as such. There is no reason why any description of grammar should avoid terms such as: *noun, verb, adjective*, etc.; *word, sentence, paragraph, text*, etc. The problem comes in how these terms are defined: it is, for example, only at best very approximately true that nouns are 'the names of persons, places or things', or that verbs are 'doing words'; and in some instances it is not true at all. Although definitions cannot be complete, teachers will have to explain terms in language pupils can understand, just as they must explain any other unfamiliar words in books that pupils read. As pupils begin systematic work on explicit knowledge about language in the secondary school they will learn through experience that some simple working definitions have to be refined to take account of the complexity of language structure and use.

There are some terms where alternatives mean almost exactly the same. There is little reason therefore to prefer one to the others, e.g.: *speech marks, quotation marks, inverted commas; borrowing, loan word*. It is, however, desirable to choose a set of terms that are widely recognised, internally consistent and as simple as possible, not introducing complex concepts unnecessarily.

There are cases where technical terms are conventionally used, but add nothing to what could be said in simpler ways: e.g. *etymology* simply means 'the history of a word', and *morphology* simply means 'word structure'.

More interestingly, there are terms which are used in everyday English, but which have more precise meanings or quite different connotations in technical discussion, e.g.: *language, accent, dialect, pidgin, creole, non-standard.* Muddles can easily arise in discussion of the relation between spoken and written English. For example, if distinctions are not clearly maintained between sounds (phonemes) and letters, it becomes impossible to say things such as:

> *English has five vowel letters, but (depending on the accent) spoken British English has around twenty-four significant vowel sounds.*

> *The word* thin *begins with a single consonant phoneme represented by two consonant letters. The word* box *ends with a single consonant letter which represents two consonant sounds /ks/. The word* locks *ends in three letters which represent the same two sounds.*

There are terms which have no equivalent in everyday English, but without which certain generalisations about English just cannot be made. For example:

> *In English spelling, if a grammatical word and a lexical word sound the same, the grammatical word tends to have the shorter spelling: e.g.* for, four; by, buy; in, inn; to, two; I, eye; etc.

For us to have proposed a standard terminology would serve no useful purpose. Textbook writers and teachers might attempt to teach this terminology irrespective of its value to pupils' learning. In any case, such a standardisation exercise would be an enormous project and could not be imposed in practice, and many decisions would remain essentially arbitrary. However, as part of a whole-school policy on language, teachers of English and of other languages (and possibly of other subjects) should meet and discuss what framework of description and which terms they propose to use in the school. This might, for example, be in the context of a marking policy for children's writing. This could be organised by the language co-ordinator in the primary school, and by the head of English in the secondary school. The LEA English adviser should have a co-ordinating role to ensure liaison between feeder primary schools and their secondary schools.

If terms should not be taught through drills, or out of context, it follows that terms should not be tested out of context. Appropriate use of terminology will be one aspect of language use which teachers will take into account when they are assessing children's spoken and written language. Learning linguistic terminology is enabling, because it forms one part of children's growing vocabulary and thinking. Use of technical terms is one aspect, for example, of how cogently pupils can talk or write about a topic, how explicitly they can express themselves, and how well they can suit their language to their audience and purpose. Linguistic terminology will therefore be implicitly assessed as part of how well children can use language. It should be assessed as part of the whole, not as something separate.

Teachers themselves will need to know enough about language to use this knowledge confidently. This had implications for teacher training, which the Kingman Report spells out in detail. Throughout our Report we stressed that the success of the National Curriculum depends on the professional abilities of teachers. Graham Frater, our HMI Observer, continually reminded us of the hordes of textbook publishers who might reduce our recommendations to a series of useless exercises if we did not make our rationale abundantly clear. This was particularly true of our proposals about knowledge about language, for some teachers might be ill at ease with this new material and might welcome programmes of study based on drills and rote-learning. We were initiating a major change in the teaching of English which would need great good will and understanding from all teachers. To show what we meant by grammatical description we included two examples of how meaning is constructed in different kinds of language, both spoken and written. We could not provide a grammatical description of the English language, for that was beyond our scope, but we wanted everyone to realise what kind of grammar is appropriate for both teachers and pupils to understand. Here are the two examples:

## Connectives

In spontaneous speech and personal writing, clauses are frequently connected by the words *and, then* and *but. Then* usually links actions or events in a chronological sequence, while *but* signals a contrast between two clauses, e.g.:

> *They played well but they lost.*

Sometimes, as in this example, the contrast is obvious in the language itself (*play well* v. *lose*); on other occasions, the contrast may be only in the speaker's mind, e.g.:

> *Their house is small but it's very clean.*

Here the use of *but* suggests that the speaker thinks small houses are likely to be dirty. So looking at clauses joined by *but* is one way of revealing a speaker's or writer's underlying, unstated assumptions.

By far the commonest of these three connectives is *and*. It is popular with both children and adults because it has a range of different meanings. Therefore, it provides a multi-purpose connective which is particularly useful when we are producing speech without pause for planning or time for selecting a precise alternative. The following edited transcript of spontaneous speech by an 8 year old boy shows *and* being used extensively to hold the narrative together:

> *there was this witch doctor* and *Scooby Doo was – he was standing by the witch doctor* and *the witch doctor went in* and *he went – he went chasing him Scooby Doo went in the cupboard with Shaggy* and *got some clothes on* and *they were acting on* and *then the witch doctor pressed the button* and *they turned on again then* and *then Scooby was acting* and *then they just take him* and *he keeped on switching it until they all came round* and *the all clothes fell off him.*

*And* frequently signals a chronologically ordered sequence, e.g.:

> *Scooby Doo went in the cupboard with Shaggy* and *got some clothes on.*

Another kind of ordering is where *and* suggests a cause and effect relationship, e.g.:

> *the witch doctor pressed the button* and *they turned on again.*

In these ordered relationships it is not possible to alter the order of the clauses. When *and* links two simultaneous actions there is no intrinsic ordering, e.g.:

> *Roger mowed the lawn* and *Linda weeded the flower beds.*

It is also possible for two actions to be conjoined in a simple additive way without any suggestion of temporal or causal relationship, e.g.:

> *On holiday last year I lost my purse* and *Di lost her passport.*

Since *and* expresses so many connective meanings and as it is so frequent in speech it is not surprising that young children sometimes overuse it in their writing, as in this piece by an 8 year old boy:

> *When I played with the Lego I built a bridge. It was a long bridge. And it had slats on it. And it had a slope for the cars to go up. And we made two cars one big and one small. And I made a garage. With a fence all the way round the garage. And we made a road. It wasn't a long road. And I like Lego because you can make things with it.* [spellings corrected]

One important function of *and* in a piece of writing like this is to signal to the reader that the sentences are meant to be read together as an integrated whole. Older and more skilful writers do not merely signal that succeeding ideas are linked; they use a number of different connectives, not only to introduce variety but also in order to make the meaning relationship as precise as possible. The common connectives *and, then* and *but* will sometimes be exactly right. But with time for planning and reflection, writers can choose from a wider range. So chronological sequence may be marked by *next, after, that, subsequently*, etc.; cause-and-effect relationships can be expressed by *so, therefore, accordingly, consequently*, etc.; simultaneous actions can be joined by *while* or *as*; additive relationships can be indicated by *also, in addition, furthermore, moreover*, etc.; and contrastive relationships can be expressed by *although, however, nevertheless, even so*, and so on. Some of these connectives would seem stilted and inappropriately formal in conversation or personal writing such as a friendly letter, but they occur frequently in formal expository writing. The reason for their use is that they make the task of interpretation easier for the reader. Particularly when the subject matter is demanding or unfamiliar (as in much academic writing), it is important that the relationship between ideas is signalled as clearly as possible. So the use of varied connectives is not just a matter of stylistic preference; it is also a mark of consideration for the reader.

Schoolchildren are often told, 'Never begin a sentence with *and*.' It is important to recognise that this should not be an absolute proscription: some fine writers of English use *and* at the beginning of a sentence when it suits their purposes, e.g.:

> And God said, Let there be light: and there was light. (Genesis 1:3, Authorised Version)

(Lest it be thought that that example does not count because it is seventeenth-century English, it is worth noting that modern translations retain the *and* at the beginning of that verse.) However, an overuse of *and* is both irritating and unhelpful. Pupils need to learn by reading a wide variety of well-written texts some of the other ways in which sentences and clauses can be joined. They will need to take account of meaning, of appropriateness to audience and purpose, and of structure – since, unlike *and*, some of the alternative connectives are not tied to the beginning of the sentence, e.g.:

> He said, moreover, *that he was not prepared to tolerate further delay.*

## Passive sentences

In an active sentence the subject of the sentence generally performs the action of the verb, e.g.:

*The policeman arrested the burglar.*

Here, the subject, the policeman, is doing the arresting and the burglar (the grammatical object) is affected by this action. In a passive sentence the person or thing affected by the action of the verb occurs as subject of the sentence:

*The burglar was arrested by the policeman.*

Now the former active subject (the policeman) occurs after the verb. It is not only the order of words that has changed, however, but also the form of the verb itself, since the active verb *arrested* becomes *was arrested* in the passive.

As both the active and the passive sentence mean the same thing, it is reasonable to ask why we need both. In fact, the passive has two particular advantages and these provide the reasons for its most characteristic uses. First it enables us to omit the word (or phrase) that is the subject in the active sentence. This is important because – apart from commands and elliptical colloquial exchanges – it is not possible to omit the subject in English, even when the meaning is completely obvious; for example, we have to say, *It is raining*, not *Is raining*. By turning an active sentence into the passive we get a new subject and are able to omit the old one, e.g.:

*The burglar was arrested.*

There are a number of reasons why we might want to omit the subject. It may be uninteresting, or even unknown, e.g.:

*The kitchen window has been broken.*

The active version of this would have to be something like:

*Someone (or something) has broken the kitchen window.*

On the other hand, we may know the subject but not want to reveal it to our listener, e.g.:

*I have been told that your work is unsatisfactory.*

Here the passive enables the speaker to conceal the identity of the informant. In academic writing (particularly in science), the convention has grown up that the writer or experimenter does not feature in the text: it is the passive that makes this possible, e.g.:

> *In the course of the survey, 50 old-age pensioners were*
> *interviewed and their housing preferences noted.*

An active sentence would have to refer to the interviewer(s). Another reason why the passive is used in writing is that it can reduce repetition. If several actions have been performed by the same people then, if the sentences describing the events are active, the same subject will have to be repeated, e.g.:

> *Members of the community association worked very hard*
> *preparing for the annual village show. They redecorated the*
> *village hall. They sanded and polished the floor. They replaced*
> *the lights and they mended all the broken furniture.*

The passive version can get rid of all the *theys* and introduce more variety in subject position:

> *The village was redecorated. The floor was sanded and*
> *polished. The lights were replaced and all the broken furniture*
> *was mended.*

The second advantage of passive sentences is that they have a different word order from active sentences. Both speakers and writers find this useful when they are referring to two things, one animate, one inanimate. That is because there is a stylistic preference in English for putting animates before inanimates. For example, the passive sentence:

> *The cyclist was knocked down by a van.*

is more likely than its active counterpart:

> *A van knocked down the cyclist.*

The fact that the passive brings about alterations of word order gives it a special function in writing, because it provides one means by which a writer can link sentences smoothly together and achieve the desired emphasis. There is a preference in written English for sentences within one paragraph to begin with an idea that has already been mentioned. (When a sentence begins with something completely new this usually signals the beginning of a new paragraph.) The corollary of this is that new information tends to occur towards the end of the sentence. Accordingly, a typical sequence of sentences in writing is:

> *Yesterday at the Royal Albert Hall there was music-making on a grand scale by young people from all over the United Kingdom, with a prize for the best overall performance. It was won by the Cheshire Youth Orchestra, who were in jubilant mood as they left for the journey home.*

Here, *a prize* is mentioned in the first sentence. The use of the passive *It was won* allows the prize to reappear at the beginning of the second sentence, and delays the introduction of the new information about the winners. A speaker might well use an active sentence and say, 'The Cheshire Youth Orchestra won it', but this would seem rather awkward and disjointed in writing.

Although there are several reasons why passive sentences can be useful for the writer, then, it is worth noticing that if passives are overused they can produce writing that is unappealingly arid.

These examples demonstrate that it is absurd to say that the Cox Report does not advocate the teaching of grammar. Journalists who repeated this accusation either had not read the Report, or were simply being malicious.

# Knowledge about language

Primary teachers and secondary English teachers regularly impart a great deal of knowledge about language to their pupils and encourage them to make explicit, and to share with others, the implicit knowledge they have already acquired as language users. For example, in many classrooms pupils can be found discussing the differences in vocabulary there would be between an on-the-spot oral account of a road accident and a newspaper report of it the following day; or considering the ways in which conventional spellings can be violated in advertisements and brand names; or listing some of the differences between their grand-parents' use of language and their own; or talking about the way a poet's choice of metaphor yokes together two dissimilar things so that something familiar is suddenly perceived in a new way; and so on. Teaching about language is then, in broad terms, not a new departure for most English teachers. However, treating knowledge about language systematically and giving it explicit mention in the syllabus is not universal in our schools.

## INTEGRATING KNOWLEDGE ABOUT LANGUAGE

My Working Group recommended that knowledge about language should be an integral part of work in English, not a separate body of knowledge to be added on to the traditional English curriculum. As pupils extend their skills, abilities, understanding and responsiveness in speaking, listening, reading and writing, the teacher's role is to highlight those aspects that will lead to a greater awareness of the nature and functions of language. This awareness should, in turn, contribute to the pupils' own sensitivity as language users. For this reason, we did not propose that knowledge about language should have its own profile component. To treat it separately would be to risk giving rise to the misconception that it should be separately timetabled, taught and assessed, rather than integrated in the speaking, listening, reading and writing activities of any English lesson. Accordingly, the content we saw as essential to knowledge about language was incorporated in the three profile components, speaking and listening, reading, and writing, both in the statements of attainment and in the programmes of study.

There are two further reasons why our recommendations took this form. First, many teachers are worried about the curriculum being overloaded. There are constant pressures from relatively new areas of study, such as information technology, film, television and so on. If we had proposed a separate profile component for knowledge about language, it might have been seen as having a weight (in terms of content, teaching time and assessment) which was disproportionate in relation to the English curriculum as a whole. The other reason is the extent of teachers' own knowledge about language. As is argued at length in the Kingman Report, substantial programmes of teacher training are required if teachers are themselves to know enough to enable them to design with confidence programmes of study about language. Such training is now under way. In the meanwhile, we did not feel it right to make aspects of knowledge about language in the programmes of study (which will be legally obligatory for every pupil working at levels 5 to 10) too extensive or demanding. Even so, we learnt from our visits to schools that, in some places, richer and broader work than we outline is already being done very successfully. For example, in some multilingual classrooms pupils carry out activities that make them aware of some of the similarities and differences among their languages; in other classrooms pupils write play-scripts in regional dialect or study the language of Chaucer. There is no need for such work to be abandoned because it does not feature explicitly in our programmes of study and, indeed, it would be the opposite of our intention if this were to happen.

However, our approach of presenting the subject matter within three profile components has the disadvantages that knowledge about language can appear fragmented and that teachers and pupils might not see the possibilities for coherent and cumulative work. In the Cox Report we therefore set out our rationale for explicit knowledge about language in a separate section, and printed as part of it the statements of attainment about knowledge about language from the three profile components, bringing them together in order to show their coherence. I shall do the same in this book.

## OUR RATIONALE

Two justifications for teaching pupils explicitly about language are, first, the positive effect on aspects of their use of language and, secondly, the general value of such knowledge as an important part of their understanding of their social and cultural environment, since language has vital functions in the life of the individual and of society. Language is central to individual human development; human society is inconceivable without it. Therefore it is intrinsically interesting and worthy of study in its own right. There are important social implications of such knowledge. Language is not merely a neutral medium for the conveying of information; it can trigger emotional responses which may spring from prejudice, stereotyping or misunderstanding. Such attitudes need to be laid open to examination and discussion. Moreover people need an informed understanding if they are to evaluate claims about language use which are widely made (in the correspondence columns of newspapers, for example).

As far as the effect of knowledge about language on pupils' own language skill is concerned, it is true that it has been difficult or impossible to show any direct cause-and-effect relation between teaching formal grammar and improved writing performance. However, most of the research has relied upon a narrow and traditional form of grammar teaching. The broader approach that we advocated covers not only sentence structure but also larger patterns of organisation, not only the forms of written academic English but also a range of stylistic and dialectal varieties, not only language structure but also meaning and use. My Working Group felt that there is evidence that such an approach should help to improve pupils' sensitivity to their own use of language.

It is also undoubtedly useful for teachers to be able to refer to features of pupils' work when they are correcting it or trying to help pupils in some way. For example, pupils who speak (and therefore possibly write) in a non-standard dialect of English may need help to see that their dialect is regular and patterned, and to recognise the systematic differences between it and formal, academic Standard English. Moreover, terminology is essential in understanding many standard reference books about language, such as dictionaries. (Such a terminology is also of use in foreign language teaching.) Technical terms are not ends in themselves, but because they facilitate discussion, they do need to be explicitly taught.

## PRINCIPLES UNDERLYING PROGRAMMES OF STUDY

Teachers and textbook writers need a framework of understanding which ensures that they avoid underestimating the complex competence which all native speakers have in their mother tongue. Helpful distinctions can be made between different kinds of knowledge about language, e.g.:

◇ implicit and explicit knowledge;
◇ monolingual and bilingual competence;
◇ prescriptive and descriptive approaches;
◇ knowledge appropriate to teachers and to pupils;

◇ what all pupils need to know contrasted with what some choose to learn.

Some of these distinctions can be discussed with pupils.

Work should start from the pupils' own linguistic competence. Many pupils in schools are bilingual and sometimes biliterate, and quite literally know more about language than their teachers, at least in some respects. All pupils are able, to some extent, to change their style of language according to their audience. This competence is a huge resource which should not be ignored but made explicit. A problem in studying language is that it is often too close to individual speakers to be observed dispassionately: it is either taken for granted and not seen at all, or is too intimately involved in individual and social identity to be discussed objectively.

Work on knowledge about language can be based on pupils' own fieldwork, collecting and classifying their own data, learning about the methodology of observation, classification, description, hypothesis making and explanation. The teacher's task will often be to help pupils to systematise knowledge which they already have or evidence which they collect, and to keep the focus clear.

Courses should not be watered-down linguistics. They should, however, be informed by principles and insights drawn from linguistics – for example, the idea that language in all its diversity can be approached in a non-prescriptive, non-judgmental way and that it is possible to treat systematically and objectively an aspect of human life which is often the focus of emotive and prejudiced reactions.

Materials should bring out the social significance of knowledge about language. It should lead to more understanding of language diversity, including multilingualism, and be closely related to pupils' experience in their own communities, and therefore be treated with great sensitivity to pupils' home backgrounds.

The preceding points imply certain desirable features in the programmes of study in knowledge about language. They should be based primarily on resource materials, which might include samples of language data (spoken, written, literary, non-literary, standard, non-standard, English and other languages) and facts and figures about languages in Britain and around the world, and associated activities which are essentially concrete and problem-based, so that the pupils can make their own enquiries, and so that the teacher can learn alongside the pupils. The data are all around, once teachers and pupils know what to look for. It is therefore possible for teachers to develop their own materials. Comparative study (of different languages, dialects, styles, etc.) can make explicit what is usually taken for granted about language.

# KNOWLEDGE ABOUT LANGUAGE IN THE SCHOOL CURRICULUM

The steady and purposeful development of pupils' language and of their skill in its use should be a constant aim of education at all stages and levels. The form in which knowledge about language is communicated will vary with the age and ability of the pupil, from play activities in pre-school to explicit systematic knowledge in upper secondary education. Some play activities, suitable for primary age children, were illustrated in my last chapter; more explicit knowledge about language, appropriate to the secondary curriculum, is discussed here.

Language topics can be studied from a number of points of view. A systematic approach to language study can be developed by considering any aspect of language in terms of its form and meanings, its social uses and effects, and how it varies.

Language is a system of sounds, meanings and structures with which we make sense of the world around us. It functions as a tool of thought; as a means of social organisation; as the repository and means of transmission of knowledge; as the raw material of literature, and as the creator and sustainer – or destroyer – of human relationships. It changes inevitably over time and, as change is not uniform, from place to place. Because language is a fundamental part of being human, it is an important aspect of a person's sense of self; because it is a fundamental feature of any community, it is an important aspect of a person's sense of social identity.

To take account of the nature and functions of language a syllabus for knowledge about language should cover the following material:

(a) **Language variation according to situation, purpose, language mode, regional or social group, etc.**
Nobody speaks – or writes – in the same way on all occasions. We alter our language according to whom we are talking to, what we are writing about, whether it is for social, transactional or literary purposes, and so on. The most obvious variations are the contrasts between speech and writing and between the formal and informal in both modes. An understanding of such variations should help pupils to select the appropriate vocabulary and grammar for a given purpose and to recognise why communication sometimes breaks down when inappropriate choices are made.

Even though no two people speak or write in just the same way, groups of people share sufficient language characteristics (of accent, vocabulary and grammar) to bind them together and to distinguish them from other groups. So language alone often allows us to tell whether someone is from Liverpool or London, from England or Scotland, or from Britain, Australia or the United States. Moreoever, the specialised language of certain occupational groups (for example, builders, doctors, lawyers, mechanics and scientists) is often distinctive. A sensitivity to this type of variation should contribute towards pupils becoming more tolerant of linguistic diversity, more aware of the richness it can provide and more able to cope with problems of communication.

Accordingly, in the speaking and listening profile component, the statements of attainment relate to children's growing ability to talk explicitly about:

> *regional and social variations in English accents and dialects; and attitudes to such variations; the range of purposes which spoken language serves; and the forms and functions of spoken Standard English.*

In the writing profile component, the statements of attainment relate to children's growing ability to talk and write explicitly about:

> *some of the main differences between speech and writing; the range of purposes that written language serves.*

### (b) Language in literature

Although there can be no clear-cut division between the use of language in literature and in everyday life (and it would not be fruitful to attempt to make such a division), we can recognise that some of the most arresting, innovative and enriching uses of language come from the poets, novelists and dramatists who practise the craft of writing. Awareness of these uses should help pupils to respond to texts with greater understanding, to recognise when language is being used manipulatively, and to strive for a creative vigour of expression in their own writing.

### (c) Language variation across time

English is changing all the time. There have been considerable changes in vocabulary and slight changes in pronunciation over the last fifty years. Grammatical change is slower but readily discernible if we take a time span of four hundred years. Knowledge about language change makes it possible for pupils to understand more fully the nature of Standard English and how it relates to other varieties.

Accordingly in the reading profile component, the statements of attainment relate to pupils' growing ability to talk and write explicitly about:

> *some of the main characteristics of literary language; and how it conveys meanings;*

*some of the ways in which English is constantly changing
between generations and over the centuries; and people's
attitudes to such change.*

All of these aspects of knowledge about language interlock – just as
speaking, listening, reading and writing themselves are interrelated –
and it is not possible or desirable to keep them apart. So the reading of a
poem by Wordsworth, for example, could raise questions concerning
the differences between poetic and everyday language, the nature of
Cumbrian place names and topographical terms, the effect of word
order alterations, changes in vocabulary during the past hundred and
fifty years, and so on.

Pupils' developing understanding is marked in several ways:

◇ it is usually easier to give examples from local varieties of
English (in the family or local community) than to discuss a
wider range of varieties, which are more distant, geographically, socially or historically;

◇ it is usually easier to talk about language, than to write about
it;

◇ it is usually easier to give examples of individual words (which
distinguish dialects, styles, etc.), than to give examples of
pronunciation, grammar and textual organisation;

◇ it is easier to give relevant, but isolated, examples than to give
more systematic and sustained descriptions and analyses; and
description is easier than discussing the principles underlying
the examples.

The ordering of the statements of attainment in knowledge about
language takes account of this pattern of development.

## THE STATEMENTS OF ATTAINMENT

After the Cox Report was published, the NCC made some revisions of
our statements of attainment and programmes of study. These did not
involve substantial changes, and often introduced useful clarifications
and examples. In this chapter I print the statements of attainment as
they are defined in the final Statutory Orders, *English in the National
Curriculum*, published by HMSO. The following descriptions are those
now enshrined in law.

In the speaking and listening profile component pupils should be able to:

| LEVEL | STATEMENTS OF ATTAINMENT | EXAMPLE |
|---|---|---|
| 5 | recognise variations in vocabulary between different regional or social groups, and relate this knowledge where appropriate to personal experience. | *Talk about dialect vocabulary and specialist terms; discuss the vocabulary used by characters in books or on television.* |
| 6 | show in discussion an awareness of grammatical differences between spoken Standard English and a non-standard variety. | *Take note of different ways in which tense and person are marked in the verb 'to be' after listening to recordings or participating in classroom improvisations.* |
| 7 | show in discussion an awareness of the appropriate use of spoken language, according to purpose, topic and audience. | *Analyse and reflect upon the language appropriate for a job interview, or an argument with a parent or another pupil following a presentation.* |
| 8 | show in discussion and in writing an awareness of the contribution that facial expressions, gestures and tone of voice can make to a speaker's meaning. | *Comment on the varied use of these features noted in a stage presentation, a television drama, or film. Comment on what may be conveyed (intentionally or inadvertently) in advertisements, speeches, interviews or in observed behaviour around the school.* |
| 9 | show in discussion and in writing an awareness of the ways in which language varies between different types of spoken communication. | *Describe how different kinds of language use, such as jokes, anecdote, conversation, commentary, lecture, etc., could be explained to a foreign visitor.* |

| LEVEL | STATEMENTS OF ATTAINMENT | EXAMPLE |
|---|---|---|
| **10** | show in discussion and in writing an awareness of some of the factors that influence people's attitudes to the way other people speak. | *Using the result of a survey, make a report on the attitudes to spoken language held by the class and the community.* |

In the reading profile component pupils should be able to:

| LEVEL | STATEMENTS OF ATTAINMENT | EXAMPLE |
|---|---|---|
| **5** | show through discussion an awareness of a writer's choice of particular words and phrases and the effect on the reader. | *Recognise puns, word play, unconventional spellings and the placing together of pictures and text.* |
| **6** | show in discussion of their reading an awareness that words can change in use and meaning over time and demonstrate some of the reasons why. | *Understand that technological developments, euphemism, contact with other languages or fashion all contribute to language change.* |
| **7** | show in discussion or in writing an awareness of writers' use of sound patterns and some other literary devices and the effect on the reader. | *In a group discussion on poems, advertisements or other materials, refer to rhyme, alliteration and figures of speech such as similes, metaphors and personification.* |
| **8** | discuss and write about changes in the grammar of English over time, encountered in the course of their reading. | *Comment on examples such as pronouns (from 'thou' and 'thee' to 'you'), verb forms and negatives.* |
| **9** | demonstrate some understanding of the use of lexical and grammatical effects in the language of literature. | *Consider the repetition of words or structures, dialect forms, archaisms, etc.* |

| LEVEL | STATEMENTS OF ATTAINMENT | EXAMPLE |
|---|---|---|
| 10 | demonstrate in discussion and in writing some understanding of attitudes in society towards language change and of ideas about appropriateness and correctness in language use. | *Comment on the arguments, attitudes and styles displayed in a running correspondence, on an issue of language usage or performance, in a newspaper or weekly periodical.* |

In the writing profile component pupils should be able to:

| LEVEL | STATEMENTS OF ATTAINMENT | EXAMPLE |
|---|---|---|
| 5 | show in discussion the ability to recognise variations in vocabulary according to purpose, topic and audience and whether language is spoken or written, and use them appropriately in their writing. | *Discuss the use of slang in dialogue and narrative in a published text and in their own writing and comment on its appropriateness.* |
| 6 | demonstrate, through discussion and in their writing, grammatical differences between spoken and written English. | *In a group, identify some of the differences between the language used in a tape recording of someone talking and a piece of writing by the same person.* |
| 7 | show in discussion and in writing an awareness of what is appropriate and inappropriate language use in written texts. | *Appreciate the need to take account of topic, purpose and audience.* |
| 8 | demonstrate knowledge of organisational differences between spoken and written English. | *Talk and write about the fact that speech is interactive, spontaneous and informal while writing is more tightly planned.* |

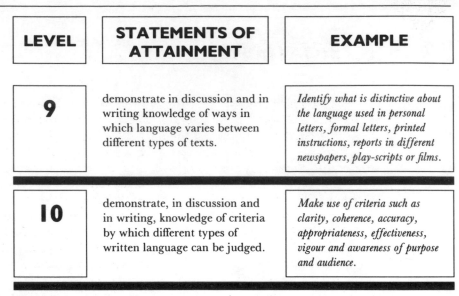

| LEVEL | STATEMENTS OF ATTAINMENT | EXAMPLE |
|---|---|---|
| 9 | demonstrate in discussion and in writing knowledge of ways in which language varies between different types of texts. | *Identify what is distinctive about the language used in personal letters, formal letters, printed instructions, reports in different newspapers, play-scripts or films.* |
| 10 | demonstrate, in discussion and in writing, knowledge of criteria by which different types of written language can be judged. | *Make use of criteria such as clarity, coherence, accuracy, appropriateness, effectiveness, vigour and awareness of purpose and audience.* |

The programmes of study for knowledge about language are printed in appendix I.

# *Literature*

*It is occasionally possible, just for brief moments, to find the
words that will unlock the doors of all those many mansions
inside the head and express something – perhaps not much,
just something – of the crush of the information that presses in
on us from the way a crow flies over and the way a man walks
and the look of a street and from what we did one day a dozen
years ago. Words that will express something of the deep
complexity that makes us precisely the way we are, from the
momentary effect of the barometer to the force that created
men distinct from trees. Something of the inaudible music that
moves us along in our bodies from moment to moment like
water in a river. Something of the duplicity and the relativity
and the merely fleeting quality of all this. Something of the
almighty importance of it and something of the utter
meaninglessness. And when words can manage something of
this, and manage it in a moment in time, and in that same
moment make out of it all the vital signature of a human being
– not of an atom, or of a geometrical diagram, or a heap of
lenses – but a human being, we call it poetry. (Ted Hughes,*
Poetry in the Making, *1967)*

Our recommendations for the teaching of literature aroused a great deal
of controversy. The dangers which threaten those who make pro-
nouncements about essential books in a National Curriculum had
already been revealed when Mr Baker in a speech in 1988 said he
thought all children aged 16 should have read George Orwell's *Animal
Farm*. This is the kind of remark on which the media thrive, and for
weeks afterwards the newspapers, radio and television were filled with
arguments and counter-arguments about essential books in a core
curriculum. If *Animal Farm*, why not *1984*? And what about Dickens's
*Oliver Twist* and *David Copperfield*, Lewis Carroll's *Alice in Wonder-
land*, Jane Austen's *Pride and Prejudice* and *Emma*, Lawrence's *Sons
and Lovers* and *The Rainbow*, Defoe's *Robinson Crusoe*, Forster's *A
Passage to India*, Shakespeare's plays and sonnets, Wordsworth's
*Lyrical Ballads*, Tennyson's *The Lady of Shalott*, the Authorised
Version of the Bible, and so on and on. It is easy to compile a list of
books for a national curriculum which are essential reading for 16 year
olds, and which is so long no average 16 year old will have time to read
them all.

# OUR LIST OF AUTHORS

As we prepared our first Report, to be published in November 1988, we wanted our document to be lively, to avoid bureaucratic jargon, and to impart enthusiasm for literature, so we included references to specific authors. We printed a list of writers who might figure in the library of a good primary school. We made it clear that the list of authors was not intended to be comprehensive: 'We stress again that we are not recommending as set texts the books of the authors listed . . . While we believe that their books do meet the criteria outlined above [in the preceding paragraphs] we have no doubt that so too do those of many authors who are favourites with children and teachers.' We left freedom for teachers to choose.

In our list of authors we did not include Enid Blyton or Captain W. E. Johns, author of the Biggles stories. Many teachers consider these two authors racist, and some find Enid Blyton's use of language narrow and undemanding. The media commentary on this first Report concentrated on this exclusion, and I was pilloried in the *Sunday Times* for blacklisting Enid Blyton's Noddy. In the tabloid press I became the villain who put his knife into Noddy and his boot into Biggles. Mr Baker told me he thought the decision to exclude Enid Blyton had proved a brilliant ploy to attract attention away from our more serious and controversial proposals.

In our final Report we decided to excise this list of authors because, as we explained, it had attracted so much unfortunate attention. We recommended that Shakespeare must figure in all syllabuses for a National Curriculum, but that teachers must be free to choose which play or plays are studied. In the crucial programmes of study for reading for key stages 3 and 4 (ages 11/12 to 14 and 14 to 16) we included this vital paragraph about the importance of the English cultural heritage:

> *Pupils need to be aware of the richness of contemporary writing, but they should also be introduced to pre-20th century literature. Teachers should introduce pupils to some of the works which have been most influential in shaping and refining the English language and its literature – for example, the Authorised Version of the Bible, Wordsworth's poems, or Dickens's novels. In particular, they should give pupils the opportunity to gain some experience of the works of Shakespeare.*

We deliberately kept these examples to the minimum to avoid controversy, and to leave teachers free to use their professional judgment in selecting texts suitable for the needs of their own pupils.

On this occasion there were objections that we should have included more names. What about Jane Austen, Dr Sheila Lawlor demanded, in the response to our Report sent in to the NCC by the right-wing Centre for Policy Studies. When the final programmes of study for key stages 3 and 4 were submitted to the House of Commons, the NCC added the novels of Jane Austen and the Brontës to our examples. I have been told that this decision was partly in response to lobbying by feminist groups. I am happy to see these names included. My Working Group was solely concerned to allow teachers the freedom to choose, and to prevent another media extravaganza about essential books in the canon. Some of our critics obviously forgot that our recommendations apply to children of all abilities. Should a teacher in an inner-city comprehensive school be forced to teach Jane Austen's *Pride and Prejudice* to children under the age of 16 from different cultural backgrounds? The teacher must decide, taking into account his or her own personal enthusiasms. We insisted strongly on the principle that children must be introduced to pre-twentieth-century literature, but we were determined to have no truck with lists of prescribed books.

We were also aware that if we published a list of set texts their names would be engraved in stone, and the canon would be unchangeable, reflecting out-of-date literary and social opinions. When I was at school in the 1930s and 1940s the canon would have included Kinglake's *Eothen*, Thomas Hughes's *Tom Brown's Schooldays*, Charles Kingsley's *The Water Babies* and the essays of Charles Lamb, all little read by the young today. If a list of modern poets suitable for children under 16 was prepared today it would probably include the popular animal and bird poems of Ted Hughes. Will his reputation survive into the twenty-first century? Will children of the future enjoy his rhetorical language? I think they will, but I cannot be sure, and I would not want the National Curriculum to force him on unwilling teachers. If a list of set books had been included in the Statutory Orders, it is easy to imagine how after ten or so years teachers would be desperately trying to change it, with old-fashioned Members of Parliament resisting in lively debates. In a collection of essays on a National Curriculum in the United States, published in the American journal *Salmagundi* in 1986, Robert Scholes insists that the establishment of a canon, a list of great masterpieces, works of genius, removes the chosen texts from history and from human actualities, placing them forever behind a veil of pieties; it fosters a reverential rather than a critical approach. This explains the bardolatry which has dominated so much writing about Shakespeare. These arguments against a prescribed list seem to me of great weight, just as applicable to Britain as to the United States.

## TEACHERS' REACTIONS

The media excitement about Enid Blyton and Captain W. E. Johns soon died away. Teachers of English offered more substantial criticisms of the literature chapter, and I have to admit that on occasions they had justification for their worries. We had allocated three chapters to the teaching of language and only one to the teaching of literature. Did that imply that literature was less important? My answer to this criticism was that teachers of English are virtually unanimous in their enthusiam for literature, but need persuasion if they are to accept our recommendations for the teaching of grammar, Standard English and knowledge about language. But I cannot deny that the literature chapter takes for granted major assumptions about the value of great literature in the curriculum, and does not engage with the many recent books which have challenged this belief (for example, Brian Doyle's *English and Englishness* [1989]). We explained how the enjoyment of reading helps to develop children's imaginative and aesthetic lives, enriches their use of language, introduces them to our cultural heritage and gives them opportunities for cultural analysis. This material, which I include later in this chapter, reflects the Working Group's basic assumptions, as I have described them in chapter 2.

Perhaps we should have written a chapter explaining our reactions to critics such as Brian Doyle or to books such as Terry Eagleton's *Criticism and Ideology* (1976), but I doubt whether the Working Group would have easily reached agreement. My own attempts in the following paragraphs may well demonstrate the difficulties facing us if we had tried to write a short response to all the great present-day debates in polytechnics and universities about the status of literature. There are so many essays and books about the so-called 'crisis' in English studies that I can do little more than simply explain my own beliefs and show how these underlie the Cox Report's recommendations for a National Curriculum. I will deal with three central issues: the desire for an English national tradition, the belief of Dr F. R. Leavis and his followers that the study of literature promotes moral sensitivity, and the claim by some post-structuralists that the privileged status accorded to 'great' literature reflects an unacceptable ideology.

## AN ENGLISH TRADITION?

A number of university teachers, particularly from Oxbridge, have written to me to complain that our National Curriculum is 'pluralist', and that we should have placed an 'English' tradition at the centre of the syllabus. In France or Germany, they say, teachers would be amazed if their own great writers were not compulsory reading for all students. We should be proud of the English qualities to be found in writers from Chaucer to Dickens, from Shakespeare to Jane Austen, from Milton to Pope.

This emphasis on an 'English' tradition has come under continuous attack during the last twenty years or so; during their undergraduate training many young teachers of English will have discussed the assumptions that underlie such concern for our cultural heritage.

The desire for a national culture is seen as damagingly con
often 'racist' and almost inevitably unsympathetic to the
women. This may surprise many people who read English literature fui
pleasure, and who would angrily reject any suggestion that they are
conservative or racist. Is not this a piece of jargon? The argument rests
no so much on the supposed responses of individual readers, but on the
effects of institutionalising an exclusive teaching of the great works of
English literature. Only so much time is available in the classroom.
Should we insist that children spend all their time with a literature
whose main non-white representatives are Othello, Man Friday in
*Robinson Crusoe* and the savages in Conrad's *Heart of Darkness*?

In his essay in *Salmagundi*, Robert Scholes argues that conservatives desire a common curriculum – any common curriculum – because
this would have a unifying effect upon a society that suffers from an
excess of pluralism, and this unifying effect, an achieved cultural
consensus, would in itself be a good thing for the country socially and
politically. In England the desire for an 'English' tradition is said to hide
a deep fear of our present multi-cultural society, a determination to
maintain our present class structure, the hierarchies of power which
give Oxbridge dons their privileged and cushioned existence. In *English
and Englishness* Brian Doyle describes a contemporary tendency of
English teachers to retreat into a museum-like or 'monumental' role as
professional curators of a residual 'national cultural heritage'. For
Doyle, such an attitude leads to a posture of cultural submissiveness, a
fear of radical political change.

In my Working Group's recommendations for the teaching of
literature we tried to balance the arguments for national unity with the
need for a curriculum which respected the present cultural diversity of
our society (the same desire for unity and diversity underpins our
recommendations on Standard English and dialects). This concept of
*balance* is of crucial importance to an understanding of our Report. A
National Curriculum must not enforce one rigid, prescriptive role on
teachers, but allow them freedom to develop their own initiatives. At
the same time they need to give due attention to this kind of balance
between different aims and purposes, in this case between the claims of
an English tradition and of multi-cultural education.

Knowledge of English literature is also of value in providing us
with a common range of reference, and is of great importance in
developing linguistic skills in Standard English. In *Salmagundi*, E. D.
Hirsch argued that literacy depends on a common background knowledge, a core of information, not of texts. He writes: 'No knowledgeable
reading researcher disputes the fact that a higher level of national
literacy will come only through a higher level of nationally shared
information.' Hirsch believes this information, about Romeo and
Juliet, for example, can be acquired by reading brief guides; there is no
need to read all the original texts. In reply to Hirsch, Scholes argues that

knowledge and information are not the same: 'literacy is very much a matter of actual experience in the production and reception of texts.' He emphasises the ability to interpret and criticise what is presented under the guise of information, the need to evaluate what purports to be information.

Both the Kingman and Cox Reports agree with Hirsch that literacy depends on shared cultural information, but also agree, with Scholes, that there is a difference between information and knowledge. In our response to the English language, both as readers and writers, we depend on an intimate feeling for words and rhythms and innuendoes and images and ironies which can only be achieved by exposure to great English literature. The Kingman Report says:

> Wide reading, and as great an experience as possible of the best imaginative literature, are essential to the full development of an ear for language, and to a full knowledge of the range of possible patterns of thought and feeling made accessible by the power and range of language. Matching book to the pupil is an aspect of the English teacher's work which requires fine judgement and sensitivity to the needs of the child. It is good for children to respond to good contemporary works, written both for children and for adults. It is equally important for them to read and hear and speak the great literature of the past. Our modern language and our modern writing have grown out of the language and literature of the past. The rhythms of our daily speech and writing are haunted not only by the rhythms of nursery rhymes, but also by the rhythms of Shakespeare, Blake, Edward Lear, Lewis Carroll, the Authorised Version of the Bible. We do not completely know what modern writing is unless we know what lies behind it. Hemingway's short sentences derive their power from their revolt against earlier, more discursive styles. The Diary of Adrian Mole is a descendant of Dickens's urgent, knowingly innocent style. The apparently 'free' verse of D. H. Lawrence is imbued with the rhythms of the Book of Common Prayer. (Chapter 2, 21)

And Kingman continues in the next paragraph:

> It is possible that a generation of children may grow up deprived of their entitlement − an introduction to the powerful and splendid history of the best that has been thought and said in our language. Too rigid a concern with what is 'relevant' to the lives of young people seems to us to pose the danger of impoverishing not only the young people, but the culture itself, which has to be revitalized by each generation. (Chapter 2, 22)

In the Cox Report we repeated the first sentence quoted above from Kingman and went on to make the following recommendation:

> *Pupils should be alerted, for instance, to literary associations such as names, quotations, and other references as part of the cultural inheritance of people in the English speaking world. Some of these literary elements are part of the language and have their place in standard dictionaries: others are quasi-proverbial and often used without an awareness of their origin. The effect is not confined to works composed in English, as consideration of Aesop's Fables or H. C. Andersen's stories will show: relevant translated works, including classical stories from Greece and Rome, may find a place in English lessons. The value of such study is clearly not only to be found in an increased familiarity with literary references. It provides a basis of fuller understanding of allusion, implication and inference. It also involves an introduction to forms of discourse which were powerful in the past and from which our own culture has developed.*

The last two sentences are important. We are not just talking about information; we are talking about the ability to respond to the living language.

These are some of the reasons why we recommend that all children should be given the opportunity to gain pleasure and critical awareness from the study of pre-twentieth-century English literature. At the same time we recommended that pupils should 'encounter and find pleasure in literary works written in English – particularly new works – from different parts of the world'. It is widely recognised that the most dynamic English today is often found outside England: from Saul Bellow, Alice Walker and Toni Morrison from the United States, Anita Desai from India, Nadine Gordimer from South Africa, V. S. Naipaul from Trinidad, Chinua Achebe from Nigeria, for example. All pupils need to be aware of the richness of experience offered by writing in English from different countries, so that they may be introduced to the ideas and feelings of countries different from their own, and so we shall help the cause of racial tolerance. In Britain today our multi-cultural society must be taken into account by anyone establishing texts for a national curriculum. Not only will children be introduced to a broader range of thought and feeling, but – through looking at litera-ture from different points of view – pupils should also be in a position to gain a better understanding of the cultural heritage of English literature itself.

In 'The Empire Strikes Back', the Collins Dictionary lecture of 1986, Robert McCrum talked optimistically and enthusiastically about how through its history 'the English language has found some of its most vigorous expression on the lips and in the writings of people whose contribution is often barely recorded in the anthologies or the archives.' He says that 'when the dictionary, the grammar and the style book seem to rule okay, we find the language of the street, of the bar, of the market-place, of the many rather than the few, striking back and changing our own, educated perceptions of what English really is.' He contends that today the dynamism which is bringing new life to the English language is coming from the periphery, not the centre. He extends this argument from spoken forms on radio and film and television to the new vitality to be found in the use of English in countries all over the world.

Similar themes were taken up in the Collins lecture of 1988 by Richard Francis, Director General of the British Council. In Britain today there are over one hundred minority languages in everyday use. Francis sees this as a source of enrichment, and notes how in recent decades many new authors, such as Timothy Mo or Salman Rushdie, demonstrate the stimulative effect of other cultures and languages on English literature written in Britain: 'Creativity in English today is increasingly multicultural.' The true danger to English today, according to Mr Francis, is not a decline in standards from some mythical golden age in the 1930s or the eighteenth century, but that the National Curriculum will stifle imagination, and mark a return to over-emphasis on rigid expository forms.

In the attainment targets for reading we included the following for levels 8, 9 and 10: 'Read a range of poetry, fiction, literary non-fiction and drama, including works written before the twentieth century and works from different cultures.' At the last minute, after the consultation exercise was completed, Mrs Rumbold changed this to read: 'read a range of fiction, poetry, literary non-fiction and drama, including pre-twentieth century literature.' When challenged in the *Times Educational Supplement* on this revision, she replied in a crucial letter which should be given maximum publicity. She pointed out that the programmes of study, which have statutory force, now say that for *all* stages reading materials should 'include works written in English from other cultures'. She insists: 'There was no decision to "downgrade the study of literature from other cultures in the English curriculum". On the contrary, the changes made in the final Order have had the effect of strengthening and extending the requirement that pupils should read works written in English from other countries and cultures' (15 June 1990). This reassurance is welcome, but it has to be said that the change gives less prominence to this requirement, and we shall need to watch with care that it is properly covered in the assessment arrangements.

# THE LEAVIS TRADITION

In the 1950s and 1960s some of the most imaginative and enthusiastic teachers of English were followers of Leavis. In recent years his ideas have been heavily criticised, and I would guess that his writings do not have great influence on young teachers of English. The idea of a great tradition, based on writers such as Jane Austen, George Eliot, Henry James, Joseph Conrad and D. H. Lawrence, has largely been rejected. The days when teachers discouraged their pupils from reading Shelley and Tennyson, because these poets were anathema to Leavis, are now long gone.

For Leavis the study of literature led to a growth of intelligence and sensibility. These qualities were reserved for a small minority of disinterested intellectuals whose insights into the great tradition of literature were said to develop in them a maturity of vision. Followers of Leavis thought themselves superior in sensibility to the debased majority who were deemed to have been corrupted by democratic industrial society. In the 1970s this 'elitist' stance was criticised because it implied that 'culture' and 'art' were inherently undemocratic. The Leavis programme for cultural renewal through the study of the great tradition seemed irrelevant to the real social and political problems of the 1970s.

Confidence in the civilising effect of the study of literature waned during this period. Since the 1939–45 war, many doubts have been expressed about the civilising effects of the arts. George Steiner's pessimistic assessment in *Language and Silence* (1967) has been quoted on numerous occasions. He asks, 'Has our civilisation by virtue of the inhumanity it has carried out and condoned . . . forfeited its claims to that indispensable luxury which we call literature?' (pp. 72–73). How can we accept Matthew Arnold's faith in the civilising influence of art, Steiner asks, now that we know that a 'man can read Goethe or Rilke in the evening, that he can play Bach and Schubert, and go to his day's work at Auschwitz in the morning' (p. 15). Is there any evidence that the ability to respond intelligently to the fiction of Henry James, for example, makes the reader less likely to embezzle funds or indulge in marital cruelty?

In the Cox Report we repeated the belief of many teachers of English that the study of literature does foster intelligence and sensibility, as Leavis so passionately argued. We were not convinced by the arguments to the contrary. In our literature chapter we wrote:

> *We do not wish to underestimate the straightforward pleasure that reading can afford. An identification of books with enjoyment and a positive readiness to devote leisure time to reading seem to us wholly desirable outcomes of primary and secondary school experience. But we would nevertheless hope*

*that by the end of their school careers as many pupils as*
*possible will have been able to 'grow' through literature – both*
*emotionally and aesthetically, both morally and socially – by*
*virtue of coming into contact with the 'range of possible*
*thought and feeling' identified above [in the quotation from*
*the Kingman Report printed on p. 72].* **An active involvement**
**with literature enables pupils to share the experience of others.**
**They will encounter and come to understand a wide range of**
**feelings and relationships by entering vicariously the worlds of**
**others, and in consequence are likely to understand more of**
**themselves.**

That civilised human beings can be responsible for acts of enormous
wickedness does not necessarily invalidate our arguments for placing
the study of literature at the centre of the National Curriculum. The
pleasure of reading offers children an extension of their being, an
enrichment of life. To deny this is to abandon all hope for liberal
education, and to condemn the schools to a narrow policy based on
vocational training.

Frank Kermode deals with these issues with lucidity and insight
in his chapter on 'The Common Reader' in *An Appetite for Poetry*
(1989). He is sceptical about the moral value of teaching the classics or
serious contemporary fiction and poetry: 'Indeed, it is immodest to
propose that by making people read these things we are improving
them, ethically or civically. All we dare claim is that we are making them
better readers' (p. 56). But his following definitions of the value of
reading are close to my own convictions: 'reading, as we ought to teach
it, can make not a good person, but a subtle, questioning one, always
with the possibility of corruption yet richer and more enriching.'
Kermode is concerned mainly with the teaching of literature in higher
education. There are other very strong arguments for the importance of
reading for pupils under the age of 16.

To foster in pupils a love of literature, to encourage their
awareness of its unique relationship to human experience and to
promote in them a sense of excitement in the power and potential of
language can be one of the greatest joys of the English teacher. It is also
one of the greatest challenges. Young people have many calls on their
time and inclinations. Children in primary school playgrounds clearly
demonstrate an instinctive pleasure in rhythm, pattern and rhyme. But
this will need constant nurturing if it is to develop into an appreciation
of the richness of poetry, where words are 'alive with a plurality of
meanings from their contexts, their associations and their sensory
qualities; they are alive with what Ted Hughes calls "the goblin in a
word"' (this quotation is from Michael Benton's essay on 'The Importance of Poetry in Children's Learning', from the NATE book *Lessons
in English Teaching and Learning* [1988]) (p. 148). Similarly, immense

skill and sensitivity are required on the part of the teacher, if very young children's natural enthusiasms for story structures and role-play are to be developed into a full and active engagement with a constantly expanding range of texts or literary genres. Narrative has been described as a primary act of mind; children construct the world through story. It is the teacher's role to recognise this, to encourage it, and to seek to develop interest in the act of reading which flows from it.

## CULTURAL ANALYSIS

In the 1970s and 1980s, as faith among British teachers in our English national heritage or in Leavis's great tradition became less influential, there was a growing fascination with problems thrown up by new methods of cultural analysis. In chapter 2 I included this as one of the five 'views' of our subject: 'A "cultural analysis" view emphasises the role of English in helping children towards a critical understanding of the world and cultural environment in which they live. Children should know about the processes by which meanings are conveyed, and about the ways in which print and other media carry values.' This means that older children must be encouraged to discuss famous texts critically, must be aware of the reasons why the traditional English canon, from Chaucer to George Eliot, has been so much under attack in recent years. There are four well-known criticisms of the established canon of the pre-1960 period:

   a) feminists argue that the canon was male-dominated. Important female writers were neglected;
   b) those concerned about multi-cultural education argue that the canon was dominated by white people, and was 'racist' (I have already mentioned the treatment of black people in English literature);
   c) writers such as Colin MacCabe have stressed the importance of the spoken language. In his Collins lecture of 1984 he described the cultural authoritarianism of Samuel Johnson's *Dictionary of the English Language*, whose acuity and precision of definition should not blind us to the fact that 'it accomplished the reduction of the language to the written and the written to the literary.' Until the 1950s written language dominated the curriculum of our schools, but in recent years teachers have increasingly recognised the importance of spoken as well as written language. The development of radio and television, of new technologies to record speech, create new emphases whose significance it is as yet difficult to grasp. But we can be certain that in the future teachers of English will regard exclusive concern with the written form as a cultural phenomenon of the past, now outdated. Many teachers are now persuaded that English lessons should not be solely

confined to 'great' literature, but should include all kinds of 'texts', spoken and written, together with popular forms such as television commercials, bestsellers and comics;

d) today many people's imaginations are dominated by film and television and video. Teachers of media studies criticise the exclusiveness of the traditional literature canon to which students are often forced to pay lip-service in examinations but which does not engage their imagination as films do. I have to admit that in my own university tutorials references to Dennis Potter's television series *The Singing Detective* or to the film *Dead Poets Society* arouse enthusiasm from students who have little to say about writers such as Spenser, Milton and Pope.

I have already quoted the Kingman Report's description of 'the range of possible patterns of thought and feeling made accessible by the power and range of language'. This concept of 'range' extends also – and very importantly – to social and cultural diversity. Pupils should gain increasing understanding that texts may be related to the interests of different groups – such as women or men, adolescents or minorities of different kinds – and that critical thinking about existing stereotypes and values can be stimulated by studying literature which expresses alternative points of view: for example, on the family, nature and industrialisation, the nation or literature itself. The recognition that there are authors who have not traditionally formed part of the literary 'canon' in the past may also lead to discussion about present-day social inequalities. For example, authors writing in dialect and authors from certain social groups have been under-represented.

Traditional teaching of English literature has been attacked because it creates in the pupil a mood of passivity, an instinctive submission to authority. Throughout their secondary school careers, pupils are often persuaded to repeat their teachers' opinions rather than to develop their own points of view. In the classroom, cultural analysis encourages students to examine for themselves the underlying assumptions in the texts they are studying. There has also been a strong movement to introduce the craft of writing into the curriculum, so pupils can create their own meanings in a variety of forms.

## CREATIVE WRITING

My own ideas about creativity were summed up in the Verbal Arts Manifesto which I wrote with Anne Cluysenaar and Alan Young in 1982. In this Manifesto, signed by Malcolm Bradbury, Richard Hoggart, Ted Hughes and Raymond Williams, among a list of forty-three, and published in the *Times Higher Educational Supplement*, we said that 'Students of English at polytechnics and universities often write dull, secondhand discursive prose and are taught to do nothing else.'

The same applies to many pupils in secondary schools. We argued that for such students practice in the craft of writing would not only be valuable for its own sake but would help them appreciate the achievements of writers of the past and take an informed interest in contemporary writing:

> Many teachers in Britain regard verbal arts, under the guise of 'creative writing', with suspicion because often there has been too much emphasis on free expression. True creativity in any art can best be developed within the framework of a thorough understanding of the nature and history of that art. The notion that verbal creation is somehow more self-indulgent, undisciplined or easy than other forms of creation is false. Responsible teaching is that which develops purposeful artistry in the handling of the medium. Verbal skill must be taught and practised in the curriculum, not left to chance, for it is one of the most important requirements for membership of a modern community.

The emphasis on the craft of writing is of central importance in the recommendations of my National Curriculum Working Group. We argue strongly that practice in writing should not be confined to the literary essay. Pupils should be given the opportunity to write in a wide range of forms: diaries, formal letters, chronological accounts, reports, pamphlets, reviews (of books, television programmes, films or plays), essays, newspaper articles, biography, autobiography, poems, stories, play-scripts, TV or film-scripts. An essential element in our proposals for the secondary school is that pupils should increasingly make their own decisions about their writing: what it is about, what form it should take, and to whom it is addressed. We oppose excessive use of decontextualised exercises written only for perusal and marking by a teacher. We want young people to write for a much wider range of purposes and audiences.

For many years the essay has dominated the syllabus, from school certificate for 16 year olds to university degree examinations. I am not denying its great importance, as a means of evaluating evidence, developing critical arguments, and organising ideas in rational form. But the essay is usually a closed form, not allowing students to admit to uncertainty in their thinking, not allowing them to explore their ideas in imaginative and open-ended ways. The essay form has been dominated by scientific models of objectivity, and, as I have already said, students have relied heavily on the repetition of the views of their teachers or the critics, views often not in accord with their own personal response to the texts being studied. Images, ambiguity, dramatic tensions, all central features of twentieth-century modern literature, are not usually allowed as the student is marked for coherence, order and objectivity.

Teaching of the craft of writing releases pupils from imprisonment in the essay form, and from passive repetition of other people's ideas.

Our recommendations for the National Curriculum emphasise the importance of drafting, the *process* of writing as well as the final product. Pupils, we say, must revise and redraft their writing in response to their own or other people's reading of their texts. This collaboration should involve both their teachers and their peers. In the past the normal essay was handed in complete in final draft, and marked with a grade and a few sentences of comment from the teacher. This is not the way professional writers engage in their task, for almost invariably drafts are discussed and heavily revised after consultation. Language comes alive when our creative writings are intended for real readers, genuinely interested in what we have to say, responding in speech or writing to our failures and successes, and this is just as important for young children as for students in higher education.

Literature and language are inseparably intertwined. The 'full development of an ear for language' encompasses a wide range of related skills, understandings and competences, underlining our belief that the language and literature facets of the English curriculum should be seen as mutually supportive rather than exclusive. Just as particularly skilful uses of language can be illustrated from literature, so deeper insights into literature can be afforded by a close examination of the language of a text. In this way, classroom discussion of – for example – the characters, themes, and moral, social or emotional issues in a work can be related to the writer's technique and craft and to the boundless potential of language for the creation of new meanings.

This vital interaction of language and literature study relates to all three of our profile components. Literature has an important role to play – in a variety of ways – in improving abilities in speaking and listening and in writing, as well as in reading. Children should experiment, for example, with dramatic improvisations of the stories they read and write; they should experience and take part in the performance of poetry; they should listen critically to radio plays. They should also be encouraged to write fiction, poetry, plays, diaries, book reviews and so on, in response to the literature they have enjoyed and shared and discussed with their teacher and classmates. Learning to read and learning to write are intimately related. By reading a wide range of literature, children become aware of new forms of discourse and modes of expression with which they may experiment in their own writing. The Kingman Report points out rightly: 'As children read more, write more, discuss what they have read and move through the range of writing in English, they amass a store of images from half-remembered poems, of lines from plays, of phrases, rhythms and ideas. Such a *reception* of language allows the individual greater possibilities of *production* of language.' (Chapter 2, paragraph 23.)

The 'creative' response to literature described above is two-fold in its effect. Pupils are able, through reading and responding to literature, to develop an understanding of and control over an ever-widening range of written forms. But the experience of writing creatively – of using the sonnet form, for example, or of imitating the characteristics of a particular writer's style – leads also to an increased critical awareness of literary technique in the writing of others. In *Teaching Through Poetry* (1988) George Marsh writes:

> *Learning about the construction of an effective text is much better done . . . through writing than through critical analysis. It has the further advantage that writing is a skill whose usefulness [pupils] can appreciate, whereas literary criticism is not. The understanding of craft and construction that develops through writing leads to a more realistic appreciation of the achievements of literary authors (p. 23).*

This approach need not replace traditional literary criticism: rather, it should be viewed as a step that may lead naturally, where appropriate, into the development of objective analytical skills as pupils learn to reflect on their own writing – and on the creative process itself – in relation to the text that inspired it. This approach is a central means of enriching the curriculum by introducing new ways of helping pupils of all abilities to enjoy literature.

## CHOICE OF BOOKS

There is an enormous variety of good material available for primary children: this was demonstrated by the length of the list of authors published in our first Report. I have already explained why this was not repeated in our final Report. We also assumed that from the age of 14 able pupils could and should be reading from a range of books written for adults, so the number of suitable authors would make any list quite impracticable. Children need to have access to well-chosen and appropriate books in school and class libraries. We therefore set out briefly the criteria which should be used in selecting children's books. When choosing books teachers may like to be reminded of the various published book guides, for example those published by the Federation of Children's Book Groups, the Signal Book Guides, the Penguin Book Guides and *Exploring Poetry 5 to 8* (NATE).

### Primary aged children

The following criteria are useful in selecting books for primary aged children:

   ◇ the language used should be accessible to children but should also make demands and extend their language capabilities;

◇ in fiction, the story should be capable of interpretation at a number of different levels, so that children can return to the book time and time again with renewed enjoyment in finding something new;

◇ print should be bold and easy to read;

◇ illustrations should be clear and attractive and, as well as being well-matched and giving helpful cues to the text, should enhance it by providing additional information, for example about the characters or setting;

◇ most important, the books selected must be those which children enjoy.

## Secondary aged children

During the years 11 to 16 pupils will be exposed increasingly to works not written specifically or exclusively for their age group. There is such a variety of good literature available for inclusion in syllabuses that we want teachers to have the freedom to make their own choice of suitable books within our broad guidelines. I have already indicated some of the principles which should guide teachers in their choice of books, and shown why both pre-1900 literature and texts from different parts of the world must be included. Too many pupils only read contemporary novels. Programmes of study should be so constructed as to give all pupils the opportunity to enjoy work in a wide range of literary forms. They should read a selection of material that includes short stories, novels, plays and poems. They should also be given the opportunity to encounter types of writing drawn from a variety of other genres – such as letters, biographies, autobiographies, diaries, film or TV scripts, travel books and other non-fictional literature. In particular, every pupil should be given at least some experience of the plays or poetry of Shakespeare. Whether this is through the study, viewing or per-formance of whole plays or of selected poems or scenes should be entirely at the discretion of the teacher.

Many teachers believe that Shakespeare's work conveys univer-sal values, and that his language expresses rich and subtle meanings beyond that of any other English writer. Other teachers point out that evaluations of Shakespeare have varied from one historical point to the next, and they argue that pupils should be encouraged to think critically about his status in the canon. But almost everyone agrees that his work should be represented in a National Curriculum. Shakespeare's plays are so rich that in every age they can produce fresh meanings and even those who deny his universality agree on his cultural importance. The 'Shakespeare and Schools' project, at the Cambridge Institute of Educa-tion, has shown that secondary pupils of a wide range of abilities can find Shakespeare accessible, meaningful and enjoyable. The project has demonstrated that the once-traditional method where desk-bound pupils read the text has been advantageously replaced by exciting, enjoyable approaches that are social, imaginative and physical. This can also be achieved by: use of film and video recordings, visits to live theatre performances, participation in songs and dances, dramatic improvisations, activities in which Shakespeare's language is used by pupils interacting with each other. Pupils exposed to this type of participatory, exploratory approach to literature can acquire a firm foundation from which to proceed to more formal literary responses, should they subsequently choose to do so.

In selecting texts teachers should take every opportunity to ensure that pupils are able to make progress as readers and to master increasingly demanding written material. However, textual difficulty is not uni-dimensional. It may lie in the subject matter, in the structure and organisation of the text, in the language, in the way meaning is presented, and in the length of the work. So, a story set in contemporary Britain is likely to be easier (for British pupils) than one set in a different period of history or in a different culture or environment. A novel with a straightforward chronological organisation is likely to be less demanding than one which makes use of flashbacks (this is one reason why young readers generally find *Jane Eyre* easier than *Wuthering Heights*, for example). A text that uses familiar everyday language is usually more accessible than one which has an archaic or literary or highly formal style. A work in which the meaning is fully apparent at a literal level is normally easier than one which depends on the interpretation of extended metaphor, analogy, symbolism, and so on. And shorter texts make fewer demands on readers' stamina, concentration and perseverance than longer ones. These different dimensions of difficulty are essentially independent. Therefore, a work may be easy in one respect and hard in others; for example, Silkin's short poem 'The Worm' is straightforward as far as the vocabulary and sentence structure are concerned but, even so, the meaning of the poem is by no means transparent. It is clear that not all pupils will, by the age of 16, be able to cope with texts which combine all such dimensions of difficulty. But if, throughout the secondary school, literature in the classroom consists chiefly of modern, chronologically organised novels, written in familiar language that is interpretable at a literal level, then not only are pupils being offered a narrowed range of literary experience, they are also being denied an important means of extending their own language and thinking. Accordingly, teachers need to choose books in such a way that all pupils have the opportunity to learn how to understand and enjoy works that make manageable but increasing demands upon them.

To summarise our position: we endorsed the statements in the National Criteria for GCSE about the choice of texts for the syllabus in English Literature. The content of the examination syllabus must consist of the detailed study of individual texts by both male and female writers as well as wider reading in all of the three main literary genres of prose, poetry and drama. Examining Groups are encouraged to extend the scope of what is traditionally regarded as the 'canon' of English Literature in recognition that awareness of the richness of cultural diversity is one of the rewards of the study of literature: 'The majority of texts studied must be literary texts originally written in English which may, for example, include American and Commonwealth writing, but works in translation may also be included.'[1] A wide personal choice may be offered in recommended reading of authors, themes, periods or genres, but works for detailed study must be of sufficient substance and quality to merit serious consideration and must be selected from at least two literary genres.

## APPROACHES TO THE TEACHING OF LITERATURE

Just as initial reading in the early years of the primary school thrives on interest and personal commitment, so the further study of literature calls for involvement and a love of reading for its own sake. As with the early stages of reading, the teaching of literature must set itself the objective of stimulating pupils' enjoyment.

Pupils should be encouraged to respond to all forms of literature in ways which they find pleasurable, and hence which are likely to promote understanding. Their response should be stimulated through a range of active strategies. For example, imitation of a writer's use of language involves an active response that requires the pupil to make meaning yet to show a grasp of the original author's craft at the same time. Most pupils will also enjoy an active presentation of plays and poetry, treated sensitively, and we include the enjoyment from reciting favourite poems aloud, whether individually or in the very successful choral speaking groups established in many schools.

It is often said that many young people lose interest in poetry, and even stories, as they go through secondary school. If this is true, it is the more important that active approaches and positive attitudes prevail, if enjoyment in books is to be kept alive in the face of more passive forms of entertainment. In poetry, pupils should experience a range of 'voices'. Many teachers exploit the possibility of comic, 'fun' poetry, or the lyrics of popular music as a way into the appreciation of a wider range of contemporary writing, beginning with writers who are easily accessible. As Michael Benton puts it in *The Importance of Poetry in Children's Learning*: 'The development of a methodology that is based upon informed concepts of reading and response rather than upon conventional, narrowly-conceived ideas of comprehension and criticism is now the priority' (p. 150). It is good news that the introduction of GCSE has endorsed this kind of methodology and response. A 'response' such as the genre transformation of a short story into a poem or one-act play may also lead some pupils towards written analysis of the more traditional kind.

The exploration of literary texts is not an elitist activity, distinct from the study of other means of communication. To take but one example of overlap, the kinds of question that are routinely asked in media education can fruitfully be applied to literature: who is communicating with whom and why; how the text has been produced and transmitted; how it conveys its meaning. And, as is often the case in the media, literary texts have the habit of not turning out to mean what might be expected at first sight. With both, it is important to keep an open mind and to be alert to the various clues and pointers to meaning that appear as the communication unfolds.

We included in an appendix a selection of teaching strategies which provide 'ways into texts' of whatever genre, period or level of difficulty. Other examples of this kind can be found in books by Michael Benton and Geoff Fox (see select bibliography). They are based on good teaching practice, and many teachers are already aware of their value as methods which neither pre-empt pupils' responses nor suggest that there is one orthodox, accepted interpretation.

## NOTE

1   1989 English Literature GCSE syllabus, Midland Examining Group, p. 19.

# Drama

I was very determined that drama activities would play a central role in the English curriculum, and I found my Working Group were unanimous in supporting this approach. In the primary school, drama is most successful when it emerges as a natural development from children's play. Successful learning often takes place when young children enjoy themselves in role-playing, which can make an important contribution to their oral and aural experience. Drama activity should continue to play a vital role in all pupils' secondary school experience.

## OUR RATIONALE

Drama deals with fundamental questions of language, interpretation and meaning. These are central to the traditional aims and concerns of English teaching, and our recommended programmes of study therefore include exploration of drama. We acknowledged, of course, that drama also has its own academic integrity and that it exists as a separate GCSE subject in many secondary schools and colleges, outside the National Curriculum. By using drama as a part of the learning process, English teachers will be providing experiences for pupils which will help them make an informed choice when considering drama as a subject option, whether for GCSE or as part of a non-examined course in combined or expressive arts. We stressed, however, that the inclusion of drama methods in English should not in any way replace drama as a subject for specialist study.

Drama makes an important contribution towards realising the overall aims of English as set out in chapter 2. For example, drama contributes to personal growth, by enabling pupils to express their emotions and by helping them to make sense of the world, and to prepare for adult life through such activities as the simulation of meetings. Role-play activities can inform other areas of the curriculum, for example history, through pupils' pretending to be living in another age, or science, through their acting out some aspects of scientific discovery.

# DRAMA IN THE PRIMARY SCHOOL

Drama – including role-play – is central in developing all major aspects of English in the primary school because:

◇ it gives children the chance to practise varieties of language in different situations and to use a variety of functions of language which it is otherwise more difficult to practise: questioning, challenging, complaining etc.;

◇ it helps children to make sense of different situations and different points of view in role-play and simulations, by allowing them to act out situations and formulate things in their own words;

◇ it helps children to evaluate choices or dilemmas, to develop the logic of different situations, to make decisions that can be put into practice, tested and reflected upon;

◇ it accustoms children to take account of audience and purpose in undertaking an activity.

Drama is of crucial importance as a learning medium, for example, in promoting collaborative talk, extending language skills and awareness of language in use, in assisting the development of voice skills in relation to reading aloud, and in extending both the form and the content of children's own writing. Drama is not simply a subject, but also – more importantly – a method; it is both a creative art form in its own right and also a learning tool. Furthermore, drama is one of the key ways in which children can gain an understanding of themselves and of others, can gain confidence in themselves as decision-makers and problem-solvers, can learn to function collaboratively, and can explore – within a supportive framework – not only a range of human feelings, but also a whole spectrum of social situations and/or moral dilemmas.

In this respect, there is a very special value to be found in drama activity for pupils for whom English is a second language. The drama process can accommodate the expression of ideas in many ways: even with limited language pupils may participate in interpreting events and emotions through visual representation. Moreover, drama activity is also a particularly powerful facilitator for pupils with special educational needs. Through drama, individuals are provided with the opportunity to perceive the world from another's position: with sensitive direction, for example, a pupil with physical handicaps can interact and learn with others on an equal level. For pupils for whom writing is difficult, drama offers a great freedom. Opportunities for problem-solving and self-expression become as open and readily accessible to them as to any other pupils. For those with emotional difficulties, drama provides an invaluable vehicle which allows the effect of behaviour to be explored. It also demonstrates that alternative behaviour patterns may well be more desirable and effective, and these can be tested out within the safety of drama. For those with severe learning difficulties drama offers a secure situation in which to examine the world. Situations can be developed that offer individuals heightened responsibility, which gives them a chance to help or encourage others. Not only does this facilitate learning of social skills from factors within the drama, but it also allows those involved to develop their self-esteem.

There is still a place within drama activity for performance to a wide range of audiences, both within the school and in the wider community. However, most drama activity should not be seen as leading to a polished end product; even where this is the result, the most significant educational value of the activity will often have been found in the process that led to that end product.

Our terms of reference suggested that we should consider drama in the context of the great dramatic works of literature. We believe that plays should be approached through the dramatic medium; children should often see or participate in the play being acted, and not just read the text. This approach will not only result in an appreciation of the literary merits, but also foster an understanding of stagecraft. There is still an important place within drama activity for the exploration and study of scripted plays, and we addressed this aspect in our statements of attainment and programmes of study. At primary level, the range of material for exploration needs to be more diverse: myth, legend, fairy stories, poems. At secondary level, such work can expand naturally into the exploration of dramatic texts. Children's own writing can also be explored – at both levels – through the medium of drama.

## DRAMA IN THE SECONDARY SCHOOL

The continued appropriateness of drama activity in the secondary school as a means of developing and broadening pupils' verbal communication skills is clear. Communicating orally involves more than reading or talking: gesture, posture, movements may all be intrinsic to it. Drawing on the fundamental drive to imitate and delving deeply into the pupil's personal experience and imaginative resources, drama may embrace all these elements of communication.

Moreover, given that the social interaction involved in drama inspires spoken language, drama activities can be structured to focus pupils' energies on experimenting with and developing control of a wide variety of language styles. Drama quickly reveals to children the effectiveness of language, building up their language resources and allowing them to develop an awareness of a whole range of linguistic choices and registers. Different situations demand different emotional and linguistic responses. In presenting pupils with a variety of different challenges and situations, drama can, for example, provide opportunities for them to:

◇ provide information, give instructions and explanations;

◇ predict and plan;
◇ narrate, recount, report on a past or present experience, real or imagined;
◇ argue, discuss, defend and justify a point of view;
◇ persuade, negotiate, mediate;
◇ come to conclusions, sum up.

As a method of developing pupils' skills in speaking and listening, drama is as important within secondary school learning as it is at primary level. Role-play, in particular, affords opportunities to practise many more varieties of language and to experience a far wider range of situations than could typically be achieved within normal classroom experience. In our speaking and listening programmes of study it is therefore recommended specifically as a learning medium.

Drama provides a discipline for the development of co-ordination, concentration, commitment, organisation and decision-making that depends upon self and group awareness, observation, imagination and co-operation. It helps pupils express emotions and explore personal feelings: it encourages them to make sense of different situations and different points of view, to practise negotiating successfully with others, and to cope with – and resolve – new situations. The importance of such skills in enabling school-leavers to present themselves with confidence and to function effectively within the world of work and as responsible citizens is clear.

The process described above is one outcome (the personal–social aspect) of the process of learning through drama. Drama is both a creative art form in its own right and an instrument of learning. Teachers who use drama are working in partnership with pupils. They are not the possessors of the 'right' answers or of a collection of facts to be imparted. Skilled teachers of drama give pupils the tools of the trade, encouraging them to become more autonomous in their handling of the dramatic medium and so to take greater responsibility for their own learning.

There is a significant parallel with the set of values inherent in the study and experience of literature. Many English teachers testify enthusiastically to the importance they attach to improvisation and role-play in exploring texts in the secondary school. Pupils use drama to gain insights into moral and social issues in works of literature. They can also use the medium to explore character or linguistic or structural features of texts. Shadow and body puppets, for example, can prove an effective way of dramatising poetry and lead to a thoughtful analysis of rhythm, form and movement.

It is obvious that drama in the English secondary curriculum is content-based, as well as process-based. At secondary school level, pupils will be involved in the study of plays and dramatic texts. As actors, audience or directors (all three, I hope) they will be the interpreters of plays written by others. As I said above, pupils should approach plays through the dramatic medium. This exploratory and performance-based approach will not only lead to a deeper understanding of the text in question (a dramatic exploration of a speech in Shakespeare, for instance, will show how the placing of different emphases can alter fundamentally one's interpretation of character or meaning), but will also lead to an understanding of the play as theatre. Performance-based activity may, of course, take place at classroom level, in small-scale improvisational sessions or in text work. Where practical, however, pupils should be encouraged to take every opportunity to widen their experience of audiences and/or co-actors. The mounting of school productions and active involvement in community or touring theatre initiatives are thus of immense value.

## CONCLUSION

The success of Theatre in Education – which brings professional actors to work with children in schools – is a particularly valuable demonstration of the ways in which pupils can learn through experience in their approach to plays. The approach that is encouraged and engendered is active and investigative, rather than passive and prescribed. This principle is at the very heart of all the recommendations relating to drama within the English curriculum that are put forward in this chapter. I have already written in the last chapter about the danger of passive repetition of the teacher's opinions, and the need to sponsor the craft of writing. Drama provides another major resource in overcoming passivity, in stimulating children to become actively involved in thinking about language, and in helping them to enjoy literature at school so that they will continue to read and to act and to attend theatrical performances for the rest of their lives.

# Media Education and Information Technology

*Round the city of Caxton, the electronic suburbs are rising. To the language of books is added the language of television and radio, . . . the processed codes of the computer. As the shapes of literacy multiply, so our dependence on language increases. (Kingman Report, Chapter 2, paragraph 7)*

In my visits to schools as a member of the Kingman Committee, I was impressed on a number of occasions by the imaginative use of word processing in the classroom. In a school in Birmingham, for example, children who were recent arrivals in this country and whose English was poor were using word processors to learn how to cope with the demands of organising a holiday through a travel agent, particularly how to write letters asking for information. They were using real brochures, choosing their holidays and working out what questions they must ask. With a word processor they enjoyed discussing their drafts with each other and with the teacher, and collaborated together on corrections and revisions.

I was pleased that the supplementary guidance for the terms of reference for my Working Group mentioned both information technology (IT) and media studies: 'English teaching will provide one appropriate context . . . for developing information handling skills, . . . and for media studies . . . The practical use of word processors in developing writing provides an introduction to information technology.'

## OUR RATIONALE

Media education and information technology alike enlarge pupils' critical understanding of how messages are generated, conveyed and interpreted in different media. First-hand use of media equipment (e.g. in making videos) and other technologies (such as desk top publishing) can contribute to children's practical understanding of how meanings are created. We already have television, video tapes and discs, word processors, desk top publishing, electronic databases, electronic mail, and experimentation in areas such as hypertext, natural language processing and so on. Their use will become more widespread. New technologies and products will develop. For schools this also implies:

- ◇ an increase in data collections of all kinds and in the use of authentic language materials for teaching about the uses of language;
- ◇ an increase in accessibility to such collectiona via CD-ROM, video disc, satellite links, etc.;
- ◇ an increase in the diversity of learning materials geared to the needs of different learners;
- ◇ a proliferation of self-access teaching materials and study packages, including interactive materials;
- ◇ the development of new study skills to access and to make best use of such materials, and the reinforcement of existing skills in new contexts.

The Working Party included in its proposals for programmes of study those aspects of media education and IT which contribute most directly to the central aim of English: to widen the range of children's understanding and use of language, and to develop their skills in it. Assessment of achievements in English should therefore be primarily concerned with such understanding and skills, rather than with pupils' knowledge about and competence in using IT and media facilities as such. Indeed, media education and IT also have their own academic integrity, particularly in the secondary school as specialised timetabled subjects outside the National Curriculum. The English curriculum should prepare pupils for possible study of these subjects as separate options, and not seek to supplant them.

Many aspects of media education and IT involve the use of machines: still cameras, video, computer terminals, etc. Our culture often regards machines as a male preserve, and girls may need opportunities and encouragement to show that they can be expert in such areas. It may sometimes be necessary, for example, to arrange for girls to have access to the technology in single-sex groups if they are to develop a confident and active understanding of the media. We wanted all pupils to be able to benefit from the opportunities that the new media and technologies offer, and we framed our proposals accordingly.

## MEDIA EDUCATION

Our terms of reference used the title 'media studies', which may be best reserved for specialist study. We interpreted our remit broadly in accordance with the following description of 'media education':

> *Media education . . . seeks to increase children's critical understanding of the media – namely, television, film, video,*

*photography, popular music, printed materials, and computer software. How they work, how they produce meaning, how they are organised and how audiences make sense of them, are the issues that media education addresses. [It] aims to develop systematically children's critical and creative powers through analysis and production of media artefacts. This also deepens their understanding of the pleasure and enjoyment provided by the media. Media education aims to create more active and critical media users who will demand, and could contribute to, a greater range and diversity of media products.[1]*

Media education should be concerned not only with modern mass media such as television, cinema and radio, but also with all public forms of communication including printed materials (books as well as newspapers) and computerised sources of information such as databases. We considered media education largely as part of the exploration of contemporary culture, alongside more traditional literary texts. Television and film form substantial parts of pupils' experience out of school and teachers need to take this into account. Pupils should have the opportunity to apply their critical faculties to these major parts of contemporary culture. Media education, like drama, deals with fundamental aspects of language, interpretation and meaning. It is therefore consonant with the aims of English teaching. In fact, media education has often developed in a very explicit way concepts which are of general importance in English. These include selection (of information, viewpoint, etc.), editing, author, audience, medium, genre, stereotype, etc. We drew on these aspects in developing our recommendations for attainment targets and programmes of study. In particular, we included the treatment of non-literary and media texts in the reading profile component.

# INFORMATION TECHNOLOGY

The English class should be one setting where pupils learn to use IT to:

◇ help in the production and reception of written language for different audiences (e.g. by using desk top publishing, spelling checkers, thesaurus, etc.);

◇ send and receive messages: electronic mail can, for example, link classes elsewhere in the country or in other countries, and can provide very powerful ways of creating real audiences for children's writing;

◇ give and respond to precise and accurate instructions, upon which successful use of the technology depends, as does language competence more generally;

◇ comprehend systems of filing and classification, including alphabetic ordering, lists of contents, indexes, symbols, etc.:

the organisation, storage and retrieval of information is, again, an important language skill generally;

◇ gain an understanding of some of the ways in which information can be manipulated (e.g. in databases, mail merge programs), and therefore show increasing discrimination in their interpretation of such information.

The word processor extends opportunities for development and reflection on ideas and meanings, for example in designing, outlining and restructuring, and through the ability of writers to engage in dialogue with their own thoughts in the form of clean hard copy (printed text). The possibilities are analogous to those in graphics that are offered to the designer by computer aided design (CAD). Since the information on a word processor or computer screen is visible to several children at once, it can be a vehicle for group discussion and exploration of the language.

In these ways English teachers have much to contribute to children's familiarity with this technology and its uses, alongside the major aim of exploiting it to promote language knowledge and skills in themselves. This is reflected in our recommendations for programmes of study in both the reading and the writing profile components.

This will not, however, be achieved as long as IT is regarded as the province of mathematics, science and technology in the curriculum, and English – or other language – teachers are seen as having little part to play. IT equipment and facilities are becoming increasingly common in schools. They can and should be made readily accessible to teachers and pupils in English as in other subjects. Our recommendations presupposed this.

## NOTE

1   Cary Bazalgette, ed. *Primary Media Education: A Curriculum Statement* (BFI Education Department, 1989).

# *Bilingual children*[1]

Our terms of reference made it clear that we were to concern ourselves with the English curriculum for all pupils, whatever their mother tongue. In particular they stressed that 'The framework [for English] should ensure, at the minimum, that all school-leavers are competent in the use of English – written and spoken – whether or not it is their first language.' The supplementary guidance said too: 'The group should also take account of the ethnic diversity of the school population and society at large, bearing in mind the cardinal point that English should be the first language and medium of instruction for all pupils in England.'

In chapter 2 I discussed one of the central aims of the English curriculum, which is to extend the range of language in which children are competent. Many children in our schools speak languages other than English. For these children, therefore, this means adding competence in Standard English to their competence in other languages. English is clearly the 'first language' of the education system. But it would be a great loss if pupils' knowledge of a range of other languages was to decline.

The distribution of bilingual children varies widely across the country, but the total numbers and diversity are certainly significant. The 1987 Language Survey conducted by ILEA found 23 per cent of the Authority's school population using a language other than or in addition to English at home, with 170 different languages spoken by its pupils. On the basis of the limited evidence available some 5 per cent of all schools in England are likely to have a significant population of children for whom English is not their mother tongue. This represents a very great pool of linguistic competence.

## ENTITLEMENT TO ENGLISH

All children should be enabled to attain a full command of the English language, both spoken and written. Otherwise they will be disadvantaged, not only in their study of other subjects, but also in their working life. In this respect my Working Group were following the path already trodden by the Swann Committee. They stated firmly: 'the key to equality of opportunity, to academic success and, more broadly, to participation on equal terms as a full member of society, is good command of English and the emphasis must therefore we feel be on the learning of English.'[2] The Swann Committee had also noted 'the views expressed very clearly to us at our various meetings with parents from the whole range of ethnic minority groups that they want and indeed expect the education system to give their children above all a good command of English as rapidly as possible'.[3]

Our initial reaction to our brief in respect of bilingual pupils was that all pupils must have access to the same attainment targets and programmes of study for English. We consulted many of those actively concerned with teaching English to bilingual pupils, who firmly endorsed this view. We recognised that the bald statement in the preceding paragraph requires amplification. The TGAT Report suggests that headteachers might exempt children with language difficulties in English from tests where the problem is so severe as to render the assessment unworkable.[4] For example, there will be some pupils who may have arrived in this country only shortly before the assessment time at one of the key ages. In such cases, we suggested that regulations made under section 19 of the 1988 Act, which allow disapplication of the provisions of the National Curriculum, should enable headteachers to exempt such pupils from the assessment requirements for English.

We were also aware of the problem that assessment in English, particularly that at age 7, could result in bilingual children reaching only a comparatively low level of achievement. If the results of assessment are used in the ways intended and if the evidence of research and HMI findings of good practice are heeded, these children should in fact benefit, because their problems with the English language will have been identified and appropriate action can be taken to help at an early stage. As the TGAT Report said: 'it should be recognised that to record a low level of performance for this reason [English as a second language (E2L)] would be no reflection on a pupil's general ability but merely an indication that the pupil needed special help in English language skills.'[5] The results of assessment should be part of a continuing process of recording a pupil's stages of language development, and this record should be available to all his or her teachers.

It may be suggested that we were inconsistent, or even guilty of unreasonable discrimination, in that we insisted on assessment in English in England for pupils whose mother tongue is not English, whereas in Wales we recommended that pupils being taught through the medium of Welsh be exempted from the key stage 1 attainment targets, programmes of study and assessment. The positions are not comparable. In Wales, Welsh is an official language and a core subject of the National Curriculum for pupils in Welsh-medium schools or classes – the only pupils for whom English is to be disapplied at key stage 1; no such language other than English is in such a position in England. These pupils in Wales do not start formally to be taught English until the age of 7 or 8; all pupils in England will be required to be taught English from age 5.

## IMPLICATIONS FOR TEACHING

There is much evidence of the ways in which bilingual children can best be helped to attain competence in English. It would be inadvisable to try to lay down too specific a strategy, because of the immense variety of English language knowledge and experience within the group loosely categorised as bilingual children. However, there are some themes which recur in the evidence of those we consulted and which were first sounded in the Bullock and Swann Reports. The latter said 'We are wholly in favour of a move away from E2L provision being made on a withdrawal basis, whether in language centres or separate units within schools.'[6] The HMI survey of English as a second language in six LEAs (published 1988) found that, on balance, the children in the survey made most progress where the programme to provide help with their English was designed to support the mainstream curriculum but with the oral component heightened. It was stressed to us that pupils having difficulty with English because it was their second language should not be equated with pupils with other special educational needs. In particular, such pupils should not be offered materials with a reduced cognitive demand. This point was made also in the reports of the mathematics and science working groups.[7] The implications are therefore that, where bilingual pupils need extra help, this should be given in the classroom as part of normal lessons and that there may be a need for bilingual teaching support and for books and other written material to be available in the pupils' mother tongues until such time as they are competent in English.

Bilingual pupils at secondary school should be helped to extend their range of English so that they can undertake high-level tasks alongside their peers. E2L teachers can contribute greatly here if they work closely with subject teachers in developing an appropriate curriculum and content. The E2L teacher has a great deal to offer subject specialists about the language approaches and assessment of the subject. Expectations need to be appropriately set and as high for bilingual pupils as for all others.

Bilingual children should be considered an advantage in the classroom rather than a problem. The evidence shows that such children will make greater progress in English if they know that their knowledge of their mother tongue is valued, if it is recognised that their experience of language is likely to be greater than that of their monoglot peers and, indeed, if their knowledge and experience can be put to good use in the classroom to the benefit of all pupils to provide examples of the structure and syntax of different languages, to provide a focus for discussion about language forms and for contrast and comparison with the structure of the English language. We endorse the view of the Kingman Committee:

> *It should be the duty of all teachers to instil in their pupils a civilised respect for other languages and an understanding of the relations between other languages and English. It should be made clear to English-speaking pupils that classmates whose first language is Bengali or Cantonese, or any other of the scores of languages spoken by the school population . . . have languages quite as systematic and rule-governed as their own.*[8]

To illustrate what can be done, here is the statement of policy of the English department of a multi-racial inner-city school: 'Pupils needs to develop full control of their language use. They therefore need to gain insight into what language is and what it can do, insights which bilingual children intuitively possess', and 'Whilst we recognise that they [bilingual pupils] need to gain access to standard forms of English – used widely as a vehicle for implementing the school curriculum, we recognise the value and importance of their own dialects and languages. Language competence is regarded as the ability to adapt language to different roles and situations.'[9]

As I point out in chapter 12, there are exciting possibilities for initiatives in knowledge about language, particularly in the areas of social and developmental linguistics. Bilingual children offer opportunities to explore language in a novel context, and a study of the different ways in which different languages convey and produce meanings should feature as an element of teachers' schemes of work, wherever this is practicable.

## LITERATURE

As I said in chapter 6, children should read literature from all parts of the English-speaking world. Children whose families come, for example, from the Caribbean, from countries in Africa or from the Indian subcontinent can greatly enrich discussion about English as a world language and about literature and drama as world concepts. Teachers need to be alive to cultural differences which may particularly affect bilingual pupils' handling of literature. Many secondary pupils are likely to be more aware than younger children of their cultural and religious frames of reference. In some cultures, critical analysis of texts is relatively unknown and may, indeed, be thought offensive. Teachers need to be sensitive to this possibility.

I have referred in chapter 2 to the need for a language policy across the curriculum; a recommendation to this effect appeared in both the Bullock and the Swann Reports. Such a policy would be of especial benefit to bilingual or multilingual children.

## NOTES

1  Excluding those in Welsh-medium schools in Wales.
2  *Education for All*, the Report of the Committee of Inquiry into the Education of Children from Ethnic Minority Groups [the Swann Committee Report], chapter 7, paragraph 3.16. (HMSO, 1985)
3  *Education for All*, chapter 7, paragraph 3.13.
4  *TGAT First Report*, paragraph 53. National Curriculum Task Group on Assessment and Testing. A Report. DES and Welsh Office, 1987.
5  *TGAT First Report*, paragraph 53.
6  *Education for All*, chapter 7, paragraph 2.10.
7  *Report of the National Curriculum Mathematics Working Group*, paragraph 10.23; *Report of the National Curriculum Science Working Group*, appendix D, paragraph 23. (1987)
8  Kingman Report, chapter 4, paragraph 33.
9  Policy Statement, English Department, Holte School, Birmingham.

# 10

# Equal Opportunities

The supplementary guidance to our terms of reference notes that 'the curriculum should provide equal opportunities for boys and girls.' It further notes that the curriculum should take account of 'the ethnic diversity of the school population and society at large', and draws attention to the principle that as wide a range of children as possible should have access to the whole curriculum.

Issues of equal opportunity may arise in a number of contexts; for example, those of gender, race, disability and religion. Such issues must be a concern of those devising the National Curriculum because the attainment targets and programmes of study must not be biased, deliberately or unwittingly, towards or against any such group. In particular, the National Curriculum assessment methods must enable all pupils to demonstrate what they can do, without the assessment of their performance being unfairly affected by the context of the task or the preconceptions of the assessor.

All pupils should pursue the programmes of study and attainment targets if they are to be able to participate fully in adult life and employment. This is their entitlement. But not all pupils enter school at age 5 with the same experience and competence: some will be further advanced than others by virtue of their family background. Schools need to ensure that all pupils, irrespective of their backgrounds, have an equal opportunity to achieve the attainment targets. Pupils with special educational needs may require particular help to pursue the programmes and targets, or in some cases modifications to those, and this problem is addressed in chapter 11. But the aim is that, wherever possible, all pupils should have access to the full range of the English curriculum.

Such principles are also advocated in the general criteria for GCSE syllabuses. Under 'Avoidance of bias' they state: 'Every possible effort must be made to ensure that syllabuses and examinations are free of political, ethnic, gender and other forms of bias.' And under 'Recognition of cultural diversity' they state: 'In devising syllabuses and setting question papers Examining Groups should bear in mind the linguistic and cultural diversity of society.'

It was beyond our brief to attempt a general statement about equal opportunities in education. There are, however, certain aspects which have particular importance in English teaching.

## THE CONTENT OF THE CURRICULUM

English teachers need to be ready to give careful introductions and support when using texts which might otherwise cause offence to some groups; for example, if a character with racist attitudes is portrayed, even though the author may not be supporting such attitudes. The choice of subjects for imaginative writing may also require care.

I discuss in chapter 6 the criteria for a balanced selection of literature in the classroom: it should include both British and non-British, both female and male authors, etc. The books chosen for study should also encompass a balanced range of presentations of other societies, and of ethnic and social groupings and life-styles within our own society.

It is well known that girls and boys tend to choose different books, and indeed that teenage boys tend to drop voluntary reading altogether. If this difference is simply accepted, it will only serve to strengthen stereotypes. All teachers should therefore enable and encourage both girls and boys to read a variety of genres by a variety of authors, including those which challenge stereotypes of the roles of the sexes and of different cultural groups. In literature and in media education, pupils should explore, for example, ways in which different groups in society are stereotyped or their viewpoints represented, and in which stories can be recast to reflect different authorial attitudes or characterisations of participants. Work on knowledge about language should involve discussion of matters such as sexist language; styles of interaction in social groups (see below); how hidden messages about social groups (such as teenagers or older people) which are conveyed by advertising etc. can be decoded for the values they contain and for the differences between what is said and what is implied.

## TASKS AND ASSESSMENT

Children should be judged on what they can do and on what they know, not on who they are. But to ignore the evidence of differences in performance between gender or ethnic groups can lead to unjust treatment of individuals. Substantial research has shown that different ethnic groups (e.g. children of Caribbean or Asian origin) display different ranges of attainment in the British education system. There are also documented differences between the average test performances of girls and boys in different curricular subjects. (See TGAT Report, appendix F.) And a strong association between social background and educational attainment is one of the best-demonstrated findings of educational research. (See TGAT Report, appendix J.) The causes of such differences are not well understood. But curricular and assessment arrangements should aim to raise expectations and to help to narrow the gap wherever possible.

As well as such differences in educational attainment, there are differences in the characteristic linguistic behaviour of various groups. Here also English teachers have particular responsibilities. The possibility of bias arises especially in the assessment of oracy, because of the difficulty of separating pupils' spoken language from perceptions of their personality and background.

Oracy involves teaching and assessing children's language behaviour with other people. Such behaviour may depend at least partly on the teacher's skill in setting up situations which will elicit the best from each child: most people are shy in some situations and confident in others, and different people's responses to the same situation may vary sharply.

Language behaviour is influenced not only by personality but also by convention and culture. Speakers of different languages and cultural backgrounds, and from different social groups, vary quite significantly in their preferred language norms. There is a growing body of research which shows that cultures differ in the way conversations and other forms of spoken discourse are conducted. Features of interaction such as body posture, gesture, preferred distance between speakers, discursive styles, the ways in which politeness is marked or attention to other speakers is signalled, differ widely across cultures. Other research illustrates the kinds of cross-cultural communication problem which can arise in interviews and other institutional settings.

There are also considerable differences between the sexes in typical speech styles, which carry implications for assessment. For example, boys are more likely than girls from the same social background to:

◇ speak with a broader regional accent and use more non-standard grammatical forms;
◇ talk about their interests and experiences with less overt enthusiasm, using a narrower pitch range, less variation in speed and volume, and fewer intensifying words and phrases;
◇ express beliefs and opinions more confidently;
◇ give direct instructions rather than negotiate, in group activities;
◇ use ritual insults, jokes, verbal bantering and aggressive argument;
◇ interrupt girls rather than boys in conversation.

Differences in speech styles may also be observed between other social groups.

Whether these characteristic differences are judged positively or negatively will depend on the context and purpose of the task. For example, in some tasks, the more direct way of speaking that is more common to boys will be advantageous; in others, the more tentative approach more frequently found in girls will be more appropriate.

## CONCLUSION

Throughout the English curriculum and in the assessment process, teachers should enable all pupils, regardless of gender, ethnic or social group, first to reflect on their performance, and then actively to seek to adapt their language characteristics to situation and purpose. For example, in some situations girls may need to strive to be more assertive, while in others boys may need to develop greater sensitivity in their use of language. The differences in language behaviour between the sexes should be specifically drawn to pupils' attention; in group work in mixed schools teachers could assist reflection, comparison and adaptation by ensuring a balance between mixed and single-sex work wherever appropriate. Similar principles should apply to the treatment of differences in language behaviour between other groups. It is not suggested that the results of assessment should be adjusted to take account of characteristic differences between groups in performance. But those preparing standard assessment tasks and other assessment instruments should consider them so as to minimise bias in the task or context and guard against any preconceptions of assessors; and any comparison of results between single-sex schools or between those with different ethnic or social class populations should be made in the light of the evidence referred to above.

# 11

# Special Educational Needs

Our supplementary guidance said, in relation to special needs:

> *The Government proposes that where a pupil has a statement of special [educational] needs under the 1981 Education Act, the statement should specify any National Curriculum requirements which should not apply or should be modified for that individual pupil. In addition, orders may define circumstances in which the application of the National Curriculum provisions to individual pupils might be modified or lifted for any foundation subject. . . . I should be grateful if you would consider whether exceptions of this kind for categories of pupils can be justified in the case of English.*

As TGAT pointed out, pupils with special educational needs make up a very diverse group. Their difficulties stem from a number of different causes and may be temporary or permanent; and they may be receiving their education, either outside the mainstream (whether in special classes or units in ordinary schools, or in special schools) or in ordinary classes in ordinary schools.

## ACCESS THROUGH ENGLISH

The Working Party believed, and those we consulted concurred whole-heartedly, that competence in English is important, both in its own right and to enable pupils to gain access to and benefit from the other subjects of the National Curriculum. Pupils with special educational needs, like all other pupils, should have the opportunity to experience as far as possible the full range of the English curriculum. For example, pupils with reading problems (including dyslexic pupils) should not be deprived of literature, but should have the opportunity of experiencing it through listening to others reading aloud, whether live or recorded, and through seeing plays and films, as well as through reading suitably simplified versions.

It is assumed therefore that virtually all children will travel along broadly the same curricular path in English, but that some will move more quickly, and further, than others; and some may be around the level 1 attainments for the whole of their school careers. Pupils will also move at different speeds for different activities. Some pupils of secondary school age who have special educational needs may continue to display some literacy skills within the lower levels associated with key stages 1 and 2, so the teaching they receive in English will need to cater for this whilst incorporating material with a range and degree of interest, and in some cases intellectual demand, more appropriate to their chronological age. In other subjects too they may need written and other materials with simplified language demands but perhaps higher demands in other respects. All of the attainment targets can be assessed at various levels, with corresponding programmes of study leading towards them. Pupils with special educational needs should therefore be able to participate in the attainment targets, programmes of study and assessment arrangements, subject where appropriate to the modifications we recommend below.

## ASSESSMENT AT LEVEL 1

Level 1 is intended to encompass a wide range of attainment, from those pupils who have barely begun to learn, to those who are very close to achieving level 2. There will be a small minority for whom achieving level 1 alone will present longer-term goals, which they work towards through a series of preliminary programmes. When such pupils attain level 1, the fact that, despite their difficulties, they have started down the curricular path should be acknowledged as a real achievement.

A level 1 assessment at age 7 is intended to signal that the child may need special help. In the majority of cases this will merely confirm what teachers already knew, and will strengthen their hands in taking appropriate action; for example, seeking assessment under the 1981 Act with a possible view to securing a statement of special educational needs. In others, it will come as something of a surprise, and there may then be a need for the child to undergo further diagnostic tests to establish the extent of the problem. A level 1 performance should always prompt further investigation. This might, for example, reveal that a child who appeared to be inattentive or a slow learner was in fact showing symptoms of specific learning difficulties (e.g. dyslexia) or a hearing impairment – possibly an intermittent one such as is associated with otitis media.

# MODIFYING THE CURRICULUM
## Pupils with 1981 Act statements

A small proportion of pupils with special educational needs will have statements made under the Education Act 1981 to specify the educational and other provisions necessary to meet these. The procedures of the 1981 Act ensure that statements are drawn up on the basis of the pupil's individual needs, but with the general aim of ensuring, as far as possible, an education comparable with that of the pupil's age group in the mainstream. The proportion of pupils with statements varies widely across the country, partly because of the LEAs' differing policies on 'statementing', but overall stands at some 1.7 per cent of the total population of statutory school age, with just over a fifth of these in ordinary rather than special schools. It is impossible to recommend blanket modifications to our proposals for pupils with statements which are, by definition, individually tailored to their needs. However, later in this chapter there are some general suggestions which may be of assistance to those who will be responsible for incorporating into statements modifications to the National Curriculum requirements.

## Pupils without statements

But most pupils with special educational needs will not be the subject of statements. Amongst the general population of children in ordinary schools, about a sixth have special educational needs of one kind or another. The Working Group's suggestions will also be relevant to some of the pupils with special educational needs but without statements, whose particular requirements could be met by statutory modifications (which the 1988 Act allows in respect of children falling within certain cases and circumstances) to or within Orders for attainment targets, programmes of study and assessment arrangements for English.

## Pupils with learning difficulties

Pupils with learning difficulties, with or without statements, are likely to make only slow progress with reading and writing. For such pupils oral work should be given greater emphasis initially, though the skills of reading and writing must not be neglected. Where such pupils also have speech impairments, there may be a case for exempting them altogether from – or modifying – some of the assessment arrangements, even if they continue to pursue the attainment targets and programmes of study.

     Pupils with specific learning difficulties (e.g. dyslexia) should, given appropriate help, achieve as well as pupils without special educational needs. Dyslexic pupils may, however, have particular difficulty with the attainment target concerned with 'secretarial' skills, and in this respect they may benefit particularly from using word processors, including spelling checkers. They will benefit especially, too, from explicit teaching about language, which is already included in the recommended programmes of study and which may need adaptation and reinforcement for such pupils. The reading attainment target contains statements of attainment for the earlier levels which relate to information retrieval. Explicit teaching of this skill should also be of special value to pupils with specific learning difficulties, who generally find it difficult to master.

## Pupils with physical disabilities

Pupils with physical disabilities should in general have the same attainment targets and programmes of study as their peers. But where their particular disability impairs their access to the curriculum, this access should be facilitated by alternative means, and it should be recognised that the problem of access may hinder their initial progress, though they may be expected to catch up later.

Some pupils with physical disabilities may require the writing attainment targets to be modified. For example, the handwriting target, which applies up to level 4, and the presentation target, which applies from levels 5 to 7, might be inappropriate. Such pupils should be enabled to produce their written work on a word processor or concept keyboard.

## Pupils with impaired vision

Pupils with impaired vision will obviously experience difficulty with reading. Depending on the degree of impairment, they may need special large-print books or optical or electronic devices for enlarging and enhancing print, or to be taught braille. Even so they may also have difficulty in covering the full range of literature suggested, though not in understanding or enjoying it. They may therefore need to be read to or to listen to 'talking book' cassettes. Where the reading skill required is that of interpreting such things as labels and road signs, they should pursue the normal targets and programmes as far as possible for their own safety, though they may need help where practicable to interpret these things through other than ordinary visual means. Such pupils may also have difficulty with writing. They might therefore be exempted from – or given modified – handwriting and presentation targets and, depending on the degree of impairment, undertake the writing tasks through alternative means of communication, using technological aids.

## Pupils with impaired hearing

Profoundly deaf pupils will almost certainly need modification of the speaking and listening component, especially if they were born deaf or lost their hearing before acquiring language. They might be allowed to use signing, or speech with signing support. It should also be recognised that their progress with reading and writing is likely to be handicapped initially if they come to school with a restricted knowledge and experience of language. Moreover, since their condition limits their ability to pick up and assimilate new words and to understand the subtleties of language, the problem becomes greater as more specialised vocabulary and abstract terms are introduced. The achievements of pupils with a hearing impairment will undoubtedly be affected by these factors, and this will need to be taken into account, for example, in the assessment of the first attainment target in writing. Pupils with less severe hearing impairments may also need modifications to the requirements, but of a less far-reaching nature.

## Pupils with temporary problems

For pupils with temporary problems, it will be for headteachers to decide whether the National Curriculum provisions should be modified temporarily. These temporary problems might include medical problems, family crises and other similar major difficulties; they might apply to pupils with special educational needs as to any other pupil. Pupils with temporary problems might also include Traveller children affected by discontinuity of schooling. In all these cases headteachers will need to consider what action is most appropriate in the circumstances.

## EXTERNAL ASSISTANCE

Some pupils with special educational needs, with or without statements, may need assistance to enable them to communicate their achievements. Such assistance may come from, for example, speech therapists, occupational therapists, medical specialists or psychologists. There may be resource implications, but the involvement of such experts is essential if the pupils concerned are to be enabled to perform in English to their full potential. For most pupils, however, assistance can be expected to be found from within the school's own resources. It should come through day-to-day teacher contact, and through language specialists' involvement in support teaching and in helping their colleagues to use appropriate language consistently across the curriculum.

# 12

# English Language and Literature in the Schools of Wales

English is the first language of five out of six pupils in Wales and is the main medium of instruction in the great majority of schools. For a very large number of primary pupils in Wales our attainment targets and programmes of study will be as appropriate as they are for pupils in England. However, in Wales there is a significant number of schools where Welsh rather than English is the main medium of instruction and where a substantial proportion of pupils may have Welsh as their first language. Some of these schools may be formally designated as Welsh schools (Ysgolion Cymraeg). Nevertheless, many of these will be attended, especially in English-speaking areas, by pupils the great majority of whom speak English as their first language. Others may not be designated as Welsh schools but may nevertheless use Welsh as the main medium because the community served is largely Welsh-speaking and a significant proportion of pupils speak Welsh as the first language. Welsh is also taught as a second language in the majority of schools in Wales, but for varying proportions of pupils' time. The National Curriculum Welsh Working Group had the remit to recommend attainment targets and programmes of study in Welsh for both Welsh- and English-speaking pupils.

## ENGLISH IN PRIMARY SCHOOLS IN WALES

The eventual aim of teaching both Welsh and English to pupils in primary schools is a degree of bilingualism which represents a worthwhile educational achievement at the age of 11 and which can be the basis for further progress in secondary school. In those schools which teach Welsh as a second language but do not use it extensively as a medium of instruction, pupils can in general properly be expected to undertake the programmes of study and attainment targets deemed appropriate for English-speaking pupils in England. Of the pupils attending those schools which aim to use Welsh as a main medium, in Welsh-speaking areas a proportion, and in the designated Welsh schools of the English-speaking areas the great majority, may be

English-speaking initially. There is in these schools an attempt to establish an early capability in Welsh and considerable emphasis on learning in and through the language. This is necessary not only to give initial English-speakers the means whereby they may learn effectively through Welsh, but also to strengthen Welsh-speaking pupils' grasp of the language. This approach usually extends to the end of the infant stage; English is formally introduced as a subject and medium at about the age of 7 in most Welsh-medium schools, though there may well be some informal use of English earlier.

Given the above circumstances, we recommended that our attainments targets, programmes of study and assessment arrangements for the first key stage should be waived for pupils taught mainly through Welsh at the infants' stage. The Secretary of State for Wales accepted this recommendation, and his formal proposal for regulations to effect it was widely welcomed.

English is taught as a subject and to a lesser extent used as a medium in all Welsh-medium schools at the junior stage. Pupils will also encounter English in the community outside school and in particular through the mass media, and many pupils become increasingly influenced by this experience of English between the ages of 7 and 11. As a result of these educational and social influences the great majority of pupils in Welsh-medium schools achieve a satisfactory degree of bilingualism by the age of 11 and it is appropriate for them to be assessed against the attainment targets set for pupils in English-medium schools. The evidence accumulated over the course of Assessment and Performance Unit surveys suggests that there are no significant differences between the performance at 11 in English of pupils educated mainly through Welsh and other pupils (whether the latter are in schools in Wales or elsewhere in the UK).

The programmes of study proposed in Welsh-medium schools for the 8 to 11 age group will need modification to accommodate the needs of pupils whose first formal teaching in and through English has been delayed until the age of 7. Such modification need only be slight, since these pupils are older and more mature when they begin English and will already have experienced a similar range of programmes of study in Welsh. In addition, many of them will be initially English-speaking and will be making continual and substantial use of English outside school, particularly in speaking and reading. Therefore the only modification we recommended was that any material in the English programmes of study for the 5 to 7 age group not covered by the Welsh equivalent should be included in the English programmes of study for these pupils in the 8 to 11 age group. This recommendation was accepted by the Secretary of State for Wales.

# ENGLISH IN SECONDARY SCHOOLS IN WALES

In secondary schools in Wales, all pupils will be learning English and Welsh. The Secretary of State for Wales accepted our recommendation that, for key stage 2, the same range of levels, statements of attainment, programmes of study and assessment arrangements as those applicable to pupils in England should apply to pupils in Wales, whether in Welsh- or English-medium schools. It therefore follows that our recommended range of levels, statements of attainment, programmes of study and assessment arrangements for key stages 3 and 4 should apply to all pupils in Wales.

It is unlikely that any modification will be required to the programmes of study for pupils in key stages 3 and 4, who have been educated mainly through the medium of Welsh. We recommended, however, that those for key stage 3 be carefully scrutinised to see whether there is any need to emphasise particular elements in the light of the modifications to the key stage 2 programmes of study. There may also prove to be areas of language study common to the programmes of study for both English and Welsh. We therefore suggested that our proposals and those of the Welsh Working Group for first language Welsh speakers be examined for overlap, with the possibility of modification in mind, so that bilingual speakers of Welsh and English may not have to study the same linguistic features twice over.

Assessment processes need to be developed which reflect the fact that there are similar developmental stages in learning both languages. Acceptance of the proposed attainment targets and programmes of study will mean in at least some Welsh-medium schools a more systematic approach to the teaching of English than is sometimes encountered. It will also entail in some schools a more explicit policy for the systematic use of both Welsh and English as media of instruction. It is essential that English staff co-operate with their Welsh-teaching colleagues to develop coherent school policies for the teaching of many aspects of language and for language use across the curriculum. The possibilities offered for initiatives in knowledge about language are exciting, particularly in the areas of social and developmental linguistics, including choice of language as well as choice of appropriate style within one mother tongue. Additional problems may have to be faced in the development of referencing skills in bilingual pupils, for whom it may be a frequent experience that information has to be extracted in one language for exploitation in the other. The skills involved are those which should be as widespread as possible in a bilingual situation. In this context a well-resourced and adequately staffed central library may well be a requirement.

## KNOWLEDGE ABOUT LANGUAGE

The Kingman Report and my earlier chapters discussed the place of knowledge about language in the teaching and learning of English. The bilingual aims of Welsh-medium schools (and to a lesser extent those of schools where Welsh is taught as a second language) offer opportunities to explore this theme in a novel context. An examination of the different ways in which the two languages convey and produce meanings should feature as an element of programmes of study in English and Welsh in all schools in Wales, and in particular in the mainly Welsh-medium schools.

## LITERATURE

In earlier chapters it is proposed that schools and individual teachers should retain a considerable measure of freedom in the choice of literature to be read by and with pupils, but that such choice should take careful account of pupils' interests. In Wales it should also take special account of pupils' cultural environment. This culture is increasingly one which is common to young people in many countries, but which none the less continues to retain local and regional characteristics. The Welsh dimension to the curriculum will be manifested in a number of subjects, and English can make a significant contribution, not least in the choice of literature for use in the classroom. The works of the so-called 'Anglo–Welsh' writers and (in English-medium schools) translations of major works in Welsh should figure in such a choice as a literary expression of the many different things it can mean to live in Wales. Nevertheless the Working Group did not think it appropriate to specify any particular literature in the programmes of study, which are intended to be given statutory force.

# *Assessment*

Our supplementary guidance invited us to offer advice in broad terms about assessment, having regard to the TGAT reports, in relation to the attainment targets we recommended, and particularly on what might appropriately be measured by nationally prescribed tests. We took to heart TGAT's comment that 'The assessment process itself should not determine what is to be taught and learned. It should be the servant, not the master, of the curriculum. Yet it should not simply be a bolt-on addition at the end. Rather, it should be an integral part of the educational process, continually providing both "feedback" and "feed-forward".'[1] Detailed advice on the assessment of each area of English is set out in chapters 14 to 16, which are concerned with the recommended profile components. It was formulated in accord with the general principles for the assessment of English described in the following paragraphs.

## LANGUAGE DEVELOPMENT AND ASSESSMENT

The problems in defining a linear sequence of language development have been the subject of a great deal of research. This has shown that children do not learn particular features of written language, for example, once and for all at any particular stage; they continually return to the same features and refine their competence. While this does not mean that it is impossible to define any linear development, it does mean that language development must be conceived, fostered and assessed in terms which are broad enough to accommodate variations between individuals in the sequences followed and the effects of iterative processes upon pupils' increasing grasp and sophistication.

Such a view of language development is still consistent with the proposition that many children can reasonably be expected to know, understand and do certain key things in language by the end of the main educational stages of infant, junior, early and late secondary schooling; and that virtually all children, other than those with special learning difficulties, can be expected to attempt those things. Although the individual paths may be different, the routes tend to converge around certain points in children's lives. The end of each educational stage – with the transition to the next being marked often by a change of school, teacher or teaching approach – then offers a suitable opportunity to take stock of what each pupil has achieved, and his or her further needs. In fact schools already plan the curriculum and schemes of work around their perception of the needs of the class as a whole: this implies a view of the present achievements, pace and direction of desired development for the class, within which variations can be devised for individual pupils. Our proposals for attainment targets and programmes of study were intended to help those assumptions to be made more explicit and acted upon.

But it is essential that they should not lead to negative judgments about individual pupils' language competence in narrow, discrete areas, and then to arbitrary decisions on the next learning steps in some artificial sequence. That is why we preferred the TGAT concept of a 10-level scale (rather than a simple 'pass/fail' system of attainment targets), with each interval broadly representing typical progression observable over a sufficient period of some two years of schooling, and by the same token a degree of differentiation at any one age-point which is not spuriously precise. It is also why we recommended progressive attainment levels within each target which wherever possible allow for gradual growth of sophistication, rather than just acquisition of additional skills; profile components which acknowledge the complex relationship between different facets of language; and programmes of study which are broad enough to accommodate a variety of paths towards the common objective. At the same time the targets and levels are pitched so as to challenge all children to extend and enrich their language development.

## RANGES OF ATTAINMENT

The range of pupil attainment within the 10-level scale will vary at the end of each key stage. We accepted TGAT's rough estimate of the median level of attainment at each key stage, i.e. key stage 1: level 2, key stage 2: level 4, key stage 3: levels 5/6, and key stage 4: levels 6/7. However, empirical evidence suggests that the range of attainment around the median is rather wider than TGAT anticipated. Less able pupils can often make comparable progress with their peers in the acquisition of reading and writing skills up to the age of 9 or 10, but have great difficulty in progressing beyond the level of attainment reached at that stage. By the end of key stage 3 or 4, some of the pupils may have reached only level 2 or 3. Whilst every help and encouragement should be given to such pupils in order that they can continue to make progress, the range of levels associated with each key stage, for the purposes of programmes of study and assessment, should reflect this characteristic of the learning process in English. It should also reflect the fact that very able pupils may well be able to reach higher levels of attainment earlier in English than in other, more content-based subjects. We recommended that the range of levels associated with each of the four key stages should be as follows:

> *key stage 1: levels 1 to 3*
> *key stage 2: levels 2 to 5*
> *key stage 3: levels 3 to 8*
> *key stage 4: levels 3 to 10*

These ranges reflect the likely span of attainment of the great majority of pupils at the end of each key stage and, consequently, the ground that programmes of study must cover in order to provide pupils working towards the levels in question with the necessary support. The ranges do not constrain the level of attainment that may be recorded for an individual pupil at the end of a key stage, which in exceptional circumstances could be outside the expected range.

## THE STRUCTURE OF ATTAINMENT TARGETS

The view of language development expressed above led us to propose the structure of profile components and attainment targets described in the following chapters. The choice of the modes of language as the basis allows objectives to be set in activities which are recognisable to teacher, pupil and parent, and for differences in the pace and sequences of development in each mode to be registered, while acknowledging the close connections that nevertheless exist between them. It also enables important constituents of English, such as literature, drama and knowledge about language, to be treated as they naturally arise in particular modes, rather than being arbitrarily consigned to some self-contained category.

We deliberately chose a limited number of attainment targets within each profile component. A balance has to be struck between, on the one hand, an exhaustive catalogue of separately identifiable language achievements, and, on the other, an undifferentiated and possibly selective description of language in the round. The former allows for detailed and unambiguous statements, but risks 'atomising' language and making a burden of assessment; conversely, the latter may be easier to monitor and report, but insufficiently comprehensive and more difficult to interpret and act upon. We judged it right to opt for the second, simpler approach, in the interests of pupils, teachers, parents and the wider public. Ways of overcoming the difficulties are discussed below, where it is argued that our attainment targets together cover all that it is important to assess and report upon formally in English.

Although the targets are few in number, each one embraces several cognate aspects of language.

## THE SCOPE OF ASSESSMENT

Assessment methods must be ones in which all concerned can have confidence because they are as valid, reliable and clearly reported as possible. By valid I mean here that the assessment should actually measure what it is intended to measure; by reliable, that it should consistently give the same result for similar performances.

We recommended that these requirements should be fulfilled for English by observance of the following principles:

◇ assessment should be a continuous process which reinforces teaching and learning. It should be conducted with due economy and not as an addition, costly in both financial and human resources, tacked on at intervals;

◇ each pupil's performance against each attainment target during each educational stage should accordingly be covered by some form of structured assessment;

◇ since the assessment of language competence is dependent on the task and context (that is, a child may show different levels of performance in the same language area when undertaking tasks of different kinds or set in different contexts), the widest practicable range of types of task and setting should be used, including where appropriate the unfamiliar as well as the familiar;

◇ assessment should pay attention to the process as well as the product of the task: to the way in which children approach and sustain it, the elements in which they have particular difficulties or strengths, as well as the quality of the finished work;

◇ finally, because it is important that the assessment process be trusted by all those concerned (pupils, teachers, parents, employers, those in further and higher education and the public at large) the criteria should be clearly understood, widely accepted as reasonable, and capable of unambiguous interpretation in operation.

## INTERNAL AND EXTERNAL ASSESSMENT

We were asked to consider the balance between internal assessment by teachers, and externally prescribed and standardised assessment. We held that both have important parts to play in each profile component. Detailed advice is included in chapters 14 to 16.

The TGAT report proposed that external assessment should be in the form of standard assessment tasks (SATs) which could involve a package of different items stemming from everyday classroom activities, a variety of methods of teacher presentation and pupil response (oral, written, graphical, practical) and a degree of choice in the context and setting of each task, and be conducted over an extended period rather than confined to a short, timed exercise. All these features are important for valid and reliable language assessment. External assessment should sample all the attainment targets applicable at each stage, though not necessarily every strand within each target.

Internal assessment for National Curriculum purposes should be carried out as an integral part of day-to-day classroom activities. It should draw upon tasks and activities related to those used in the SATs. Differentiation by task should be used more extensively here than in SATs, although teachers should guard against persistent use of tasks making inappropriate demands based on wrongly pitched expectations of pupils' performance. While internal assessment should give teachers more scope to select activities and contexts to meet the current circumstances of the class or individual pupils, and to explore outcomes in greater depth, it should nevertheless be planned, structured, conducted and recorded so that it supports and informs National Curriculum requirements. It should also be moderated, generally by other teachers in the school. For these reasons teachers will need professional guidance and training in internal assessment for English, and we recommended that the DES and the School Examinations and Assessment Council (SEAC) should commission this.

Self-assessment by pupils themselves, even at the primary stage, has a part to play by encouraging a clear understanding of what is expected of them, motivation to reach it, a sense of pride in positive achievements, and a realistic appraisal of weaknesses that need to be tackled. It should be given due weight as part of the evidence towards the teachers' internal assessments.

## ASSESSMENT IN THE PRIMARY SCHOOL

TGAT recommended that each pupil should undertake not more than three SATs at age 7, covering at least the three core subjects and perhaps technology; and three or four SATs at age 11, supplemented where appropriate by more specific short tasks. A SAT could include topics relating to mathematics, science and language; and where attainment targets in these subjects have elements in common – for instance, in aspects of communication – they could be assessed by the same items. This should be done wherever practicable. However, we assumed that, at each key stage, the equivalent of about one SAT would be designed to sample all three English profile components. The proposals below related to that 'SAT-equivalent', whether in one single SAT or spread over several.

The SAT-equivalent of age 7 should be an extended task, consisting of a series of related sub-tasks sampling each of the individual attainment targets. A combination of modes of teacher presentation should be used, but pupils' responses should be mainly oral or practical except where the target requires some writing or graphical work by the pupil. The sub-tasks should reflect a range of types of process and of contexts, set in a project which is coherent as a whole and involves group as well as individual activity. Schools and teachers should have some choice of alternative contexts from a bank of SATs covering the same broad mixture of processes and making the same level of demand on pupils.

Similar principles should apply to the SAT at age 11, but it should incorporate a few separate short tasks as well as an overall extended task, and greater weight should be given to individual activity and to written pupil response.

In both cases the tasks should be designed to resemble, and build on, normal classroom activities. Differentiation should be mainly by outcome, not by giving different pupils different tasks pitched at their expected level of performance, though the latter may be appropriate to a small extent in the additional short tasks for pupils aged 11 at the extremes of the range. The tasks should all be capable of being administered, recorded and marked by the class teacher, occasionally with help where needed from another teacher in the school. They should not generally require the presence of an external assessor, although we assume that the combined outcome of internal and external assessment will be subject to some form of moderation.

## ASSESSMENT IN THE SECONDARY SCHOOL

As TGAT said: 'Assessment in the secondary phase must take account of emerging subject emphases at 11, and reflect a very largely subject-based organisation in the pre-14 stage and later up to 16 when it must articulate with GCSE and Records of Achievement (RoA).'[2] There may therefore be less scope for a pupil's knowledge and use of English to be assessed through other subjects.

TGAT did not make recommendations for the number of SATs at age 14. We suggested that, overall, the SAT (or SATs, depending on the precise arrangements) for pupils aged 14 should comprise an extended task, covering all attainment targets, with some separate short, timed tasks in addition. We recommended that in the SAT at age 14 greater weight than at age 11 should be given to individual activity and to written pupil response.

## ASSESSMENT AT AGE 16 – GCSE

In the supplementary guidance given to us by the Secretary of State, it was suggested that we assume that all pupils would take GCSE in English (or an equivalent examination). We therefore did not suggest any alternative assessment arrangements for pupils at age 16 not taking GCSE, and we assumed that the National Curriculum assessment arrangements for key stage 4 will, in their final form, be taken as the basis for a revision of the GCSE criteria.

The arrangements whereby GCSE is awarded on the basis of 100 per cent coursework in English have been much welcomed by teachers. However, we recognised also that some anxieties have arisen from these arrangements on account of the scope for outside assistance with coursework. We wished to preserve and build on the immense enthusiasm generated by the introduction of GCSE while introducing SATs which are fair to all pupils. We therefore suggested that assessment in English at age 16 should comprise coursework assessed by teachers, some coursework undertaken under controlled conditions (e.g. for a prescribed task, within a given time limit, with certain restrictions on access to reference materials), and SATs including end-of-course assessment and written examinations.

## DUAL CERTIFICATION

There has been concern that the introduction of GCSE has had the unintentional effect of squeezing English Literature, as a separate subject for examination, out of some schools. In response to this concern some examining groups have been developing syllabuses for double awards in English and English Literature, entailing the assessment of the same pieces of work against both the English and the English Literature criteria. To enable such syllabuses to be pioneered, the groups obtained from the Secretary of State a temporary dispensation from the English Literature national criterion 4.4.3, which specifies that: 'Although the same reading material may be used in courses leading to examinations in English and English Literature, the same pieces of work may not be submitted for assessment of Course Work in both examinations.'

The attainment targets and programmes of study overall reflect the balance between language and literature which we wish to see in the National Curriculum in English, to be undertaken by all pupils. We also recognised that there may be some pupils who would derive benefit from a wider study of literature than that embodied in our recommendations. This would be undertaken outside the National Curriculum, but, because of the pressures on the timetable, it would none the less be advantageous if some of the work undertaken to meet the National Curriculum requirements could be assessed against the additional literature criteria and so count towards the additional qualification. We were unable in the time available to us to formulate specific recommendations concerning such a course, but we hoped that SEAC would encourage the pioneering work of the GCSE examining groups on dual certification and that this will lead to proposals for a course which some pupils could take in addition to that provided to meet the National Curriculum requirements, but where the same pieces of work might be assessed against different criteria contributing towards a separate grade.

# RECORDING AND REPORTING OF PERFORMANCE

We offered the following explanations of our thinking about issues of recording, aggregating and reporting assessments, as guidance to SEAC and the developers of SATs. Our overall concern was that the curriculum intentions expressed in our attainment targets and programmes of study, and teaching practice in the classroom, should not be distorted by the procedures agreed for recording, aggregation and reporting. We strongly recommended that the consequences of the chosen procedures should be evaluated by means of a pilot study, simulation exercise or trialling before the first fully reported national assessments, and that they should be kept under review thereafter.

There are several points at which some aggregation of an individual pupil's assessment results may be required; for example, when reporting to his or her parents: first, in defining the overall level reached in an attainment target covering several strands; second, in combining the attainment targets within a profile component; and third, in summing the results of profile components for English as a whole. Aggregation procedures will also be required when publicly reporting results for groups of pupils – in a class, school, LEA or nationally.

## Assessment and reporting of strands within attainment targets

In deciding a pupil's level of achievement within any one attainment target, it is not valid or practicable to decide on the level of each individual strand, add those levels together, and produce an average. Such averaging can work only if there is the same number of strands at each level and if each strand is continuous from level 1 to level 10. Our attainment targets do not have the same number of strands at each level, nor are the strands continuous, because we were very keen that our presentation of the content, skills and processes of the English curriculum should reflect good practice as far as possible and not be distorted by assessment requirements. (Discontinuities in strands are described in the chapters on each profile component.)

Another problem with averaging is that it gives equal weight to each strand within a given level, and this was emphatically not our intention. Our view was that strands are essentially an organisational convenience for dealing with the subject matter in each attainment target – not a theoretical construct, nor a guide to the weight that material should be given in either teaching or assessment. Furthermore, because there are different numbers of strands at different levels, if averaging were applied the weighting of a given strand would vary arbitrarily from level to level, not because of its changing importance within the curriculum but merely by virtue of the number of other strands accompanying it.

Accordingly, a pupil's reported level of attainment within each attainment target should normally be the level at which he or she has achieved every strand. For example, a pupil who had achieved all the strands at level 2 in the reading target and who had progressed to level 3 in two of them would be reported as being at level 2 in reading, with the pupils and his or her parents being told that particularly good progress was being made in the two 'advanced' aspects. We set much store by full reporting: it is only fair to the pupil that good performance in particular strands should be noted and reported both to parents and to future employers etc.

Provided that the allocation of strands to levels is right (and only empirical experience can confirm this), a pupil should normally be able to reach roughly the same level of performance in each strand within a target, and our approach to the recording of attainment should work equitably. However, there must be some scope for flexibility to cope with the 'near-miss'. A near-miss at, say, level 5 in one strand of attainment, when a pupil has clearly achieved level 5 in all the other strands, should not result in the pupil being deemed to have reached level 4 overall. That would be too mechanistic – particularly given the scope for interpretation that inevitably exists in judging whether a pupil has reached a level. So we wished to see allowances made for the near-miss in one strand, and to rely on moderation to ensure that this flexibility works fairly for all pupils.

In exceptional cases, there may be a pupil who, in one particular strand, is at a level very much below his or her overall ability in that attainment target. For example, an excessively shy child might not be able to read aloud expressively and yet might be a highly competent reader in all other respects. In such a case, it would be a distortion of the assessment arrangements if the pupil were recorded as being level 2 overall in reading, reflecting level 2 performance in reading aloud, when in all other reading strands he or she was, say, at level 7. We strongly urged that this issue should be given serious attention and that the system of moderation (perhaps leading to 'endorsement' of a record of achievement) should be designed to deal sensibly and justly with such cases.

One implication of our holistic approach to assessment (in which competence is required in all the strands of an attainment target) is that the standard achieved in English may appear to be lower than that in other subjects. This is because there is a problem peculiar to English in trying to express the overall level of attainment reached in the subject in terms which are fair and convey meaning. The English profile components, attainment targets and programmes of study cover a very wide span of human activity including aesthetic, expressive, analytical and descriptive abilities as well as interpersonal skills, in ways which those for other, more content-based subjects will not. We stressed the high degree of overall achievement that is involved in reaching each level in our attainment targets – demanding equal proficiency in a range of skills and understanding.

Any such under-reporting may not matter too much provided that it is consistent for all schools, LEAs and nationally, and provided that the basis for aggregation is not changed over time. But the fact should be recognised in any statements about, for example, our national performance in English, and in comparison of 'before' and 'after' the introduction of the National Curriculum. If, in practice, there seems to be understatement of performance to a marked degree, then that may suggest that some strands of attainment need to be modified or the levels to which they are allocated changed.

Strands in each attainment target should be taught together since most are closely interwoven. This should be reflected in the assessment process. There is likely to be a single context in which attainment in all the strands is assessed and it would make no sense to try to assess each strand in a separate context. We firmly recommended against strand-specific assessment or testing: there should not be SATs or examinations designed to assess performance solely in any part of an attainment target rather than in the whole target. We did, however, expect that teachers and assessors should form a clear impression of a pupil's attainment within each strand rather than just seek an overall impression for the target as a whole. This is essential if reporting to parents is to bring out particular strengths or weaknesses in a pupil's performance.

## Aggregation of attainment targets in profile components

When a pupil's performance is being reported to his or her parents, particular strengths and weaknesses among strands should be highlighted. Schools may need guidance on appropriate ways of doing this. As a minimum national requirement the parents should be informed of the levels attained in individual attainment targets. For most other reporting purposes, the level of detail provided by the three profile components will suffice. We included in this assumption the reporting of pupils' attainment at the end of key stage 4 through GCSE. We believed that the information needs of further and higher education establishments and of employers for their recruiting exercises will be better met if GCSE results are presented in terms of the three profile components rather than aggregated into a single grade for English as a whole, as at present.

A method of weighting will be required in the case of the writing profile component which contains more than one attainment target. We recommended that the writing, spelling and handwriting targets should be weighted 70/20/10 respectively for key stages 1 and 2; and that the writing and presentation targets should be weighted 80/20 respectively for key stages 3 and 4. This reflected our view of the relative significance of each of these aspects, at each stage, for the purpose of summarising assessment results in writing as a whole. In particular, it takes account of the substantial importance of the skills of composition, especially in secondary schooling, and of the tendency to achieve the bulk of the progress in 'secretarial skills' during primary schooling. The specific weightings should not, however, be seen as measures of the amount of time and effort that should be devoted to teaching each aspect, which must depend upon pupils' needs.

## Aggregation of profile components for English overall

The unit 'score' which should be used as a basis for aggregating pupils' results to produce figures for English as a whole should be the level recorded for each pupil in each attainment target or profile component. Any attempt to take account of better performance in some strands within targets for these aggregations would be impracticable and would lead to distortion. But, like TGAT, we do not favour quoting a single average level for the whole group of pupils: it will almost always be more informative to show the spread of results among the group; for example, by a percentage distribution, level by level. Whenever statistics are produced for a class or school, they should be accompanied by a description of where the strengths and weaknesses lie in relation to particular attainment targets, so that those responsible for taking action for example, in management and in service training areas can best judge what steps are needed.

The reporting of assessment will need, especially in the early stages, to be accompanied by clear explanations, not only for the education service but also for parents and others, of what is meant by the targets and the levels awarded. But it is important to remember that reporting performance in the currency described above is only the beginning, not the end of the process. Schools should supplement this by more detailed information about the English curriculum followed, the way it is delivered, the different facets of language achievement which underlie the aggregate figures, and the next steps planned for pupils to build on that. If richness and variety of language development are to be encouraged, and excellence promoted and weaknesses tackled with the support of all concerned, schools should make such communication a priority.

# NOTES
1   TGAT, First Report, paragraph 4.
2   TGAT, First Report, paragraphs 1–58.

# 14

# Speaking and Listening

*Where children are given responsibility they are placed in situations where it becomes important for them to communicate – to discuss, to negotiate, to converse – with their fellows, with the staff, with other adults. And of necessity they are likely to develop oral skills. This basically is how oracy grows: it is to be taught by the creation of many and varied circumstances to which both speech and listening are the natural responses. (Andrew Wilkinson,* Spoken English, Educational Review, *1985)*

*We learnt that it is hard to build models to scale from a drawing as they are not very accurate in size. We learnt that working together was a lot easier than going solo; but arguing brought out the better ideas. (Project reported by children aged 10 to 11)*

The inclusion of speaking and listening as a separate profile component in our recommendations reflected the Working Group's conviction that they are of central importance to children's development. The value of talk in all subjects as a means of promoting pupils' understanding, and of evaluating their progress, is now widely accepted. For instance, the Cockcroft Report (1982) on the teaching of mathematics drew attention to the importance of learning through talk. This emphasis has been endorsed by the mathematics and science teachers' associations and by the National Association for the Teaching of English, as well as by cross-subject movements such as the Association for Primary Education. In *Better Schools* (1985) the government drew attention to the need to reconsider traditional teaching techniques in order to promote and encourage the development of oral skills. In a majority of primary and middle schools it was found that there was an over-concentration on practising skills in literacy and numeracy, that much work was too closely directed by the teacher and there was little opportunity for oral discussion (pp. 5–6).

In addition to its function as a crucial teaching and learning method, talk is also now widely recognised as promoting and embodying a range of skills and competence – both transactional and social – that are central to children's overall language development. In 1982 and

1983, the APU carried out surveys of standards in oracy among pupils of 11 and 15. The theoretical framework underlying the APU's oracy tests is echoed in the GCSE national criteria for assessing oral communication. For the first time in this country, for many pupils, the assessment of oracy has been made compulsory: by GCSE.

## OUR RATIONALE

Recent surveys have drawn attention to the importance of talking and listening both in obtaining employment and in performing well in it. The surveys[1] report the significant finding that in interviews employers attached importance to candidates' answers to open questions which invited them to express and develop ideas in a sustained way, and to their ability to engage in discussion and to exchange views. Conversely, they attached little value to questions to which there were simply short right or wrong answers. Employers also identified the ability to relate to the interviewer as a key factor. Howe,[2] reflecting on the results of his survey in Marks and Spencer, drew attention to the importance of employees being able to cope – in both work and other activities – with a variety of complex situations through talk. He emphasised the consequent need for schools to ensure that adequate opportunities were provided for improving accomplishments in speaking and listening.

Employment apart, there are very many other areas of adult life in which teenagers will need increasingly sophisticated competence in speaking and listening. Through such media as TV, radio and the cinema, for instance, they will see and hear an abundance of information which they will need to evaluate and use judiciously for their own purposes. As consumers, they will need to know how to conduct oral transactions effectively – how to seek information, how to negotiate, how to complain. As potential jurors or witnesses, voters or representatives of political or interest groups, they will need to know how to judge or present a spoken case, how to recognise emotive language and arguments that are specious or selective, and how to marshal facts with clarity and precision. As members of smaller groups within a larger community – a trade union or residents' association, for instance – they will need to be able to function collectively through discussion; for example, to represent or protect their interests. English departments in secondary schools should take some of the responsibility for preparing pupils for such purposes of spoken language in public life by providing firm foundations on which they will be able to build as adults with increasing maturity and experience. Moreover, as patrons or practitioners of the arts and as future adult learners in all spheres of life, pupils should be given every opportunity to become familiar with – and derive pleasure and understanding from – the widest possible range of oral presentations: from plays, films and broadcasting to debates and public lectures.

# SOCIAL AND TRANSACTIONAL LANGUAGE

The development of children's spoken language in the English curriculum is concerned with the relations between language, speaker and listener. Some talk (e.g. casual conversation) is predominantly listener-related: it is social or interpersonal in its functions, rather than aiming to convey particular information in a precise way. No particular outcome may be expected from such talk at all: it does not have a definable purpose, beyond maintaining social relations. Clarity and efficiency are, for example, not criteria by which we judge social talk, and the world would be a very unpleasant place if they were. But in some other types of spoken language, it is predominantly the context which matters: it is information-related or transactional in its functions, and characteristically has a definable purpose. Communication will have failed if the listener does not discover which platform the train leaves from or how to load the program into the computer.

These two orientations are not entirely separate: most speech involves some information and it is couched differently according to the audience. But in most circumstances, the focus will tend to be either more on the maintenance of social relations, or more on the conveying of information clearly, concisely and unambiguously.

Under normal circumstances, children's social talk will develop naturally, without teacher intervention. But not all children will automatically acquire all the forms of transactional spoken language which are necessary and highly valued in education and in society. Most children will need the skilled and active support of their teachers, in all subjects, in building their confidence and developing the transactional skills and language which are necessary both across the curriculum and in adult life. An adequate transactional competence should be a real achievement of lasting value.

# TALKING AND LISTENING SKILLS

The effectiveness of talking and listening is determined not only by the ability to use speech appropriately, but also by the ability to listen actively. The former includes being able to adjust ways of speaking – such as tone and vocabulary – according to audience, context and purpose; the latter involves skills of concentration and assimilation. The use and interpretation of silence can also be important.

The structure and patterns of spoken language are distinct from those of writing: it is rare, for example, for a speaker continuously to use complete sentences as we understand them in writing – particularly in a situation where interruption is both accepted and expected. Similarly, oral language differs significantly from written language in its complex interactive nature: non-verbal communication, such as body language, is also a part of the process.

## DIALECT

Teachers should never treat non-standard dialect as sub-standard language but should recognise the intimate links between dialect and identity and the damage to self-esteem and motivation which can be caused by indiscriminate 'correction' of dialect forms. All children should be supported in valuing their own dialects and in using them where they are appropriate to context and purpose, but they should also be able to use Standard English when it is necessary and helpful to do so in speaking as well as writing. We did not, however, see it as the school's place to enforce the accent known as Received Pronunciation (see chapter 3).

## DEVELOPMENT OF ORAL SKILLS

Development of oral skills will involve increased sensitivity to the nuances of language and presentation, and to the implications of context. Pupils should demonstrate their growing competence as both speakers and listeners by:

- ◇ developing increasing clarity and precision in describing experience and expressing opinions, and sensitivity in articulating personal feelings;
- ◇ formulating – and making appropriate responses to – increasingly complex instructions and questions;
- ◇ developing an increasing capacity to organise or sequence information and response;
- ◇ demonstrating an increasing ability to evaluate and to reflect;
- ◇ increasingly adjusting language and delivery to suit audience and purpose, and being able – as an audience with others – to understand, respond to and reflect on correspondingly wider modes of address;
- ◇ showing an increasing ability to function collaboratively – e.g. involving others in a discussion; listening to and giving weight to the opinions of others; perceiving the relevance of contributions; timing contributions; adjusting and adapting to feedback;
- ◇ showing an increasing ability to be explicit about how written and spoken language can support each other.

## THE ATTAINMENT TARGET

The range of communication purposes for the spoken word is extensive. It may be used, for example, to persuade; to explain; to instruct; to entertain; to narrate; to speculate; to argue a case; to report; to describe; to find out; to clarify or explore an issue; to solve a problem; to interpret; to summarise; to evaluate; to reflect; to announce; to criticise and to respond to criticism. The proposed attainment target is therefore deliberately broad and the associated programmes of study should enable children to develop confidence and competence as speakers and listeners in a wide variety of situations.

We proposed the following single attainment target for the speaking and listening profile component:

> *the development of pupils' understanding of the spoken word and the capacity to express themselves effectively in a variety of speaking and listening activities, matching style and response to audience and purpose.*

## STRANDS WITHIN LEVELS OF ATTAINMENT

In defining the statements of attainment we have, wherever possible, grouped speaking and listening skills into broad strands:

◇ the skills enabling pupils to put forward (and interpret) clear and properly supported statements of personal feeling, opinion or viewpoint;

◇ the skills, enabling pupils to give accurately – and to assimilate and act appropriately on – information, explanations and instructions;

◇ the skills enabling pupils to communicate imaginatively and effectively as performers or readers;

◇ the skills enabling pupils to function collaboratively and to participate positively and with understanding in general discussion;

◇ the skills enabling pupils to develop and express an awareness of varieties of spoken language and of the relationship between spoken and written language.

The separation of skills into these groupings is simply an organisational device. The broad lines of development which are proposed in our descriptions of the ten levels under this attainment target will require flexible interpretation since language development is not linear but recursive, with pupils returning repeatedly to the same aspects of competence and reinforcing their skills on each occasion. In addition, what is difficult will vary for different individuals and according to circumstances: some topics will themselves vary in difficulty; some people will perceive the difficulty of the same task very differently; and circumstances may make an otherwise easy task seem very hard.

Beyond level 6 there are no statements of attainment which relate to dramatic performance; it is at level 7 and beyond that the claims of drama as a separate subject become specific. We also believed that it would be inappropriate for performance in drama at those levels to detract from a higher level of performance for spoken English as a whole.

# PROGRAMMES OF STUDY

The range of activities recommended for programmes of study is drawn up in general terms and, for the most part, gathered in clusters to enable schools to match their particular planned activities to our specifications. In suggesting programmes according to level we have taken account of a range of dimensions of difficulty. Topics will vary in difficulty in a variety of ways according especially to their familiarity, their controversial or uncontroversial character, in degrees of abstraction and complexity and much else. Similarly, the challenges of talking and listening may increase as one's audience ranges outwards from intimates to strangers and upwards in group size. What we may expect, know or not know about our audience can present other dimensions of difficulty and challenge. This is a condensed account of the factors which complicate the business of speaking and listening – readers will easily add for themselves their own accounts of the personal and emotional features which make for vulnerability or call for sensitivity.

In drawing up the list of activities below we aimed to recommend programmes of study that reinforce the links between English and drama, and between English and media education, which we sought to emphasise throughout this Report:

◇ we see role-play as a valuable means of broadening pupils' mental and emotional horizons and of developing social and personal confidence: it provides an ideal medium for much of the exploratory and/or performance-based elements of programmes of study;

◇ media work has a particular significance, leading naturally to discussion of how spoken language and visual accompaniment are interpreted; this leads to an understanding of the processes of selection, omission and editing which take place when any programme is prepared. For example, in advertising can pupils distinguish the aesthetic from the transactional? In news broadcasts, panel discussions or documentaries can they distinguish how fair or balanced are the points of view presented?

# ASSESSMENT

The list of activities suggested in the programmes of study, combined with the variety of suggested groupings, is wide in its implications. Assessment in individual areas through SATs will necessarily be a sampling process. The SATs should nevertheless include as much speaking and listening, in a wide a range of representative activities, as is practicable. But the bulk of assessment in speaking and listening should be conducted locally and recorded by teachers in a common format.

We listed five important criteria which informed our recommendations and which we expected those constructing internal and external assessment arrangements to take into full account. These criteria were:

◇ the assessment of speaking and listening should, where possible, be informal, continuous and incidental, applied to tasks carried out for curricular purposes;

◇ the tape recording of individual children's oral performance for assessment purposes might not be part of normal classroom activity and thus not in line with TGAT recommendations. Given the technical and administrative problems that such a method would present in many classrooms and the artificiality which would be introduced, we recommend that tape recordings (audio or video) should not be used to moderate the assessment of oral performance for SATs (though it may, of course, be used by teachers or pupils, as part of their planned activities). We were aware of the implications of this recommendation regarding the moderation of assessment, but urged that alternative means of establishing common standards in oracy should be explored (in line with current developments in GCSE oral assessment);

◇ although there are some widespread non-reciprocal speaking and listening situations (such as radio, television, public address systems and lectures), the processes of listening and speaking are primarily reciprocal and integrated. The ability of a listener to respond appropriately to instructions is heavily dependent on the ability of the instructor to speak plainly. Tests of listening which by their nature place all responsibility for comprehension upon the listening should therefore be avoided;

◇ oral assessment methods should both reflect and promote the variety of classroom activities recommended in the Report;

◇ particular attention should be paid, by task-setters, teachers and moderators alike, to the danger that oral assessment might be influenced by cultural or social bias. There are differences in the verbal and non-verbal behaviour of members of different social groups, whether defined by ethnicity, gender or social class; and consequently assessors' own expectations may vary.

# ENDNOTE

We stressed that what we suggested in this chapter treads some new ground. It will undoubtedly need further refinement and modification in the light of consultations and of experience. We recommended that teachers should be given training in the assessment of speaking and listening and in moderation methods. We also recommended that there should be a central bank of specially compiled examples for training in the moderation process.

## NOTES

1   P. Jones, *Lip Service* (OUP 1986); A. Howe, *Oracy in the Work Place* (Wiltshire Oracy Project 1983); P. D'Arcy, *Language in Operation in Industry* (Wiltshire County Council 1983).
2   Howe, *Oracy in the Work Place*.

# 15

# *Reading*

*Learning to read is a satisfying activity. What encourages children to read and thus to learn to read is not some 'intrinsic reward' like praise or high marks or a special treat, but being able to read. Watch children engrossed in a book from which they are learning about reading, and there will be no need to ask where the fundamental satisfaction lies. (Frank Smith, Reading, 1978)*

Our proposals for attainments in reading covered three related forms of development:

◇ the development of the ability to read, understand and respond to all types of writing;
◇ the development of reading and information-retrieval strategies for the purpose of study;
◇ the development of knowledge about language.

## OUR RATIONALE

Reading is much more than the decoding of black marks upon a page: it is a quest for meaning and one which requires the reader to be an active participant. It is a prerequisite of successful teaching of reading, especially in the early stages, that whenever techniques are taught, or books are chosen for children's use, meaning should always be in the foreground.

Reading takes pupils beyond first-hand experience: it enables them to project themselves into unfamiliar environments, times and cultures, to gain sympathetic understanding of other ways of life and to experience joy and sadness vicariously. Much of this imaginative experience stems from literature whose quality influences the depth and range of the pupil's imaginative experience. In addition, literature provides examples of different kinds of language use and may be used as a stimulus for a variety of learning activities.

Pupils can be helped to develop emotionally, aesthetically and intellectually by means of the pleasurable activity of reading. The pleasure principle should motivate the programmes of study, and always be given high priority. There is a danger, particularly in the final years of compulsory schooling, that little time is given to promoting reading for fun. Too much concentration on set texts for assessment purposes can turn pupils against reading.

The requirement to make time for independent reading, not least as a source of pleasure, remains crucial, whatever the total curriculum demands. It should be seen as a definite part of a school's total reading programme in English: it is not an interruption of it. Indeed, if necessary, it can be integrated into other classroom activities. Independent reading need not be solitary, but it can include reading silently a book selected by personal preference. Such reading in the classroom may still be the only occasion when some pupils experience this activity: in which case, they may well value it very highly indeed.

There should be opportunities for individual and group reading activities, which might lead to 'performance readings' of texts of different genres, especially drama and poetry. Teachers should continue the practice of reading aloud in class; there is plenty of evidence that this simple activity can interest and enthuse. It is a valuable means of conveying the pleasure of reading, and as valid at secondary as at primary level. The widespread enjoyment derived from hearing stories well read is clearly apparent in the continuing popularity of programmes devoted to this on radio and television.

Reading is also one of the means by which we interact with the society in which we live. The transactional uses of print can differ sharply in style and form from the various genres of imaginative writing and may, indeed, vary extensively themselves according to type and purpose. These variations can include the use of signs and diagrams to replace, or partly replace, written text. Pupils need to be able to respond to such forms, and schools have an obligation to help them to read everything from labels and slogans to the subject textbooks of the secondary school curriculum.

# READING IN THE PRIMARY SCHOOL

We hoped parents would share books with their children from their earliest days, read aloud to them, and talk about the stories they have enjoyed together. Many parents will also have shown by their own reading of newspapers, periodicals, lists, calendars, instructions and leaflets and by their sending and receiving of letters and cards that reading plays an important role in their daily lives. Many pre-school children will have played spontaneous games in which the pretended reading (and writing) of stories, lists, letters and so on shows their own recognition of the pleasurable and purposeful nature of reading. Reading is best taught in the classroom when teachers build on this basis.

A prime objective of the teaching of reading must be the development of the pupil's independence as a reader. But 'there is no one method, medium, approach, device, or philosophy that holds the key to the process of learning to read . . . Simple endorsements of one or another nostrum are of no service to the teaching of reading.'[1] In their quest for meaning, children need to be helped to become confident and resourceful in the use of a variety of reading cues. They need to be able to recognise on sight a large proportion of the words they encounter and to be able to predict meaning on the basis of phonic, idiomatic and grammatical regularities and of what makes sense in context; children should be encouraged to make informed guesses. Teachers should recognise that reading is a complex but unitary process and not a set of discrete skills which can be taught separately in turn and, ultimately, bolted together.

The environment provided by the school should promote the reading development of all pupils. Examples of purposeful and pleasurable uses of print should be displayed in classrooms, foyers and school libraries. Well-chosen picture books, poetry collections, folk tales, stories, novels, reference books and non-fiction should be available for use in all primary classrooms. Well-presented notices, labels and children's own work should also be displayed to stress the communicative character of the written word.

As independence is strengthened, pupils should be encouraged to read more difficult texts and to look not only at what is said, but at how meaning is expressed and how effects are achieved in writing. Progress will be shown by increased reading fluency; an increase in the range of types of texts which the pupil can tackle without frustration; an increase in the range of approaches which readers can apply to particular texts according to their own purposes and those of the texts – skimming, scanning, close reading and so on. On these points, teachers need clear and agreed guidelines. They also need well-informed assessment procedures for recording pupils' progress; the support of well-chosen and well-supplied book stocks in classrooms, in school libraries and from local authority school library services.

## READING IN THE SECONDARY SCHOOL

In the secondary school, pupils should continue to read, understand and respond perceptively to an increasingly wide range of texts. Pupils learn to read, in the deepest sense of that word, by reading widely and often. It remains very important at secondary level that reading should also be encouraged outside the classroom, at home, in libraries at school or in the locality. This will help pupils to develop a personal love of reading which will continue after compulsory schooling. We have already stressed the importance of silent reading in the classroom. In addition, reading programmes should certainly include shared experiences, whether in small groups, or within a whole class. The shared fun, or criticism, of a text can bring its own satisfaction.

At secondary school, pupils should be increasingly encouraged to think critically about the texts they encounter, as a means of enlarging their understanding of the worlds of others, and in this way to examine and develop their own responses. They should also analyse, through a variety of approaches, the form and style of a writer as the method of conveying meaning. Learning to read involves recognising that writing is made: poets were originally called 'makers', craftsmen and women. Pupils should be encouraged to question the intentions behind a text, the reasons for choice of vocabulary, image or genre, and to become increasingly aware of the richness and complexity of literature. They should be aware of the importance of refining and substantiating their opinions by the use of precise textual reference.

In chapter 6 I say that literature plays an important role in improving abilities in speaking and listening, and in writing, as well as in reading. The Working Group particularly urged that children should be encouraged to write fiction, poetry, plays, diaries, book reviews and so on, in response to the literature they have enjoyed and have shared and discussed with their teacher and classmates. This applies just as much at secondary as at primary level.

Poetry needs to be a central part of the reading programmes throughout the secondary sector, and this assumption needs reinforcing especially at 14 to 16. Evidence suggests that some teachers are least happy about teaching poetry to this age group, in comparison with the other main literary genres. Clearly, pupils will sense a teacher's unease in presenting poetry to them, and are then likely to respond negatively. It is crucial that teachers' attitudes to poetry communicate enthusiasm for it. In chapter 6 I describe ways of bringing literature to life for pupils of all abilities. I hope that these methods will help teachers themselves to enjoy poetry and to share their pleasure with their pupils.

## THE ATTAINMENT TARGET

We proposed the following single attainment target for the reading profile component:

> the development of the ability to read, understand and respond to all types of writing, as well as the development of information-retrieval strategies for the purposes of study.

## STRANDS WITHIN LEVELS OF ATTAINMENT

At level 3 there are statements of attainment that refer to the ability to read silently with sustained concentration, and to listen attentively to stories read aloud. These strands do not continue through the levels because it is not possible to specify further measurable stages of development in these abilities, and it would be cumbersome to repeat them unchanged throughout the remaining seven levels. Nevertheless, it is clearly important that pupils should have opportunities both to read silently and to listen to well-written books read aloud throughout their school years.

Strand (i) at levels 3 and 4 refers to the ability to read aloud fluently and expressively. Again, this strand is not continued into the higher levels because further development of this ability would move into areas such as acting and public speaking, which are not appropriately assessed within a reading component.

From level 5, the statements of attainment are presented in five strands: the range of literature read, responses to literature, understanding and interpreting non-literary and media texts, study skills and information-retrieval strategies, and knowledge about language.

From level 5, strand (i) in the statements of attainment describes in broad terms the kinds of literature that pupils will read at successive levels. By level 8, the reading material is as demanding as it can be. Therefore, levels 8, 9 and 10 are identical since there can be no differentiation in the material itself. The same argument applies to strand (iv) (from level 5 onwards), which deals with study skills and information-retrieval strategies, which is repeated from levels 8 to 10.

# ASSESSMENT
## General

Assessment should be both internal and external, with suitable moderation arrangements. Internal assessment should be continuous, conducted through a variety of methods and contexts, and based on structured observation by the teacher. External assessment, in the form of SATs, should:

◇ generally be conducted by the pupils' own teachers;
◇ observe the principle of fitness for purpose;
◇ be intrinsically rewarding and enjoyable for pupils and accord with good classroom practice.

## Assessment in primary school

For internal assessment, a common national format for record-keeping should be devised and employed. We recommended that SEAC, in consultation with NCC and Curriculum Council for Wales, develop an assessment format and handbook and that the approach exemplified by the 'Primary Language Record' (1988: Centre for Language in Primary Education) be adopted as a starting point. What is devised should not make excessive demands upon time or resources. The continuous assessment element should commence when the child starts school, and continue throughout the primary phase.

Within this continuous assessment, the teacher's structured observation should have regard to all the strands in the attainment target and should look for: children's growing confidence and independence as readers; the ways they read aloud; the reading and information-retrieval strategies they employ; their responses to reading; and the range and difficulty of the texts they are able to handle and comprehend. The record of the continuous assessment should cover:

what the child has read; the child's reading strategies and approaches when handling a familiar text; levels of comprehension; retrieval of information; and reading tastes and preferences.

External assessment through the SAT should cover reading comprehension. There are many types of reading test currently used in primary schools: most of them, however, are norm-referenced rather than criterion-referenced, and so do not relate directly to our levels of attainment. In addition, many existing tests use decontextualised approaches which do not adequately assess children's understanding of meaning. It will be necessary to develop new methods of testing reading comprehension which build on the experience of the best of the existing tests and of the APU's work, but which should also meet the following criteria.

First, they should be designed to arise naturally out of good primary practice. The choice of texts should draw on reading material of the kind children will encounter in schools through the programmes of study we have recommended. If extracts rather than complete texts are used, they should be free-standing and coherent in structure and content. The test question should be what experienced teachers would be likely to ask, taking account of the character of the reading material, its context and the purposes for which it would normally be encountered. The tests should be practicable to administer in the classroom context, and to mark and moderate. The marking should give credit for children's grasp of meaning and allow 'positive' errors to be distinguished from 'negative'. The results should be capable of being used formatively and to indicate any particular need for support for the child, or for more specific diagnostic assessment. For more able readers, the test results may point to the need for further enrichment.

At age 7, the pupil's response to the SAT might be mainly but not exclusively oral. At age 11, the SAT should be of greater length and complexity, and the pupil's response might be mainly but not exclusively written.

## Assessment in secondary school

Internal assessment of pupils in key stages 3 and 4 should be continuous and record their progress across all aspects of the attainment target. The record should build upon those which have been maintained for pupils in key stages 1 and 2. The principles we advocate for record-keeping at the primary phase are also applicable for the record for pupils in key stages 3 and 4. We recommended that SEAC be invited to design and pilot national guidelines and a format for assessing and recording pupils' reading attainments, which can be readily administered and maintained by teachers.

For external assessment, we recommended that the SAT and SATs at key stages 3 and 4 should sample all the strands. They should cover in particular the pupils' response to literature, and their competence in using information and reference materials, and should meet the general criteria described above. At the end of key stage 3 the pupils' response should be mainly in written form but may include some oral work. At the end of key stage 4 the response should be in written form only. As with external assessment in the primary phase, we believe that new methods of testing pupils' reading skills may need to be devised, building on the best of GCSE practice.

## NOTE
1   Bullock Report, paragraph 6.1.

# 16

# *Writing*

*The evidence gathered from successive surveys of pupils'
attitudes to reading and writing suggests that the language
experience of many pupils is concentrated in a relatively
narrow range of types of writing. (APU, Pupils' Attitudes to
Writing, 1987)*

## OUR RATIONALE

The term 'writing' is ambiguous: in the first place, it can refer either to
the process of writing or to the written product. The term is also
ambiguous between the composing aspects of writing and the secretarial aspects, such as good handwriting and spelling. For example, it is
possible now for word processors with spelling checkers to take over
some of the proof-reading aspects of writing and to produce impeccable
print-out.

Attainment targets and programmes of study must therefore
cover both these aspects of writing, here called for convenience 'composing' and 'secretarial'. Our main principle was that the secretarial
aspect should not be allowed to predominate in the assessment while
the more complex aspects of composition are ignored. It is evident that
a child may be a poor speller, but write well-structured and interesting
stories, or be a good speller, but write badly structured and boring
stories.

## FUNCTIONS OF WRITTEN LANGUAGE

Written language serves many purposes both for individuals and for
society as a whole, and is not limited to the communication of information. For the individual author, writing can have cognitive functions in
clarifying and supporting thought. (Spoken language also allows
thoughts to be formulated in one's own words, but written language has
the added advantage of making a detached reflection on them possible.)
Such writing is essentially private. At the level of whole societies,
written language serves the functions of record-keeping and of storing
both information and literary works. It therefore supports and trans-
mits the culture. Such writing is essentially public and intended for an
audience.

These points are relevant both to the programmes of study and to
assessment, since they show that linguistic forms cannot be corrected or
assessed independently of their purpose. The nature of the assessment
should be geared to the purpose of the writing. For example, it is

perfectly appropriate to demand neatness, correct spelling, and features of Standard English in work which has a public purpose. But this may be less appropriate for work with essentially private purposes. The different functions of written language are an important topic for knowledge about language and part of an understanding of how society works.

## THE RELATIONS BETWEEN SPOKEN AND WRITTEN LANGUAGE

There is no simple transition from spoken to written language. In the development of their writing, children have to move from casual to formal language, from spontaneous to planned language; and from a known to an unknown audience. Further, some children have to add the forms of Standard English to their own non-standard forms, and others have to move from their mother tongue to English. In each case, the language competence acquired is additive: it does not replace earlier competences. Children also have to acquire forms of written language which are rarely or never used in spoken English, since written language is not just spoken language written down. Children cannot be expected to learn everything at once. A measure of tolerance of errors in different language tasks is essential.

Spoken and written language are closely related both developmentally and theoretically. Spoken language tends to be informal, spontaneous and interactive with the speakers face-to-face, whereas written language tends to be formal, edited and non-interactive, with writer and reader separated. But these are only the most typical configurations. All combinations are possible. For example, a letter to a friend may be informal; a telephone conversation is not face-to-face; interactive written communication is possible via computer terminals; a speech may be a carefully edited and rehearsed monologue; etc. Even so, the various features characteristically associated with casual conversation and with formal writing provide a way of organising programmes of study. The basic principle is so to organise teaching that children have experience of producing written language across these various forms. Language experiences which will ensure this are set out in the programmes of study.

## ASSUMPTIONS

When children first come to school they have a large body of language experience to draw on. This will differ according to the richness of the environment provided by the home and the wider community, but all children live and grow up in a print-rich world full of writing and people who write.

Just as many young children come to school believing that they can read, so they will come willing to try to be writers. The very youngest children, given the opportunity to use what they know, are able to demonstrate considerable knowledge of the forms and purposes of writing. This may at first be simple 'draw writing', but as they develop and learn more about how written language works, their writing comes increasingly close to standard adult systems. It is normal for their early attempts to consist of strings of letters, with words represented by the initial letter or by clusters of consonants. Children's early invented spellings often demonstrate logical consistency; this grasp of regularity should be recognised as an initial achievement and children should be helped to be confident in attempting to spell words for themselves without undue dependence on the teacher.

In early writing we see errors of letter formation, spelling and composition occurring as children make hypotheses about the rules that govern the writing system. Teachers provide the greatest encouragement for children to communicate in writing when they respond more to the content of what is written than to such errors, and when they share a child's writing with other children.

Through increasing encounters with a range of examples children make sense of literary experiences and it is the responsibility of the teacher to provide and foster that range in the classroom. Teachers will have diverse roles to play in the development of young writers: they will be observers, facilitators, modellers, readers and supporters. Through these roles the teacher intervenes in the child's learning, most often by a careful structuring of the contexts for writing.

During the early years of the secondary school, and as they grow into adolescence, pupils will increasingly be able to take a more objective view and develop greater understanding of the writing process. In so doing they will be building on their earlier writing experiences, which should have given them a positive view of themselves as writers who are capable of making and receiving meanings using a variety of forms depending on audience and purpose.

The programmes of study should, above all, enable pupils to exercise more conscious and critical control over the writing process. It is possible to identify a number of strands which should feature in their development as writers during these years. These are to do with an increasing ability to:

  ◇ write in different forms for different purposes and audiences;
  ◇ write coherently about a wide range of topics, issues, ideas, incidents, etc.; organising different kinds of text in ways which help the reader;
  ◇ craft writing which is significantly different from speech, showing a developing control of grammatical structure and of a differentiated vocabulary; and write in a style which is appropriate for the purpose, audience and subject matter;

◇ know when and how to plan, draft, redraft, revise and proof-read their work;

◇ understand the nature and functions of written language.

It is important that teachers should help pupils in this process by recognising the interrelatedness of writing, reading and speaking and listening. I have already stressed the need for younger pupils to have increasing encounters with a range of examples through which they make sense of literary experiences, and this should continue into the secondary stages. By careful planning of schemes of work to integrate programmes of study for speaking and listening, reading and writing, teachers should be able to foster the writing development of their pupils, helping them to develop an ear for language through reading or listening to works in a wide variety of styles written by really fine authors. Both literary and non-literary writing will often develop from the interaction between the pupils' own insights and what they have read (or heard read) in the classroom.

An essential aspect of development in the secondary stages is that pupils should increasingly make their own decisions about their writing – what it is about, what form it should take and to whom it is addressed. The written essay – usually 400–500 words long – has dominated the English language and literature curriculum for many years because it has been seen as the main vehicle for the transmission of knowledge in written examinations. The advent of GCSE and the more widespread development of continuous assessment of coursework in all English examination syllabuses have provided opportunities for pupils in secondary schools to use writing for a much wider range of purposes and audiences. This is a development to be welcomed and encouraged.

All pupils should be expected to keep a file containing work in progress, as well as completed pieces, which may need to be selected and filed separately for the purposes of moderation and final assessment. It is most important that teacher assessment should take account of the way pupils tackle writing tasks – that is, it should be sensitive to the writing process as well as to the finished product. Consequently, pupils should keep in their files the necessary range and variety of types of writing, including where appropriate any rough notes, plans or early drafts. They should play an active part in assessing their own progress through discussion with those who read their writing – their peers, teachers or other adults.

Much writing in English will be attempted by pupils to record their thoughts on topics of personal or public importance. Through discussion or role-play, teachers should seek to provide frequent oppor-tunities for this type of writing to occur, and should respond to the meanings that their pupils strive to convey.

Pupils should know that their writing need not always be formal or follow literary models; it can also effectively capture and record first thoughts and immediate responses and can be used for note-making, collecting and shaping information etc. Equally, however, it should be recognised that some writing is about communicating with the outside world and having a say in that world. In the Kingman Report we wrote:

> *People need expertise in language to be able to participate effectively in a democracy. There is no point in having access to information that you cannot understand, or having the opportunity to propose policies which you cannot formulate. People receive information and misinformation in varying proportions from, among others, family and friends, work mates, advertisers, journalists, priests, politicians and pressure groups. A democratic society needs people who have the linguistic abilities which will enable them to discuss, evaluate and make sense of what they are told, as well as to take effective action on the basis of their understanding. The working of a democracy depends on the discriminating use of language on the part of all its people. Otherwise there can be no genuine participation, but only the imposition of the ideas of those who are linguistically capable. As individuals, as well as members of constituencies, people need the resources of language both to defend their rights and to fulfil their obligations. (chapter 2, paragraph 2)*

Teachers should both create and respond to opportunities to focus on aspects of knowledge about written language and about some of the differences between speech and writing.

The full development of both reading and writing in the secondary years requires a broad definition of text to encompass both literary and non-literary forms. Pupils should continue to develop in their dual roles as makers of meanings in their own texts and as receivers and makers of meaning in the texts of others.

## THE ATTAINMENT TARGETS

We proposed the following attainment targets:

> *attainment target 3: a growing ability to construct and convey meaning in written language matching style to audience and purpose;*
>
> *attainment target 4: spelling (levels 1 to 4 only);*
>
> *attainment target 5: handwriting (levels 1 to 4 only);*
>
> *attainment target 4/5: presentation (levels 5 to 7).*

# STRANDS WITHIN LEVELS OF ATTAINMENT

If proposals for assessment are to have coherence, they must be based on a theory of difficulty. Bearing in mind some caveats below, it is possible to predict the relative difficulty of a writing task (and of a language task more generally). Other things being equal, a writing task is easier if the organisation is chronological; if the subject matter is drawn from personal experience; if the subject matter is concrete rather than abstract; and if the audience is known to the writer. The first distinction is usually clear-cut: the organisation is either chronological or not. (Texts which are typically chronological are narratives and reports; texts which are typically non-chronological are descriptions and arguments for a point of view.) The other distinctions are relative rather than absolute; for example, the subject matter may be more or less abstract, the audience may be very well known or less well known.

As I have already pointed out, children do not learn particular features of written language once and for all at a particular stage. Development is recursive. This means that writing development must be defined in broad terms and cannot be measured solely by one-off tests at particular ages. Language competence is dependent on the task: children will show different ability on tasks of different kinds. Therefore only a relatively broad range of tasks can hope to assess children's performance. The general line of development extends from emergent writing, through the early stages of composition, towards growing fluency and control and finally to full independence. We share the view of the National Writing Project that 'To try to put ages against these expectations produces great problems.' However, bearing these caveats in mind, it is still reasonable to expect children to have made demonstrable progress along the developmental path when they reach key stages in the education system.

The attainment targets proposed in this chapter fall into two main categories. One covers the composing aspects and concerns language meaning, use and structure: the organisation, form and patterns of writing. The other is secretarial, as defined above, and concerns the pupil's competence in spelling and handwriting. The reason for separating these two aspects in the attainment targets is that they are independent abilities: people with good spelling and neat handwriting are not necessarily good writers, and vice versa. Attainment targets form the basis of assessment. For assessment purposes it is clearly important that independent abilities should not be grouped under the same target. For example, if both composing and secretarial abilities were included in one global writing attainment target, a pupil who had achieved level 6 in the composing aspect but only level 3 in the secretarial aspect would have to be recorded as being at level 3 in writing. Establishing separate attainment targets, however, makes it possible to record separately a pupil's performance in different aspects of the writing task. This separation should not be interpreted as giving special standing to the secretarial aspect. The composing aspect is obviously by far the more important and this is reflected in the recommended weighting.

In the primary school, children have a great deal to learn about both spelling and handwriting. Some will be noticeably better at one than the other. For this reason, we recommended that there should be two separate targets, one for spelling and the other for handwriting, covering ages 5 to 11 (levels 1 to 4). By the time they reach the secondary school, the majority of children will have developed their own style of handwriting. To extend statements of attainment for handwriting beyond level 4 would entail entering the field of calligraphy. Therefore, we did not recommend that there should be a handwriting attainment target after level 4. Nevertheless, fluent and legible handwriting continues to be important, so the one secretarial attainment target that we propose from level 5 onwards is called presentation and includes both spelling and handwriting.

One aspect of development as a writer is the growing ability to handle successfully different forms such as stories, poems, accounts, reports, instructions, essays, etc. In order to learn the conventional ways in which subject matter is organised and presented in these different forms, it is necessary for children to have plenty of opportunities to read or hear read good examples of a range of different types of texts. Young children hear stories either told or read from a very early age and, as soon as they have the skill, they read them themselves. In this way, they internalise the elements of story structure – the opening, setting, characters, events and resolution. Similarly, they come to realise that, in satisfying, well-structured stories, things that are lost will be found, problems will be solved, mysteries will be explained, and so on. It is partly because of this early extensive experience of stories that so much writing in primary schools is in story form. In responding to children's writing, teachers are well able to distinguish between an embryonic attempt at a story and a more developed example; indeed, there is substantial research available on the stages of story-writing through which young writers progress. So, because children know and use the story form and because it is possible to discern a sequence of development, we specified various aspects of story structure in the statements of attainment from level 2 to level 4. From the beginning, though, children should be learning to write in other forms and for other purposes. In the early stages we distinguished between 'other chronological writing' and 'non-chronological writing'. We have not continued the story strand in the statements of attainment beyond level 4, although many pupils will continue to write stories of increasing complexity throughout the secondary school, because by then it will be just one of the many types of writing that pupils might undertake.

Throughout the school years, all children should have ample

opportunities to write poetry, either singly or in groups; this is made explicit in the programmes of study. However, we did not include a poetry strand in the statements of attainment because we did not feel that any pupil should be required to write a poem in order to achieve a particular level of attainment.

An important part of the composing process is the choice of appropriate and lively vocabulary. Nevertheless, we have not included vocabulary in our statements of attainment until level 7. This is partly because vocabulary is the most individualistic part of a person's knowledge of language, and continues to develop throughout life, although its growth is clearly fastest in the early years. It is also because the choice of vocabulary is determined by the subject matter. It can be assessed only by its appropriateness, but this depends entirely on what the pupil is writing about and for what purpose (and so has a cross-curricular dimension). The main line of development is that vocabulary becomes increasingly differentiated according to the purpose of the writing (e.g. whether it is everyday or technical) and to its style (e.g. formal or informal). There is also growing differentiation between colloquial and literary vocabulary. This aspect of writing development is one in which it is relatively easy to specify the direction of develop-ment, and achievements at higher levels, but where the precise specifica-tion of intermediate levels is much more difficult. It makes little sense, for example, to require that children have a command of formal vocab-ulary before they are competent in technical vocabulary or vice versa.

The best writing is vigorous, committed, honest and interesting. We did not include these qualities in our statements of attainment because they cannot be mapped on to levels. Even so, all good class-room practice will be geared to encouraging and fostering these vital qualities. In their revisions the NCC tried to include these qualities, but everyone agrees this is very difficult.

Development in attainment target 3 is marked by:

◇ increasing control over the structure and organisation of different types of text;
◇ a growing ability to handle complex or demanding subject matter;
◇ a widening range of syntactic structures and an expanding vocabulary, as the pupil begins to use language that is charac-teristic of writing rather than speech and to strive for a style that is appropriate to the subject matter and the readership;
◇ a growing capacity to write independently and at length;
◇ an increasing proficiency in re-reading and revising or redraft-ing the text, taking into account the needs of the audience;
◇ a developing ability to reflect on and talk about the writing process.

Punctuation is included in this attainment target because it helps the reader to identify the units of structure and meaning that the writer has constructed.

With regard to spelling, the aim should be that by the end of compulsory schooling pupils should be able to spell confidently most of the words that they are likely to need to use frequently in their writing; to recognise those aspects of English spelling that are systematic; to make a sensible attempt to spell words that they have not seen before; to check their work for misspellings and to use a dictionary appropriately. The aim cannot be the correct unaided spelling of any English word – there are too many words in English that can catch out even the best speller. For this reason, the presentation attainment target stops at level 7 (the level that should be achieved by the average 16 year old) because there is no way of extending it to level 10, other than by specifying lists of increasingly irregular and unusual words – which would be absurd.

# ASSESSMENT
## General

The attainment targets suggested above should be assessed through a variety of writing, using a combination of internal and external assessment. Those aspects of the targets which relate to the writing process, as distinct from the product, should be covered by mainly internal assessment – for example, probing pupils' ability to reflect upon and discuss the organisation of their own writing. For these purposes teachers will need to keep samples of children's writing in order to monitor its range and development over the course of a key stage; and they will need systematic means of recording and appraising the ways in which pupils approach writing tasks, including talking about what they are doing and why. As part of the internal assessment process, some self-assessment should be involved, through children's discussing a piece of writing with the teacher or with their peers, and then redrafting it. The children could use a standard pro forma to assess their own performance against the relevant parts of the attainment targets. We therefore recommended the development by SEAC of a national format and guidelines for internal assessment of these aspects of writing, to parallel our similar recommendation in the case of reading.

Extended tasks in external assessment SATs may also, however, be capable of monitoring aspects of the writing process, as well as the product of composition and its physical presentation: we recommended that SEAC should commission development work with this in mind.

## Assessment in primary school

Assessment in the primary school should incorporate internal assessment as above from the outset. In addition, chapter 13 suggests an extended task for the SAT at age 7, sampling each of the individual attainment targets. Within this task, pupils should be asked for three contrasting pieces of writing; for example, a short narrative based on a personal experience, a poem, a list of some kind (e.g. for a recipe), or a factual account based on observation. All of the writing attainment targets should be assessed in the context of those pieces of work; spelling and handwriting should not be assessed through decontextualised tests or exercises.

At age 11, the same requirements should apply, but with the addition of two short, timed tasks, one perhaps consisting of a factual account or description and the other of a short, imaginative piece of prose.

## Assessment in secondary school

Internal assessment and recording in the secondary school should build on that of the primary school. More particularly, pupils should compile a folder of coursework containing writing of a range of types on a variety of topics for different and clearly specified audiences. In both key stages 3 and 4 they should have the opportunity to present an extended piece of work that has been planned, drafted, revised and polished over a period of time.

The SATs at ages 14 and 16 should provide pupils with a wide choice, but should require them to produce a number of contrasting pieces of writing within both long and short timed tasks and spanning the range from imaginative literary uses of language to the clear and orderly presentation of information and argument. As in the earlier key stages, we recommended that where the 'secretarial' aspects (presentation, spelling, handwriting) apply, they should not be assessed in isolation, but through purposeful writing activities.

## Marking policy

I have discussed the process of continuous assessment and the function of the samples of children's work in providing a basis for further development. In this context it may be helpful to include a section here on the teacher's response to children's written work, and in particular to the marking policy adopted. As James Britton and his colleagues put it:

> *very close reading of children's writing is essential, because that is the best means we have of understanding their writing processes. Children value perceptive comments, responses and*

*questions on their writing, but they quickly see through
perfunctory approval and generalised faint praise. And it's
worth remembering that for very many children, for many
years, their teachers are the only readers of the bulk of their
work.*[1]

It is axiomatic that the context of children's learning is significant. The teacher's ability to react sympathetically, to welcome a pupil's
contribution, written or spoken, in a supportive manner, is especially
important. Such a response nurtures trust in the relationship. 'The
encouraging comment, sincerely meant, however brief, is the English
teacher's most powerful weapon. It is utterly at variance with this to
adopt what Andrew Wilkinson has nicely described as the role of "the
teacher as self-appointed proof reader . . . GRowling and SPitting and
hiSSing from the margin".'[2] Negative methods of responding in marking are likely to produce sterile, cumulative consequences in a child's
writing: pupils quickly discern what is acceptable to the teacher and
merely aim to fulfil those expectations.

The teacher's response to written work should aim to foster a
child's confidence in the exploration of ideas and the manner of their
presentation. Pupils benefit from the opportunity to shape and reformulate their thinking in a helpful, non-threatening atmosphere, where
experiments in language are not only acceptable, but encouraged. The
marking response can play a vital part in promoting this linguistic
growth through establishing a dialogue, and not merely concerning
itself with surface features of the writing, or the routine correction of
technical errors. 'Assessment is not in question; it is when it becomes an
automatic and unvaried process that it loses its value for both teacher
and pupil.'[3] The process should encourage the pupils to play an active
role in learning.

Schools should formulate marking guidelines, as one feature of a
cross-curricular language policy. These might establish:

◇ the purpose, style and tone of written comments;
◇ the basis for pointing out technical errors, and the manner of
   their correction;
◇ the techniques to encourage successful examples of language
   use;
◇ the part played by discussion with individual pupils in marking their work;
◇ the way marking will be used in connection with further
   learning, and hence as a crucial link in a coherent programme
   of study;
◇ the contribution of the assessment to a pupil's record of
   achievement.

Such guidelines can help to clarify aims and objectives in setting, and responding to, written work, for the benefit of pupils, staff and parents. Pupils, especially, might increase their understanding of how they learn. In addition, the clarification of such issues could well provide the initial stimulus for a whole-school language policy.

## NOTES

1  James Britton *et al.*, *The Development of Writing Abilities. 11 to 18* (Macmillan 1975), p. 44.
2  Anthony Adams and John Pearce, *Every English Teacher* (Oxford University Press 1974), p. 92.
3  Bullock Report, paragraph 11.10.

# Conclusion

And so children in state schools in England and Wales are beginning to follow the programmes of study. The Report has been generally welcomed in independent schools, and will certainly influence their teaching methods and aims. The next stage is the assessment of the children, about which teachers are naturally worried. The ways in which assessment is introduced will very much affect how our Report is implemented, but I have not been involved in any way with the arrangements for assessment, and can only look on and hope for the best. This book gives the rationale on which the assessment should be based. In my talks to teachers I continually stress that the attainment targets and programmes of study must not be set in stone, and that, as we move through the 1990s, they must be re-evaluated. Similarly, the assessment process must proceed by trial and error, for we have much to learn about the best methods of conducting this huge experiment of a National Curriculum. It would be absurd to suggest that in the brief period during which my Working Group prepared the Report we solved every problem. At the very least we must have made mistakes of emphasis, and these will need correction as the years go by.

In the 1990s the National Curriculum in English should bring about revolutionary changes in the schools, and indeed have some influence on our national character. The teaching of English is not just a matter of developing skills in speaking and listening, reading and writing, but affects the individual and social identity of us all. The Report is especially controversial in its recommendations on speaking and listening, knowledge about language, grammar, Standard English, creative writing and multi-cultural education, and I will say a word or two in conclusion about all of these.

The decision to give speaking and listening one-third of the weighting in the assessment is of considerable significance. Extrovert pupils will be given more credit than in the past, and in sixth forms and higher education students should be more ready to contribute in tutorials and seminars. In my teaching career in provincial universities I have often been confronted by first year students who arrived at their first tutorial determined not to speak. It has not been easy to persuade them to participate, and obviously their passive attitude derives from inadequate teaching in the schools (which often boast excellent examination results). In the wider society young people in future should be more ready to speak up and engage in discussion when facing the challenges of work or citizenship or politics. Drama and role-playing will become central in the classroom activities, as they already are in many courses for business executives. It is possible that the traditional view of the English as reserved, taciturn and silent will become a thing of the past.

Our recommendations on knowledge about language should increase understanding of the varieties of English, and so promote tolerance. Pupils should be helped to understand that clear, accurate English is of vital importance, but also that Standard English is not a form fixed immutably for eternity, but changes slightly from decade to decade. They should appreciate the status of dialect and value the richness of those other languages which in our multi-cultural society many children speak at home.

The decline in the teaching of grammar in the 1950s and 1960s was a great misfortune. In our Report we reintroduce the teaching of grammar, as part of a wider understanding of discourse, in ways which should make the subject less forbidding for pupils of all abilities. Children ought to be excited by the extraordinary diversity of the English language; they ought to enjoy language games, and even drafting can become a deeply satisfying activity. To produce a piece of clear prose, after revision and discussion with friends or teacher, can be a form of personal fulfilment. Similarly, an understanding of the rules by which language works can be an enriching experience; it need not be a useless chore.

I say again that all children need to be able to speak and write Standard English, where appropriate. I utterly reject the views of those educationalists who would confine the Cockney or the Scouse to their own dialects. We can respect dialect, and yet also grant every child the opportunity to speak and write in a manner comprehensible to everyone else who speaks English from whatever part of the world. To deny pupils this opportunity is to leave them in deprivation for the rest of their lives. In our Report we make clear that this does not involve the teaching of Received Pronunciation; it certainly does not mean that we are imposing a 'middle-class' language. Standard English is an international resource, of vital importance for all children.

If these recommendations about language are to succeed, children must be encouraged to write for themselves, and teachers must also participate. In some schools children and teachers join together at some point in the day for silent reading. Children are convinced that reading matters when they see teachers themselves reading and enjoying their own choice of books. Similarly, they need to be in touch with teachers who write, and who share with their pupils their own pieces of work. The Report argues strongly that enjoyment of literature is encouraged when children are experimenting with their own texts, showing their drafts of stories or reports or reviews or verse to their peers and revising them, where possible, for publication in class or school magazines. Children need to engage regularly in the craft of writing, to use language in structured ways to communicate their own emotions and ideas. And, as I stressed in chapter 6, the books they read should be taken from different genres, and include both pre-1900 English literature and texts in English written from other cultures. If we are to live together harmoniously in a multi-cultural society, we must tolerate each other's ways of life, learn to compromise and even to admire, where appropriate, forms of behaviour and feeling and thought very different from our own.

The innovations in the National Curriculum in English ought to be carried forward into sixth forms, polytechnics and universities. In the Ludwig Mond lecture at Manchester University in 1989, George Steiner talked about how scientists in their normal activities usually work in groups, undertaking research as a team, and how they can hope optimistically that they will solve problems, that by next week they may have moved forward in their understanding of their subject. In contrast, literary scholars often appear to be walking backwards, looking across history to the great works of Shakespeare or Racine or Goethe. As a result teachers of the arts often succumb to nostalgia for a lost golden age, and this can develop into a profound distrust of any form of change in the literary canon or in their teaching practices.

We can overcome passivitity (and boredom in many students) only if we change our teaching practices. All my proposals – that students should write in a variety of forms, that they should develop abilities in speech and drama, that they should read new works from different cultures – would bring about new collaborations and co-operations, new extensions of sympathy and imagination. We should transform our students from passive consumers to active makers. They would become members of a working community. They would look forward to next week, when they might publish a magazine or take part in a play or complete a piece of writing which they have discussed with friends. I think this transformation, already taking place in some institutions of higher education, is inevitable, and expect to see this quiet revolution in teaching practices triumphant throughout education in the 1990s.

# Appendix I:
# Attainment targets and programmes of study

# Attainment target 1: speaking and listening[1]

Knowledge, skills and understanding in speaking and listening (AT1).

● ● ● ● ● ● ● ● ● ● ● ● ● ● ● ● ● ● ● ● ● ● ● ● ● ● ● ● ● ● ● ● ● ● ● ● ●

The development of pupils' understanding of the spoken word and the capacity to express themselves effectively in a variety of speaking and listening activities, matching style and response to audience and purpose.

From level 7, pupils should be using Standard English, wherever appropriate, to meet the statements of attainment.

| LEVEL | STATEMENTS OF ATTAINMENT | EXAMPLE |
|---|---|---|
| | Pupils should be able to: | |
| **1** | a) participate as speakers and listeners in group activities, including imaginative play. | *Suggest what to do next in a practical activity; tell stories; play the role of shopkeeper or customer in the class shop.* |
| | b) listen attentively, and respond, to stories and poems. | *Ask questions about a story or poem; retell a story; enact a poem; draw a picture to illustrate a story or poems.* |
| | c) respond appropriately to simple instructions given by a teacher. | *Follow two consecutive instructions such as 'Choose some shells from the box and draw pictures of them.'* |
| **2** | a) participate as speakers and listeners in a group engaged in a given task. | *Compose a story together; design and make a model; assume a role in play activity.* |
| | b) describe an event, real or imagined, to the teacher or another pupil. | *Tell the listener about something which happened at home, on the television or in a book.* |
| | c) listen attentively to stories and poems, and talk about them. | *Talk about the characters; say what they like or dislike about a story or poem.* |

| LEVEL | STATEMENTS OF ATTAINMENT | EXAMPLE |
|---|---|---|
| **2** | d) talk with the teacher, listen, and ask and answer questions.<br><br>e) respond appropriately to a range of more complex instructions given by a teacher and give simple instructions. | *Talk about events or activities in or out of school – such as a school trip, a family outing or a television programme.*<br><br>*Follow three consecutive actions such as 'Write down the place in the classroom where you think your plant will grow best, find out what the others on your table think and try to agree on which is likely to be the best place.'* |
| **3** | a) relate real or imaginary events in a connected narrative which conveys meaning to a group of pupils, the teacher or another known adult.<br><br>b) convey accurately a simple message.<br><br>c) listen with an increased span of concentration to other children and adults, asking and responding to questions and commenting on what has been said.<br><br>d) give, and receive and follow accurately, precise instructions when pursuing a task individually or as a member of a group. | *Tell a story with a beginning, middle and end; recount a series of related incidents that happened at home or in a science activity.*<br><br>*Relay a simple telephone message in role-play or real life; take an oral message to another teacher.*<br><br>*Listen to the teacher or to a radio programme on a new topic, then discuss what has been said.*<br><br><br>*Plan a wall display or arrange an outing together.* |
| **4** | a) give a detailed oral account of an event, or something that has been learned in the classroom, or explain with reasons why a particular course of action has been taken.<br><br>b) ask and respond to questions in a range of situations with increased confidence. | *Report on a scientific investigation, or the progress of a planned group activity, to another group or the class.*<br><br><br>*Guide other pupils in designing something; conduct an interview on a radio programme devised with other pupils.* |

| LEVEL | STATEMENTS OF ATTAINMENT | EXAMPLE |
|---|---|---|
| **4** | c) take part as speakers and listeners in a group discussion or activity, expressing a personal view and commenting constructively on what is being discussed or experienced. | *Draft a piece of writing, with others, on a word processor; contribute to the planning and implementation of a group activity.* |
| | d) participate in a presentation. | *Describe the outcome of a group activity; improvise a scene from a story or poem or of the pupils' own devising.* |
| **5** | a) give a well-organised and sustained account of an event, a personal experience or an activity. | *Describe a model which has been made, indicating the reasons for the design and the choice of materials.* |
| | b) contribute to and respond constructively in discussion, including the development of ideas; advocate and justify a point of view. | *Explain the actions taken by a character in a novel; work in a group to develop a detailed plan of action; provide arguments in favour of an approach to a problem.* |
| | c) use language to convey information and ideas effectively in a straightforward situation. | *Provide an eye witness account of an event or incident; explain how a personal possession was lost, describing the item in question.* |
| | d) contribute to the planning of, and participate in, a group presentation. | *Compile a news report or a news programme for younger children; perform a story or poem by means of improvisation, making use of video, or audio recorders where appropriate.* |
| | e) recognise variations in vocabulary between different regional or social groups, and relate this knowledge where appropriate to personal experience. | *Talk about dialect vocabulary and specialist terms; discuss the vocabulary used by characters in books or on television.* |

| LEVEL | STATEMENTS OF ATTAINMENT | EXAMPLE |
|---|---|---|
| **6** | a) contribute, to group discussions, considered opinions or clear statements of personal feeling which are clearly responsive to the contributions of others. | *Present or develop a line of reasoning in discussion of an issue raised by a story and comment on other viewpoints.* |
| | b) use language to convey information and ideas effectively in a variety of situations where the subject is familiar to the pupils and the audience or other participants. | *Explain a technical aspect of a hobby to someone with a general interest; present a news report on a local issue.* |
| | c) contribute to the planning and organisation of, and participate with fluency in, a group presentation or performance. | *Participate in a group presentation of a scripted or improvised episode from a story or novel; present to the class the results of a group investigation.* |
| | d) show in discussion an awareness of grammatical differences between spoken Standard English and a non-standard variety. | *Take note of different ways in which tense and person are marked in the verb* to be *after listening to recordings or participating in classroom improvisations.* |
| **7** | a) express a point of view clearly and cogently to a range of audiences and interpret accurately a range of statements by others. | *Present a personal opinion or a belief to younger pupils, another teacher, or another adult.* |
| | b) use and understand language which conveys information and ideas effectively on occasions where the situation or topic is less readily familiar to the pupils and/or their audience. | *Explain to a younger pupil how to construct a model, or make a book; describe the reasons why a character in a book, or in improvised or text-based drama, behaved in a particular way.* |
| | c) take an active part in group discussions, contributing constructively to the development of the argument. | *Introduce a new, relevant idea to a group discussion about the planning of a visit, or the making of a database; show respect for the contributions of others.* |

| LEVEL | STATEMENTS OF ATTAINMENT | EXAMPLE |
|---|---|---|
| **7** | d) show in discussion an awareness of the appropriate use of spoken language, according to purpose, topic and audience. | *Analyse and reflect upon the language appropriate for a job interview, or an argument with a parent or another pupil following a presentation.* |
| **8** | a) express points of view on complex matters clearly and cogently and interpret points of view with accuracy and discrimination. | *Debate a contentious issue and summarise the main arguments.* |
| | b) convey information and ideas in a variety of complex situations involving a range of audiences and in language which is matched to context and purpose. | *Explain causes and effects; speculate upon outcomes of a policy or a given course of action; take part in interviews for, or on behalf of, a school mini company.* |
| | c) take an active part in group discussions, contributing constructively to the sustained development of the argument. | *Take part in a real or simulated committee discussion which requires an agreement; express views and cite evidence in group discussions of books or poems.* |
| | d) show in discussion and in writing an awareness of the contribution that facial expressions, gestures and tone of voice can make to a speaker's meaning. | *Comment on the varied use of these features noted in a stage presentation, a television drama, or film. Comment on what may be conveyed (intentionally or inadvertently) in advertisements, speeches, interviews or in observed behaviour around the school.* |
| **9** | a) give a presentation expressing a personal point of view on a complex subject persuasively, cogently and clearly, integrating talk with writing and other media where appropriate, and respond to the presentations of others. | *Introduce a researched environmental topic for discussion, using slides, OHP transparencies, notes or diagrams in the presentation.* |

| LEVEL | STATEMENTS OF ATTAINMENT | EXAMPLE |
|---|---|---|
| 9 | b) take an active part in group discussion, displaying sensitivity, listening critically and being self-critical. | *Discuss a film or television programme, recognising and helping to develop the views of others, accepting and offering alternatives in positive ways.* |
|  | c) show in discussion and in writing an awareness of the ways in which language varies between different types of spoken communication. | *Describe how different kinds of language use, such as jokes, anecdote, conversation, commentary, lecture, etc., could be explained to a foreign visitor.* |
| 10 | a) express a point of view on complex subjects persuasively, cogently and clearly, applying and interpreting a range of methods of presentation and assessing their own effectiveness accurately. | *Devise and mount an advertising campaign concerned with a matter of principle.* |
|  | b) take a variety of leading roles in group discussion, including taking the chair, listening with concentration and understanding and noting down salient points. | *Summarise an argument and help to formulate a conclusion.* |
|  | c) show in discussion and in writing an awareness of some of the factors that influence people's attitudes to the way other people speak. | *Using the results of a survey, make a report on the attitudes to spoken language held by the class and the community.* |

**Note:** Pupils unable to communicate by speech may use other means including the use of technology, signing, symbols or lip-reading as alternatives to speaking and listening.

# Attainment target 2: reading²

Knowledge, skills and understanding in reading (AT2).

●●●●●●●●●●●●●●●●●●●●●●●●●●●●●●●●●●●●●●●●

**The development of the ability to read, understand and respond to all types of writing, as well as the development of information-retrieval strategies for the purposes of study.**

| LEVEL | STATEMENTS OF ATTAINMENT | EXAMPLE |
|---|---|---|
| | Pupils should be able to: | |
| 1 | a) recognise that print is used to carry meaning, in books and in other forms in the everyday world. | Point to and recognise own name; tell the teacher that a label on a container says what is inside or that the words in a book tell a story. |
| | b) begin to recognise individual words or letters in familiar contexts. | In role-play, read simple signs such as shop names or brand names; recognise 'bus-stop', 'exit', 'danger'. |
| | c) show signs of a developing interest in reading. | Pick up books and look at the pictures; choose books to hear or read. |
| | d) talk in simple terms about the content of stories, or information in non-fiction books. | Talk about characters and pictures, including likes and dislikes. |
| 2 | a) read accurately and understand straightforward signs, labels and notices. | Read labels on drawers in the classroom; read simple menus. |
| | b) demonstrate knowledge of the alphabet in using word books and simple dictionaries. | Turn towards the end to find words beginning with s, rather than always starting from the beginning. |
| | c) use picture and context cues, words recognised on sight and phonic cues in reading. | Use a picture to help make sense of a text; recognise that 'Once' is often followed by 'upon a time'; use initial letters to help with recognising words. |
| | d) describe what has happened in a story and predict what may happen next. | Talk about how and why Jack climbs the beanstalk and suggest what may be at the top. |

| LEVEL | STATEMENTS OF ATTAINMENT | EXAMPLE |
|---|---|---|
| **2** | e) listen and respond to stories, poems and other material read aloud, expressing opinions informed by what has been read. | *Talk about characters, their actions and appearance; discuss the behaviour of different animals described in a radio programme.* |
| | f) read a range of material with some independence, fluency, accuracy and understanding. | *Read something unprompted; talk with some confidence about what has been read; produce craftwork related to reading work.* |
| **3** | a) read aloud from familiar stories and poems fluently and with appropriate expression. | *Raise or lower voice to indicate different characters.* |
| | b) read silently and with sustained concentration. | |
| | c) listen attentively to stories, talk about setting, story-line and characters and recall significant details. | *Talk about a story, saying what happened to change the fortunes of the leading characters.* |
| | d) demonstrate, in talking about stories and poems, that they are beginning to use inference, deduction and previous reading experience to find and appreciate meanings beyond the literal. | *Discuss what might happen to characters in a story, based on the outcome of adventures in other stories.* |
| | e) bring to their writing and discussion about stories some understanding of the way stories are structured. | *Refer to different parts of the story such as 'at the beginning' or 'the story ends with'; notice that some stories build up in a predictable way, e.g. 'The Three Little Pigs', 'Goldilocks and the Three Bears'.* |
| | f) devise a clear set of questions that will enable them to select and use appropriate information sources and reference books from the class and school library. | *Decide that the wildlife project needs information about the size and colour of birds, their food and habitat, and look it up.* |

| LEVEL | STATEMENTS OF ATTAINMENT | EXAMPLE |
|:---:|:---|:---|
| **4** | a) read aloud expressively, fluently and with increased confidence from a range of familiar literature. | *Vary the pace and tone of the voice to express feelings, or to represent character or mood.* |
| | b) demonstrate, in talking about a range of stories and poems which they have read, an ability to explore preferences. | *Describe those qualities of the poem or story which appeal and give an indication of personal response.* |
| | c) demonstrate, in talking about stories, poems, non-fiction and other texts, that they are developing their abilities to use inference, deduction and previous reading experience. | *Recognise and use those clues in a text which help the reader predict events.* |
| | d) find books or magazines in the class or school library by using the classification system, catalogue or database and use appropriate methods of finding information, when pursuing a line of inquiry. | *Use search reading to contribute to an inquiry into health and safety at school or in the home.* |
| **5** | a) demonstrate, in talking and writing about a range of stories and poems which they have read, an ability to explain preferences. | *Make simple comparisons between stories or poems; offer justification for personal preference.* |
| | b) demonstrate, in talking or writing about fiction, poetry, non-fiction and other texts, that they are developing their own views and can support them by reference to some details in the text. | *Discuss character, action, fact and opinion, relating them to personal experience.* |
| | c) show in discussion that they can recognise whether subject matter in non-literary and media texts is presented as fact or opinion. | *Look for indications which suggest the difference: whether evidence is offered or whether persuasion is used in the absence of facts.* |

| LEVEL | STATEMENTS OF ATTAINMENT | EXAMPLE |
|---|---|---|
| **5** | d) select reference books and other information materials and use organisational devices to find answers to their own questions and those of others. | *Decide what information is required for a project on a topic of their own choice and locate it by reference to chapter titles, sub-headings, typefaces, symbol keys, etc.* |
| | e) show through discussion an awareness of a writer's choice of particular words and phrases and the effect on the reader. | *Recognise puns, word play, unconventional spellings and the placing together of pictures and text.* |
| **6** | a) read a range of fiction and poetry, explaining their preferences through talking and writing, with reference to details. | *Show involvement and independent choice over a range of genres.* |
| | b) demonstrate, in talking and writing about literature, non-fiction and other texts, that they are developing their own insights and can sustain them by reference to the text. | *Make judgments about characters and their actions, developing those characters and events in their own writing or drama.* |
| | c) show in discussion or in writing that they can recognise whether subject matter in non-literary and media texts is presented as fact or opinion, identifying some of the ways in which the distinction can be made. | *Look for indications which will help determine the difference: unsupported assertion, the use of statistics, attacks upon character which distract from an opponent's reasoning or evidence.* |
| | d) select from a range of reference materials, using appropriate methods to identify key points. | *Research a public figure using posters, interviews, publicity material, databases, etc.* |
| | e) show in discussion of their reading an awareness that words can change in use and meaning over time and demonstrate some of the reasons why. | *Understand that technological developments, euphemism, contact with other languages or fashion all contribute to language change.* |

| LEVEL | STATEMENTS OF ATTAINMENT | EXAMPLE |
|---|---|---|
| **7** | a) read a range of fiction, poetry, literary non-fiction and drama, including pre-twentieth-century literature, explaining their preferences through talking and writing, with reference to detail. | *Read letters, diaries and autobiographies; works from a range of cultures, and in translation* |
| | b) talk and write about literature and other texts giving evidence of personal response and showing an understanding of the author's approach. | *Write further episodes of a book under discussion; write journals or letters in character; compose imaginary letters to characters in books or to their authors; assess the development of a relationship in a play or novel.* |
| | c) show in discussion that they can recognise features of presentation which are used to inform, to regulate, to reassure or to persuade, in non-literary and media texts. | *Note the effect of the enhancement or suppression of colour, page layout, illustration, style and size of print, verbal emphasis through repetition, exclamation or vocabulary.* |
| | d) select, retrieve and combine information independently from a wide range of reference materials. | *Write a background briefing for a group presentation, drawing upon an encyclopaedia or database.* |
| | e) show in discussion or in writing an awareness of writers' use of sound patterns and some other literary devices and the effect on the reader. | *In a group discussion on poems, advertisements or other materials, refer to rhyme, alliteration and figures of speech such as similes, metaphors and personification.* |
| **8** | a) read a range of fiction, poetry, literary non-fiction and drama, including pre-twentieth-century literature. | *Read texts whose content, length, organisation or language make demands on the reader.* |
| | b) talk and write about literature and other texts, giving evidence of personal response and showing an understanding of the devices and structures used by the writers, with appropriate reference to details. | *Write essays commenting upon points of style, character or plot in comparison with other texts; show how or why a dramatist or novelist used questions and/or repetition to build up emotion in an episode involving two characters.* |

| LEVEL | STATEMENTS OF ATTAINMENT | EXAMPLE |
|---|---|---|
| **8** | c) show in discussion and writing an ability to form a considered opinon about features of presentation which are used to inform, regulate, reassure or persuade, in non-literary and media texts. | *Compare two reports of the same event, or devise two texts which serve contrasting purposes or audiences.* |
|  | d) select, retrieve, evaluate and combine information independently and with discrimination, from a comprehensive range of reference materials. | *Write a short study drawing upon ideas from different parts of a text or different texts.* |
|  | e) discuss and write about changes in the grammar of English over time, encountered in the course of their reading. | *Comment on examples such as pronouns (from* thou *and* thee *to* you*), verb forms and negatives.* |
| **9** | a) read a range of fiction, poetry, literary non-fiction and drama, including pre-twentieth-century literature. |  |
|  | b) talk and write clearly about literature and other texts giving sustained evidence of personal response and showing an understanding of the devices and structures used by the writer, making comparisons within texts and between different texts. | *Analyse the differences and similarities between two novels, showing a sustained personal response to both texts.* |
|  | c) show in discussion and in writing an ability to recognise techniques and conventions of presentation in non-literary and media texts, and judge the effectiveness of their use. | *Recognise the structure of news stories or the ways in which television programmes and newspapers match style and content to specific audiences; produce text in a number of media, drawing on these techniques.* |

| LEVEL | STATEMENTS OF ATTAINMENT | EXAMPLE |
|---|---|---|
| 9 | d) select, retrieve, evaluate and combine information independently and with discrimination, from a comprehensive range of reference materials, making effective use of the information. | *Prepare a well-argued report drawing on information from a variety of sources.* |
|  | e) demonstrate some under-standing of the use of lexical and grammatical effects in the language of literature. | *Consider the repetition of words or structures, dialect forms, archaisms, etc.* |
| 10 | a) read a range of fiction, poetry, literary non-fiction and drama, including pre-twentieth-century literature. | |
|  | b) talk and write cogently and knowledgeably about literature and other texts giving sustained evidence of personal response and showing an understanding of the devices and structures used by the writer, making detailed comparisons within texts and between different texts. | *Compare the treatment by different authors of similar themes, providing detailed evidence and a clear grasp of relevant background.* |
|  | c) show in discussion and in writing an ability to evaluate techniques and conventions of presentation in non-literary and media texts, and judge the effectiveness of their use. | *Compare the presentation of news or commentary in similar broadcasts on two television channels or between radio and television; compare the treatment of the same event in two newspapers.* |
|  | d) select, retrieve, evaluate and combine information independently and with discrimination, from a comprehensive range of reference materials, making effective and sustained use of the information. | *Make appropriate use of a variety of techniques, and, in devising a presentation, make use of a range of media consistently and appropriately for the audience.* |

| LEVEL | STATEMENTS OF ATTAINMENT | EXAMPLE |
|---|---|---|
| 10 | e) demonstrate in discussion and in writing some understanding of attitudes in society towards language change and of ideas about appropriateness and correctness in language use. | *Comment on the arguments, attitudes and styles displayed in a running correspondence, on an issue of language usage or performance, in a newspaper or weekly periodical.* |

**Note:** Pupils who need to use non-sighted methods of reading, such as braille, may use alternatives which do not demand a visual approach. Pupils unable to read aloud may use other means such as signing.

# Attainment target 3: writing[3]

Knowledge, skills and understanding in writing (ATs 3–5).

● ● ● ● ● ● ● ● ● ● ● ● ● ● ● ● ● ● ● ● ● ● ● ● ● ● ● ● ● ● ● ● ● ● ● ● ● ● ● ●

**A growing ability to construct and convey meaning in written language matching style to audience and purpose.**

| LEVEL | STATEMENTS OF ATTAINMENT | EXAMPLE |
|---|---|---|
| | Pupils should be able to: | |
| **1** | a) use pictures, symbols or isolated letters, words or phrases to communicate meaning. | *Show work to others, saying what writing and drawings mean.* |
| **2** | a) produce, independently, pieces of writing using complete sentences, some of them demarcated with capital letters and full stops or question marks. | |
| | b) structure sequences of real or imagined events coherently in chronological accounts. | *An account of a family occasion, a practical task in mathematics or an adventure story.* |
| | c) write stories showing an understanding of the rudiments of story structure by establishing an opening, characters, and one or more events. | *A story with an opening which suggests when or where the action takes place and which involves more than one character.* |
| | d) produce simple, coherent non-chronological writing. | *Lists, captions, invitations, greetings cards, notices, posters, etc.* |
| **3** | a) produce, independently, pieces of writing using complete sentences, mainly demarcated with capital letters and full stops or question marks. | |

| LEVEL | STATEMENTS OF ATTAINMENT | EXAMPLE |
|:-----:|:------------------------|:--------|
| **3** | b) shape chronological writing, beginning to use a wider range of sentence connectives than *and* and *then*. | *but when after so because* |
| | c) write more complex stories with detail beyond simple events and with a defined ending. | *Stories which include a description of setting and the feelings of characters.* |
| | d) produce a range of types of non-chronological writing. | *Plans and diagrams, descriptions of a person or place, or notes for an activity in science or design.* |
| | e) begin to revise and redraft in discussion with the teacher, other adults, or other children in the class, paying attention to meaning and clarity as well as checking for matters such as correct and consistent use of tenses and pronouns. | |
| **4** | a) produce, independently, pieces of writing showing evidence of a developing ability to structure what is written in ways that make the meaning clear to the reader; demonstrate in their writing generally accurate use of sentence punctuation. | *Make use of titles, paragraphs or verses, capital letters, full stops, question marks and exclamation marks; set out and punctuate direct speech.* |
| | b) write stories which have an opening, a setting, characters, a series of events and a resolution and which engage the interest of the reader; produce other kinds of chronologically organised writing. | *Write, in addition to stories, instructions, accounts or explanations, perhaps of a scientific investigation.* |
| | c) organise non-chronological writing for different purposes in orderly ways. | *Record in writing an aspect of learning; present information and express feelings in forms such as letters, poems, invitations, posters, etc.* |

| LEVEL | STATEMENTS OF ATTAINMENT | EXAMPLE |
|---|---|---|
| **4** | d) begin to use the structures of written Standard English and begin to use some sentence structures different from those of speech. | *Begin to use subordinate clauses and expanded noun phrases.* |
| | e) discuss the organisation of their own writing; revise and redraft the writing as appropriate, independently, in the light of that discussion. | *Talk about content and those features which ensure clarity for the reader.* |
| **5** | a) write in a variety of forms for a range of purposes and audiences, in ways which attempt to engage the interest of the reader. | *Write notes, letters, instructions, stories and poems in order to plan, inform, explain, entertain and express attitudes or emotions.* |
| | b) produce, independently, pieces of writing in which the meaning is made clear to the reader and in which organisational devices and sentence punctuation, including commas and the setting out of direct speech, are generally accurately used. | *Make use of layout, headings, paragraphs and verse structure; make use of the comma.* |
| | c) demonstrate increased effectiveness in the use of Standard English (except in contexts where non-standard forms are needed for literary purposes) and show an increased differentiation between speech and writing. | *Understand that non-standard forms for literary purposes might be required in dialogue, in a story or play-script; use constructions which reduce repetition.* |
| | d) assemble ideas on paper or on a VDU, individually or in discussion with others, and show evidence of an ability to produce a draft from them and then to revise and redraft as necessary. | *Draft a story, a script, a poem, a description or a report.* |

| LEVEL | STATEMENTS OF ATTAINMENT | EXAMPLE |
|---|---|---|
| **5** | e) show in discussion the ability to recognise variations in vocabulary according to purpose, topic and audience and whether language is spoken or written, and use them appropriately in their writing. | *Discuss the use of slang in dialogue and narrative in a published text and in their own writing and comment on its appropriateness.* |
| **6** | a) write in a variety of forms for a range of purposes, presenting subject matter differently to suit the needs of specified known audiences and demonstrating the ability to sustain the interest of the reader. | *Write an illustrated story which is suitable for a younger reader.* |
| | b) produce, independently, pieces of writing in which the subject matter is organised and set out clearly and appropriately and in which sentences and any direct speech are helpfully punctuated. | *Employ a wider range of uses of the comma and make use of brackets or pairs of dashes, where necessary.* |
| | c) demonstrate the ability to use literary stylistic features and those which characterise an impersonal style, when appropriate, using Standard English (except in contexts where non-standard forms are needed for literary purposes). | *Alter word order for emphasis or deliberately repeat words or sentence patterns.* |
| | d) recognise when redrafting and revising are appropriate and act accordingly, either on paper or on a computer screen. | *Write a second draft of an account of a group activity following the group's discussion of the first draft.* |
| | e) demonstrate, through discussion and in their writing, grammatical differences between spoken and written English. | *In a group, identify some of the differences between the language used in a tape recording of someone talking and a piece of writing by the same person.* |

| LEVEL | STATEMENTS OF ATTAINMENT | EXAMPLE |
|-------|--------------------------|---------|
| **7** | a) write in a wider variety of forms, with commitment and a clear sense of purpose and awareness of audience, demonstrating an ability to anticipate the reader's response. | *Write notes, personal letters, formal letters, instructions, essays, newspaper articles, reviews, biographies, stories, poems, play-scripts, radio and TV scripts. Plan, formulate hypotheses, inform, explain, compare and contrast, persuade, entertain, express attitudes or emotions, describe experience imaginatively.* |
| | b) produce well-structured pieces of writing, some of which handle demanding subject matter; punctuate their writing so that meaning and structure are clear to the reader. | *Devise a news broadcast of topical interest for a particular channel or develop a play-script from an improvisation. Go beyond first-hand experience.* |
| | c) make a more assured and selective use of a wider range of grammatical and lexical features, characteristic of different styles, that are appropriate for topic, purpose and audience; use Standard English (except in contexts where non-standard forms are needed for literary purposes). | *In transactional writing, choose neutral vocabulary; in imaginative writing, choose vocabulary which conveys attitudes, responses and emotions.* |
| | d) demonstrate an increased awareness that a first draft may be changed, amended and reordered in a variety of ways. | *Change the form from a story to a film-script; restructure text on a VDU or alter sentence structure or choice of vocabulary.* |
| | e) show in discussion and in writing an awareness of what is appropriate and inappropriate language use in written texts. | *Appreciate the need to take account of topic, purpose and audience.* |

| LEVEL | STATEMENTS OF ATTAINMENT | EXAMPLE |
|---|---|---|
| **8** | a) write in a wide variety of forms, with a clear sense of purpose and audience, demonstrating an ability to judge the appropriate length and form for a given task and to sustain the interest of the reader. | *Produce editorial columns for a broadsheet newspaper and for a tabloid.* |
| | b) produce, independently, well-structured pieces of writing, providing evidence that the function of paragraphing has been grasped; punctuate writing so that meaning and structure are clear to the reader. | *Separate distinct ideas and events and unify related ones in their writing.* |
| | c) make an assured and selective use of a wide range of grammatical constructions, which are appropriate for topic, purpose and audience; use Standard English (except in contexts where non-standard forms are needed for literary purposes) | *Forms of writing might include: alteration of word order, lexical or structural repetition, passive constructions, adverbial connectives and varied and appropriate vocabulary such as colloquial, formal, technical, poetic or figurative.* |
| | d) demonstrate knowledge of organisational differences between spoken and written English. | *Talk and write about the fact that speech is interactive, spontaneous and informal while writing is more tightly planned.* |

| LEVEL | STATEMENTS OF ATTAINMENT | EXAMPLE |
|---|---|---|
| **9** | a) write in a wide variety of forms, with an assured sense of purpose, organising and presenting subject matter appropriate for specified audiences, both known and unknown, showing awareness of the need to sustain the interest of the reader; present subject matter from a point of view other than their own, showing evidence of commitment to the topic; produce a sustained piece of writing when the task demands it. | *Write an essay justifying the actions of a character in a novel or play of whom they disapprove.* |
| | b) organise and present complex subject matter in coherently linked sentences within paragraphs; punctuate writing so that meaning and structure are clear to the reader. | *Present an investigative report about a contentious issue, drawing on a number of conflicting points of view; weave more than one strand into a story.* |
| | c) make an assured and selective use of a wide range of grammatical constructions which are appropriate for topic, purpose and audience, demonstrating awareness of the means whereby a writer may choose to achieve a desired emphasis; show an ability to sustain the chosen style; use Standard English (except in contexts where non-standard forms are needed for literary purposes). | *Vary sentence beginnings; alter word order; use lexical or structural repetition, passive constructions, adverbial connectives, elliptical constructions, non-finite subordinate clauses and choose varied and appropriate vocabulary such as colloquial, formal, technical, poetic or figurative.* |
| | d) demonstrate in discussion and in writing knowledge of ways in which language varies between different types of texts. | *Identify what is distinctive about the language used in personal letters, formal letters, printed instructions, reports in different newspapers, play-scripts or films.* |

| LEVEL | STATEMENTS OF ATTAINMENT | EXAMPLE |
|---|---|---|
| **10** | a) write, selecting an appropriate length, in a wide variety of chosen forms, demonstrating an assured sense of purpose and audience and a commitment to the topic. | *Write a report of their chosen investigation into language use, which is well-judged in length and form for the audience and uses a range of techniques of presentation, including accounts of interviews, descriptions of people, analyses of tabulated data and summary conclusions.* |
| | b) organise complex, demanding or extended subject matter clearly and effectively; produce well-structured pieces of writing in which the relationship between successive paragraphs is clear; punctuate their writing so that meaning and structure are clear to the reader. | *Present the similarities and differences between conflicting points of view or handle elements of a story which involve characters in very different contexts.* |
| | c) sustain a personal style, making an assured, selective and appropriate use of a wide range of grammatical constructions and an extensive vocabulary, choosing to use Standard English (except in contexts where non-standard forms are needed for literary purposes) and maintaining the interest and attention of the reader. | *Use a variety of sentence lengths, structure and openings and achieve striking effects through an apt choice of words.* |
| | d) demonstrate, in discussion and in writing, knowledge of criteria by which different types of written language can be judged. | *Make use of criteria such as clarity, coherence, accuracy, appropriateness, effectiveness, vigour and awareness of purpose and audience.* |

**Note:** At each level of attainment the use of technological aids by pupils who depend on them physically to produce their written work is acceptable.

178

# Attainment target 4: spelling[4]

Knowledge, skills and understanding in writing (ATs 3–5).

| LEVEL | STATEMENTS OF ATTAINMENT | EXAMPLE |
|---|---|---|
| 1 | Pupils should be able to:<br><br>a) begin to show an understanding of the difference between drawing and writing, and between numbers and letters.<br><br>b) write some letter shapes in response to speech sounds and letter names.<br><br>c) use at least single letters or groups of letters to represent whole words or parts of words. | <br><br><br><br>*Initial letter of own name.* |
| 2 | a) produce recognisable (though not necessarily always correct) spelling of a range of common words.<br><br>b) spell correctly, in the course of their own writing, simple monosyllabic words they use regularly which observe common patterns.<br><br>c) recognise that spelling has patterns, and begin to apply their knowledge of those patterns in their attempts to spell a wider range of words.<br><br>d) show knowledge of the names and order of the letters of the alphabet. | <br><br>see car man sun hot cold thank<br><br><br>coat goat feet street<br><br><br>*Name the letters when spelling out loud from a simple dictionary or word book.* |

| LEVEL | STATEMENTS OF ATTAINMENT | EXAMPLE |
|:---:|:---|:---|
| **3** | a) spell correctly, in the course of their own writing, simple polysyllabic words they use regularly which observe common patterns. | because after open teacher animal together |
| | b) recognise and use correctly regular patterns for vowel sounds and common letter strings. | -ing -ion -ous |
| | c) show a growing awareness of word families and their relationships. | grow growth growing grown grew |
| | d) in revising and redrafting their writing, begin to check the accuracy of their spelling. | *Use a simple dictionary, word book, spell checker, or other classroom resources; make spelling books or picture books.* |
| **4** | a) spell correctly, in the course of their own writing, words which display other main patterns in English spelling. | *Words using the main prefixes and suffixes.* |

**Note:** At each level of attainment the use of technological aids by pupils who depend on them physically to produce their written work is acceptable.

# Attainment target 5: handwriting[5]

● ● ● ● ● ● ● ● ● ● ● ● ● ● ● ● ● ● ● ● ● ● ● ● ● ● ● ● ● ● ● ● ● ● ● ● ● ● ● ●

| LEVEL | STATEMENTS OF ATTAINMENT | EXAMPLE |
|---|---|---|
| 1 | Pupils should be able to:<br><br>a) begin to form letters with some control over the size, shape and orientation of letters or lines of writing. | |
| 2 | a) produce legible upper and lower case letters in one style and use them consistently (i.e. not randomly mixed within words).<br><br>b) produce letters that are recognisably formed and properly oriented and that have clear ascenders and descenders where necessary. | *Produce capital letters and lower case letters which are easily distinguishable.*<br><br><br>b *and* d,<br>p *and* b |
| 3 | a) begin to produce clear and legible joined-up writing. | |
| 4 | a) produce more fluent joined-up writing in independent work. | |

**Note:** Pupils may be exempted from this target if they need to use a non-sighted form of writing such as braille or if they have such a degree of physical disability that the attainment target is unattainable.

# Attainment target 4/5: presentation

| Knowledge, skills and understanding in writing (ATs 3–5). |
| --- |

●●●●●●●●●●●●●●●●●●●●●●●●●●●●●●●●●●●●●●●

| LEVEL | STATEMENTS OF ATTAINMENT | EXAMPLE |
| --- | --- | --- |
| | Pupils should be able to: | |
| **5** | a) spell correctly, in the course of their own writing, words of greater complexity. | *Words with inflectional suffixes, such as -ed and -ing, where consonant doubling (running) or -e deletion (coming) are required.* |
| | b) check final drafts of writing for misspelling and other errors of presentation. | *Use a dictionary or computer spelling checker when appropriate.* |
| | c) produce clear and legible handwriting in printed and cursive styles. | |
| **6** | a)) recognise that words with related meanings may have related spellings, even though they sound different; recognise that the spelling of unstressed syllables can often be deduced from the spelling of a stressed syllable in a related word. | Sign, signature; medical, medicine; muscle, muscular; history, historical; grammar, grammatical; manager, managerial. |
| | b) check final drafts of writing for misspelling and other errors of presentation. | *Use a dictionary or computer spelling checker when appropriate.* |
| | c) write fluently and legibly. | |
| | d) show some ability to use any available presentational devices that are appropriate to the task, so that finished work is presented clearly and attractively. | *Handwriting, typewriting, computer print-out, artwork, computer graphics, desk top publishing.* |

| LEVEL | STATEMENTS OF ATTAINMENT | EXAMPLE |
|---|---|---|
| **7** | a) spell (and understand the meaning of) common roots that have been borrowed from other languages and that play an important role in word-building; recognise that where words have been borrowed in the last 400 years, there are some characteristic sound–symbol relationships that reflect the word's origin. | micro-, psych-, tele-, therm-; ch- *in French words like* champagne, chauffeur, charade, *and* ch *in Greek words like* chaos, chiropody, chorus; *compared with the* ch- *in long-established English words like* chaff, cheese, chin. |
| | b) check final drafts of writing for misspelling and other errors of presentation. | *Use a dictionary or computer spelling checker when appropriate.* |
| | c) write fluently and legibly. | |
| | d) show an increased ability to present finished work appropriately, clearly and attractively. | |

**Note:** At each level of attainment the use of technological aids by pupils who depend on them physically to produce their written work is acceptable. Pupils may be exempted from the statements of attainment which require handwriting if they need to use a non-sighted form of writing such as braille or if they have such a degree of physical disability that those statements of attainment are unattainable.

# Programmes of study for key stages 1 to 4

The examples printed in italics serve to illustrate the programmes of study and are non-statutory.

The programmes of study include elements which must be experienced by pupils in order to achieve a particular level. This should <u>not</u> be interpreted as meaning that pupils working at earlier or later levels should be debarred from those elements.

# Programmes of study for certain groups of children in Wales

The programmes of study at key stage 2 for groups of pupils who are excepted from the National Curriculum requirements with regard to the teaching of English at key stage 1[6] are set out in the Schedule to these programmes of study.

# Programmes of study for speaking and listening:

## support attainment target 1

●●●●●●●●●●●●●●●●●●●●●●●●●●●●●●●●●●●●●●

1   Provision should be made to ensure that pupils unable to communicate by speech may use other means including the use of technology, signing, symbols or lip-reading as alternatives to speaking and listening.

---

### PROGRAMME OF STUDY FOR KEY STAGE 1[7]

---

### General introduction

2   Through the programme of study, pupils should encounter a range of situations, audiences and activities which are designed to develop their competence, precision and confidence in speaking and listening, irrespective of their initial competence or home language.

3   These planned situations and activities should cover:

- working with other children and adults – involving discussion with others; listening to, and giving weight to, the opinions of others; perceiving the relevance of contributions; timing contributions; adjusting and adapting to views expressed;

- development of listening (and, as appropriate, reactive) skills in non-reciprocal situations, *e.g. radio programmes*;

- development of speaking and listening skills, both when role-playing and otherwise – when describing experiences, expressing opinions, articulating personal feelings and formulating and making appropriate responses to increasingly complex instructions and questions;

- development, by informal means and in the course of purposeful activities, of pupils' powers of concentration, grasp of turn-taking, ability to gain and hold the attention of their listeners, and ability to voice disagreement courteously with an opposing point of view.

4   All activities should:

- help to develop in pupils' speaking and listening their grasp of sequence, cause and effect, reasoning, sense of consistency, clarity of argument, appreciation of relevance and irrelevance, and powers of prediction and recall;

- by informal and indirect means, develop pupils' ability to adjust the language they use and its delivery to suit particular audiences, purposes and contexts and, when listening to others, to respond to different ways of talking in different contexts and for different purposes. Pupils should therefore be encouraged to reflect on and evaluate their use of spoken language and to reformulate it to help the listener;

- draw on examples from across the curriculum, and in particular those existing requirements for mathematics and science which refer to use of spoken language and vocabulary, asking questions, working in groups, explaining and presenting ideas, giving and understanding instructions;

- include provision for pupils to talk and listen in groups of different sizes and to a range of audiences;

- emphasise the importance of clear diction and audibility.

## Detailed provisions

**5** The range of activities designed to develop pupils' ability to speak and listen should include:

- listening and responding to stories, rhymes, poems and songs – familiar and unfamiliar. These should include examples from different cultures and authors and from pupils' own work;

- securing responses to visual and aural stimuli, *e.g. pictures, television, radio, computer, telephone*, making use of audio and video recordings as appropriate;

- discussion of their work with other pupils and the teacher;

- collaborative planning of activities in a way which requires pupils to speak and listen;

- talking about experiences in or out of school, *e.g. a school trip, a family outing, a television programme seen*;

- telling stories, and reciting poems which have been learnt by heart;

- collaborative and exploratory play;

- imaginative play and improvised drama;

- giving and receiving simple explanations, information and instructions; asking and answering questions.

## PROGRAMMES OF STUDY FOR KEY STAGES 2 TO 4

**6** Pupils should be given the opportunity to learn how to:

- express and justify feelings, opinions and viewpoints with increasing sophistication;

- discuss increasingly complex issues;

- recount events and narrate stories;

- assess and interpret arguments and opinions with increasing precision and discrimination;

- present their ideas, experiences and understanding in a widening range of contexts across the curriculum and with an increasing awareness of audience and purpose;

- give increasingly precise instructions;

- ask increasingly precise or detailed questions;

- respond to increasingly complex instructions and questions;

- present factual information in a clear and logically structured manner in a widening range of situations – discriminate between fact and opinion and between relevance and irrelevance, and recognise bias;

- listen and respond to an increasing range of fiction, non-fiction, poetry and plays, including those which have been seen;

- recite and read aloud in a variety of contexts, with increasing fluency and awareness of audience;

- work with or devise an increasing range of drama scripts, taking on a variety of dramatic roles;

- use, and understand the use of, role-play in teaching and learning, *e.g. to explore an aspect of history, a scientific concept or a piece of literature*;

- communicate with other group members in a wide range of situations, *e.g. an assignment in science or mathematics where a specific outcome is required*;

- discuss issues in small and large groups, taking account of the views of others, and negotiating a consensus;

- report and summarise in a range of contexts;

- reflect on their own effectiveness in the use of the spoken word;

- engage in prediction, speculation and hypothesis in the course of group activity.

**7** The range of opportunities provided should:

- not be restricted to English lessons but be available across the curriculum;

- allow pupils to work in groups of various size, both single-sex and mixed where possible, with and without direct teacher supervision;

- encourage pupils to contribute individually in class discussions;

- enable pupils to talk with wider audiences, *e.g. in representing the views of a group or taking part in group or class presentations*;

- include the use, where appropriate, of audio and/or video recorders, radio, television, telephone and computer;

- allow pupils to undertake activities on behalf of others, *e.g. by making use of the telephone, or in representative roles*.

**8** The range of activities should include:

- the preparation of presentations, *e.g. to the class, the school assembly or to parents*;
- planning and problem-solving activities across the curriculum;
- assignments where specific outcomes are required;
- talking about stories, poems, play-scripts and other texts;
- taking part in shared writing activities;
- role-play, simulations and group drama.

**9** Teaching about language through speaking and listening, which should have started by the time pupils are working towards **level 5**, should focus on:

- regional and social variations in accents and dialects of the English language and attitudes to such variations;
- the range of purposes which spoken language serves;
- the forms and functions of spoken Standard English.

**10** Pupils should have increasing opportunities to develop proficiency in spoken Standard English, in appropriate contexts.

**11** Pupils should be encouraged to respect their own language(s) or dialect(s) and those of others.

## Detailed provisions for key stage 2

**12** For pupils working towards **levels 2 and 3**, teachers should refer to relevant material in the programme of study for key stage 1.

**13** In order to achieve **level 4**, pupils should be encouraged to express their opinions and to argue a point of view; to be receptive to the contributions of others and make their own contributions effectively.

**14** In order to achieve **level 5**, pupils should be helped to make more extended contributions to group or class discussions and to informal or formal presentations, *e.g. dramatic improvisation, role-play or scripted scenes*. They should be helped to make their questions more probing, and contributions to discussion more reasoned.

Activities designed to develop pupils' knowledge about language should encourage discussion of vocabulary that is specific to:

- local communities, *e.g. words for local places, buildings, institutions, etc.*;
- local usages such as *bairn (cf. child), baps (cf. rolls), outwith (cf. outside)*;
- particular age groups, *e.g. frock (cf. dress), wireless (cf. radio)*;
- certain occupations, *e.g. the specialist terms and acronyms used by groups such as doctors, mechanics, builders, computer experts and lawyers.*

## Detailed provisions for key stages 3 and 4

**15** For pupils working towards **level 3**, teachers should refer to relevant material in the programme of study for key stage 1.

**16** For pupils working towards **levels 4 and 5**, see level-related material in detailed provisions for key stage 2.

**17** In order to achieve **level 6**, pupils should be encouraged to work in a wider range of situations in which their individual contributions are given greater emphasis, for example:

- giving instructions to others in a group;
- problem-solving activities related to the school or local community;
- planning and taking part in a group presentation, which at this level might include performance of a play-script for a school production;
- the undertaking, where feasible, of small representative roles on behalf of a group, a class, or the school – *with visitors to the school for example*.

Pupils should be guided towards the use of spoken Standard English in public or formal situations.

Pupils should be given the opportunity to consider:

- people's sensitivity to features of pronunciation that differentiate the speech of one area from others;
- any grammatical differences between the speech of the area and spoken Standard English, *e.g. in verb forms, pronoun use, prepositions*.

**18** In order to achieve **level 7**, pupils should participate extensively in widely varied group work in a range of groupings. They should be encouraged to take on an increasingly responsible role, *e.g. by taking notes of the discussion and checking them with the group, representing group views in plenary sessions*. The topics for discussion should vary widely and involve the development and probing of argument and evidence. It should also require the presentation of the main issues. Literary texts (including drama scripts), the use of language, responses to the media, pupils' own written work and the use of information technology might furnish many of the materials and topics for discussion for which planned outcomes, *e.g. in written work or presentations*, might emerge.

Pupils should consider:

- language appropriate to situation, topic and purpose;
- how inappropriate language can be a source of humour (either intentional or unintentional), or may give a false impression of the speaker or writer.

Pupils should be taught:

- that Standard English is the language of wide social communication;
- that Standard English is generally required in public or formal settings;

- through discussion, about the situations and purposes for which people might use non-standard varieties rather than Standard English: *e.g. in speech with friends, in a local team or group, in television advertising, folk songs, poetry, dialogue in novels or plays.*

*It is important that pupils working towards* **level 7** *and beyond have increasing opportunities to use spoken Standard English, and in particular that those who do not speak it as a native dialect should be helped to extend their language competence so that they can use Standard English with confidence.*

**19** Pupils working towards **levels 8 to 10** should be involved in much the same programmes of work as those for **level 7**, but will need increased opportunities, where feasible, for undertaking individual, responsible and formal roles. At **level 8**, this might include some debating activities within a formal structure, opportunities to give talks on a topic of individual interest or expertise, leading a group activity towards a planned outcome or presentation (which might include a wider audience than the class). At **levels 9 and 10**, the activities themselves will not differ significantly in kind, but pupils will require teaching which helps them to act with increasing confidence and fluency, to take leading and discerning roles in discussion, to encourage others to make contributions and respond to them with understanding and appreciation, to prepare presentations effectively (including the use of audio-visual aids and handouts), to be rigorous in argument and the use of evidence, and to take effective account of audience and context.

**20** In order to achieve **level 9**, pupils should be helped to recognise that speech ranges from intimate or casual spontaneous conversation, *e.g. jokes, anecdotes, banter, gossip, argument*, through discussion, commentary and debate to more formal forms, such as *lectures and sermons, toasts and oaths*.

**21** In order to achieve **level 10**, pupils should be helped to recognise that attitudes to Standard English and to non-standard varieties, *e.g. as expressed in letters to newspapers*, can be based on stereotypes and prescriptive judgement. Teaching at this level should make more explicit what has been previously noted incidentally, i.e. how language can be a bond between members of a group, a symbol of national pride, a barrier and a source of misunderstandings, and can be used to alienate, insult, wound, offend, praise or flatter, be polite or rude. At this level these matters might be the subject of more systematic analytical and historical study.

# Programmes of study for reading

## support attainment target 2

●●●●●●●●●●●●●●●●●●●●●●●●●●●●●●●●●●●●●●●●●●

**1** Provision should be made to ensure that pupils who need to use non-sighted methods of reading, such as braille, may use alternatives which do not demand a visual approach, and that pupils who are physically unable to read aloud may use other means such as signing.

| PROGRAMME OF STUDY FOR KEY STAGE I[8] |
|---|

### General provisions

**2** Reading activities should build on the oral language and experiences which pupils bring from home. Teaching should cover a range of rich and stimulating texts, both fiction and non-fiction, and should ensure that pupils regularly hear stories, told or read aloud, and hear and share poetry read by the teacher and each other.

**3** Reading should include picture books, nursery rhymes, poems, folk tales, myths, legends and other literature which takes account of pupils' linguistic competences and backgrounds. Both boys and girls should experience a wide range of children's literature. Non-fiction texts should include those closely related to the world of the child and extend to those which enable children to deepen an understanding of themselves and the world in which they live, *e.g. books about weather, wildlife, other countries, food, transport, the stars.* Pupils should encounter an environment in which they are surrounded by books and other reading material presented in an attractive and inviting way. The reading material should include material which relates to the real world, such as labels, captions, notices, children's newspapers, books of instructions, plans and maps, diagrams, computer print-out and visual display.

**4** Pupils' own writing – either independently written, or stories dictated to the teacher or composed in collaboration with other pupils – should form part of the resources for reading.

**5** Teachers should take account of the important link between home and school, actively encouraging parents to participate and share in their child's reading, and supporting pupils where this is not possible.

## Detailed provisions

**6** Activities should ensure that pupils:

- hear books, stories and poems read aloud or on radio, tape or television and take part in shared reading experiences with other pupils and the teacher, using texts composed and dictated by the pupils themselves, as well as rhymes, poems, songs and familiar stories (including traditional stories from a variety of cultures);

- read in the context of role-play and dramatic play, *e.g. in the home play corner, class shop, or other dramatic play setting such as a café, hospital or post office. Such reading might include a menu, a sign on a door, a label on a packet, or a sign above a counter.* For pupils working towards **level 1**, the settings should include individual letters, *e.g. 'P' for Parking*, and individual words, *e.g. 'Exit'*, which pupils can be encouraged to recognise;

- retell, re-read or dramatise familiar stories and poems;

- make their own books about particular experiences, areas of interest or personal stories, *e.g. guide books, instructions, favourite poems or stories*;

- talk to the teacher and each other about the books and stories they have been reading or listening to;

- widen their range of reading, turning readily to books, choosing those which they would like to hear or read and saying why;

- ask and answer questions about what has been heard or read – how characters feel, their motives, the endings of stories;

- talk about the ways in which language is written down, in shared reading or writing sessions or in discussion with the teacher, identify words, phrases, patterns of letters and other features of written language which they recognise, and notice how words are constructed and spelled;

- refer to information books, dictionaries, word books or simple data on computers as a matter of course. Pupils should be encouraged to formulate first the questions they need to answer by using such sources, so that they use them effectively and do not simply copy verbatim;

- talk about the content of information texts.

**7** Through the programme of study pupils should be guided so as to:

- appreciate the significance of print and the fact that pictures and other visual media can also convey meaning, *e.g. road signs, logos*;

- build up, in the context of their reading, a vocabulary of words recognised on sight;

- use the available cues, such as pictures, context, phonic cues, word shapes and meaning of a passage to decipher new words;

- be ready to make informed guesses, and to correct themselves in the light of additional information, *e.g. by reading ahead or looking back in the text*;

- develop the capacity to convey, when reading aloud, the meaning of the text clearly to the listener through intonation and phrasing;

- develop the habit of silent reading.

## PROGRAMME OF STUDY FOR KEY STAGE 2

**8**  Pupils should read an increasingly wide range and variety of texts in order to become more experienced readers. They should be encouraged to develop their personal taste in reading with guidance from the teacher and to become more independent and reflective.

**9**  The reading materials provided should include a range of fiction, non-fiction and poetry, as well as periodicals suitable for children of this age. These should include works written in English from other cultures. School and class libraries must provide as wide a range as possible. The material available must pose a significant challenge to pupils; for example, poetry should not be confined to verse written for children; folk tales and fables might include translations from original sources. Pupils should discuss with others and with the teacher what has been read.

**10**  Pupils should:

- hear stories, poems and non-fiction read aloud;

- have opportunities to participate in all reading activities, *e.g. preparing and reading a selection of poems, reciting some from memory, or taking part in storytelling, sessions or dramatic activities*;

- select books for their own reading and for use in their work;

- keep records of their own reading and comment, in writing or in discussion, on the books which they have read;

- read aloud to the class or teacher and talk about the books they have been reading;

- be encouraged to respond to the plot, character or ideas in stories or poems, and to refer to relevant passages or episodes to support their opinions;

- be encouraged to think about the accuracy of their own reading and to check for errors that distort meaning;

- be shown how to read different kinds of materials in different ways, *e.g. 'search' reading to find a scientific or geographical fact*;

- learn how to find information in books and databases, sometimes drawing on more than one source, and how to pursue an independent line of inquiry.

## Detailed provisions

**11** For pupils working towards **levels 2 and 3**, teachers should refer to relevant material in the programme of study for key stage 1.

**12** In order to achieve **level 4**, pupils should be taught how to use lists of contents, indexes, databases, a library classification system and catalogues to select information.

**13** In order to achieve **level 5**, pupils should be helped to:

- look in a text for clues about characters or actions, and to use these clues to reach conclusions, evaluate and predict what may happen;

- distance themselves, when appropriate, from a text, *e.g. no longer misattributing sex or age to a character because of self-identification*.

Pupils should be taught how to interpret and use organisational devices such as chapter titles and headings, sub-headings, changes in print or typeface, and keys to symbols or abbreviations.

They should be shown how to distinguish between fact and opinion.

Teachers should discuss texts which make imaginative use of English – literature, advertising, songs, etc. – in order to bring out the ways in which the choice of words affects the impression given by the text. Pupils should consider: the way word meanings can be played with, *e.g. in riddles, puns, jokes, spoonerisms, word games, graffiti, advertisements, poems*; the use of nonsense words and deliberate misspellings, *e.g. in poems and advertisements*.

## PROGRAMMES OF STUDY FOR KEY STAGES 3 AND 4

**14** Teachers should encourage pupils to read a variety of genres, *e.g. autobiographies, letters, diaries or travel books*, as well as short stories, novels, poetry and plays. These should include literature from different countries written in English.

**15** Pupils should be introduced to:

- the richness of contemporary writing;

- pre-twentieth-century literture;

- some of the works which have been most influential in shaping and refining the English language and its literature, *e.g. the Authorised Version of the Bible, Wordsworth's poems, or the novels of Austen, the Brontës or Dickens*;

- some of the works of Shakespeare.

**16**   Teachers should encourage pupils to read in their own time, and to discuss their favourite reading. Pupils should be helped to tackle texts of increasing difficulty.

**17**   Pupils should be taught how to handle, and be given experience in using, a range of information texts in a variety of media. Teachers should use texts of increasing difficulty to develop pupils' powers of discrimination and perseverance so that they become confident and efficient in using and interpreting such material. The texts used should include some of the following: guide books, consumer reports, textbooks, instructions and manuals, stage directions, brochures, forms, contracts, information leaflets, the highway code, publicity materials, newspapers and magazines, radio and television programmes, electronically stored information, dictionaries, thesauruses, atlases, and encyclopaedias. Pupils should be taught how and when to adapt the speed and closeness of their reading for specific purposes, *e.g. finding a fact, getting the gist of a passage or making a summary.*

**18**   Pupils should be introduced to a range of media texts, and be encouraged to consider their purpose, effect and intended audience.

**19**   Teaching of knowledge about language through reading should focus on:

- some of the main characteristics of literary language and how it conveys meanings;

- some of the ways in which English is constantly changing between generations and over the centuries; and people's attitudes to such change.

**20**   Pupils should:

- use the evidence in a text to interpret and form judgments about characters' motives and be able to quote evidence in support of their views;

- be shown how to recognise that the attitudes and behaviour of a character or narrator are not necessarily the attitudes or beliefs of the author;

- continue to read aloud, highlighting meaning in a sensitive way;

- be shown how to find and select information for themselves and use it effectively;

- discuss the themes, settings and characters of the texts they read in order to make a personal response to them.

## Detailed provisions

**21**   For pupils working towards **level 3**, teachers should refer to relevant material in the programme of study for key stage 1.

**22**    For pupils working towards **levels 4 and 5**, see level specific material in detailed provisions for key stage 2.

**23**    In order to achieve **level 6**, pupils should be reading some texts not written specifically for children or young people.

Pupils should be taught how to respond to the way information is structured and presented so that they are able to identify key points. The texts should include reference books, brochures and consumer reports.

Pupils should be taught how to skim-read so that they are able to discover the structure and gist of a text quickly. They should be shown how to put together material from different sources and to make a synthesis.

Pupils should discuss:

- examples of words and expressions which tend to undergo very rapid change in use or meaning, *e.g. terms of approbation ('wicked', 'brill')*;

- differences in the use and meanings of words used by pupils, their parents and grandparents, *e.g. wireless, radio, tranny, receiver*;

- new words that have become part of the English vocabulary during the last fifty years or so, *e.g. computer, astronaut, macho*;

- the reasons why vocabulary changes over time, *e.g. contact with other languages because of trade or political circumstances, fashion, effects of advertising, need for new euphemisms, new inventions and technology, changes in society*;

- where new words come from, *e.g. coinages, acronyms, or borrowings from other languages ('glasnost', 'catamaran', 'chic')*.

**24**    In order to achieve **level 7**, pupils should read some texts written for adults, including pre-twentieth-century fiction, poetry and drama, including Shakespeare. Discussion of those texts should include the literary style, as well as themes, settings and characters.

In both fiction and non-fiction texts, they should be taught to use information or contextual clues to deduce authorial points of view. Non-literary texts used should include persuasive writing, *e.g. advertisements, leader columns from newspapers, campaign literature from pressure groups*, and reference books, *e.g. where the subject matter has a logical structure rather than following a chronological order*.

Pupils should discuss a variety of works so as to bring out the range and effects of different types of sound patterning, *e.g. alliteration, assonance, rhymes, onomatopoeia*, and of figures of speech, *e.g. similes, metaphors, personification*.

**25**    Pupils working towards **levels 8 to 10** should be reading from a wide range of literature written for adults.

They should be taught how to:

- compare surface meaning in a text with an implied sub-text;

- interpret and evaluate characterisation, ideas and themes across a range of texts;

- cross refer and make comparisons between texts;

- be flexible in reading, *e.g. skimming, reading closely or back-tracking as necessary.* The texts should include information texts of different kinds, articles on the same subject from different newspapers, short stories and poems;

- distinguish between the structural characteristics of different types of verse and poetry, *e.g. nursery rhymes, concrete poetry, haiku, limericks, ballads, sonnets, etc.*;

- analyse, over a wide range of texts and with some sophistication, the differences between attitudes or assumptions displayed by a character and those of the author;

- select appropriate reading methods for various purposes.

**26** In order to achieve **level 8**, pupils should be taught how to:

- scrutinise a text for details of characterisation, settings and attitudes;

- quote accurately from a text to support their opinions;

- recognise the author's viewpoint and – where relevant – persuasive or rhetorical techniques in a range of texts;

- use evidence when explaining conclusions;

- find material from a range of sources, *e.g. subject-specific reference books, adult encyclopaedias and databases*;

- select material by using the appropriate method of reading;

- evaluate material and draw it together coherently.

From their reading of pre-twentieth-century literature, pupils should be encouraged to identify some of the major changes in English grammar over the centuries, *e.g. the loss – except in some dialects and in religious uses – of 'thee' and 'thou'; the simplification of the verb system, e.g. from 'have', 'hast', 'hath', to 'have' and 'has';* the change in structure of negatives, *e.g. from 'I know not' to 'I don't know'.*

**27** In order to achieve **level 9**, pupils should be taught how to analyse documents critically. Teachers should discuss the cogency and clarity of such documents and should encourage pupils to improve them. Pupils should be made aware of the subtler uses of language, and of the appropriate use of figures of speech.

Pupils should discuss:

- the effects, in context, of different types of vocabulary, *e.g. archaic, literary, figurative, emotive, dialectal, colloquial, scientific, etc.*;

- grammatical features such as structural repetition, *e.g. in scripted speeches, advertisements, literary prose, poems, etc.*;

- ambiguity, either of vocabulary or grammatical structure;

- the use of grammatical deviance for special effect, *e.g. in advertisements, slogans, poems, etc.*

**28** In order to achieve **level 10**, pupils should discuss the possibility of multiple meanings in the texts studied and be taught how to recognise and describe some of them.

Pupils should consider not only the extent to which English has changed from the earliest written records, but also ways in which it is changing now. From this, they will be helped to recognise that judgments about what is appropriate or correct do not remain constant. They should be shown how to recognise when people's attitudes to language use, *e.g. as expressed in letters to newspapers*, reveal misunderstandings about the nature of language change.

# Programmes of study for writing, spelling and handwriting:

## support attainment targets 3, 4 and 5

●●●●●●●●●●●●●●●●●●●●●●●●●●●●●●●●●●●●●●●

**1** Provision should be made to ensure that pupils throughout the key stages 1 to 4 who depend physically on the use of technological aids to produce written work, are able to follow as much of the programmes of study as possible. Pupils who need to use a non-sighted form of writing such as braille or whose physical disability is such that handwriting is impossible may be exempted from the handwriting aspects of the programmes of study.

---

### PROGRAMME OF STUDY FOR KEY STAGE 1[9]

---

### General provisions

**2** Pupils should have frequent opportunities to write in different contexts and for a variety of purposes and audiences, including for themselves.

**3** Pupils should write in a wide range of activities. Early 'play' writing, *e.g. in a play house, class shop, office, hospital*, should be encouraged and respected.

**4** *Pupils will have seen different kinds of writing in the home – their names on birthday cards or letters, forms, shopping lists and so on. Those whose parents are literate in a language other than English may have observed writing in their own first language, for which there may be a different writing system. Such awareness of writing in any form can help pupils to understand some of the functions of written language and should be used to promote their understanding of the functions of the English writing system.*

**5** Pupils should see adults writing. Teachers should write alongside pupils, sharing and talking about their writing, *e.g. in journals, notes and diagrams*, so that the range of uses of writing is brought out. Pupils should be made aware of how pieces of work they have produced relate to adult uses of writing.

## Detailed provisions

**6** Pupils should be taught the conventional ways of forming letter shapes, lower case and capitals, through purposeful guided practice in order to foster a comfortable and legible handwriting style.

**7** Pupils should be enabled to compose at greater length than they can manage to write down by themselves, by:

- dictating to their teacher or another adult, or into a tape recorder; or

- working with other children; or

- using a word processor. Pupils should be able to produce copies of work drafted on a computer, and encouraged to incorporate the print-out in other work, including displays.

**8** As they become familiar with the conventions of writing, pupils should be introduced to the most common spelling patterns of consonant and short vowel sounds. Pupils should be taught how to spell words which occur frequently in their writing, or which are important to them, and those which exemplify regular spelling patterns. They should be encouraged to spell words for themselves, and to remember the correct spelling, *e.g. by compiling their own list of words they have used*. They should be taught the names and order of the letters of the alphabet.

**9** Pupils should:

- undertake a range of chronological writing including some at least of diaries, stories, letters, accounts of tasks they have done and of personal experiences, records of observations they have made, *e.g. in a science or design activity*, and instructions, *e.g. recipes*;

- undertake a range of non-chronological writing which includes, for pupils working towards **level 2**, some at least of lists, captions, labels, invitations, greetings cards, notices, posters and, for pupils working towards **level 3**, plans and diagrams, descriptions, *e.g. of a person or place*, and notes for an activity, *e.g. in science or designing and making*;

- play with language, for example by making up jingles, poems, word games, riddles, and games which involve word and spelling patterns.

**10** Pupils should write individually and in groups, sharing their writing with others and discussing what they have written, and should produce finished pieces of work for wider audiences, *e.g. stories, newspapers, magazines, books, games and guides for other children*.

**11** Pupils should be asked to write in response to a range of well-chosen stories, poems, plays or television programmes.

**12** Pupils should discuss their writing frequently, talking about the varied types and purposes of writing, *e.g. list, poem, story, recipe*. Teachers should talk about correct spelling and its patterns, about punctuation, and should introduce pupils to terms such as punctuation, letter, capital letter, full stop, question mark.

**13** Pupils should be taught to help the reader by leaving a space between words and by ending sentences with a full stop or question mark and by beginning them with a capital letter.

**14** Pupils working towards **level 3** should be taught to recognise that writing involves:

- decision-making – when the context (the specific situation, precise purpose and intended audience) is established;

- planning – when initial thoughts and the framework are recorded and ordered;

- drafting – when initial thoughts are developed, evaluated and reshaped by expansion, addition or amendment to the text.

They should be taught to look for instances where:

- ideas should be differently ordered or more fully expressed in order to convey their meaning;

- tenses or pronouns have been used incorrectly or inconsistently;

- meaning is unclear because of insufficient punctuation or omitted words;

- meaning would be improved by a richer or more precise choice of vocabulary.

**15** They should be taught, in the context of discussion about their own writing, grammatical terms such as sentence, verb, tense, noun, pronoun.

## PROGRAMME OF STUDY FOR KEY STAGE 2

**16** Pupils should continue to have varied and frequent opportunities to write. They should know for whom they are writing, *e.g. themselves (to help in their thinking, understanding or planning of an activity), their classmates, their teacher, younger children in the school, their parents or other trusted adults.* In writing for others they will learn that writing for a public audience requires more care to be taken with the finished product than writing for oneself as an aid to memory.

**17** As children become more fluent and confident as writers, there should be increased attention to the punctuation which demarcates sentences (capital letters, full stops, question marks and exclamation marks) and to the conventions of spelling. These should be taught in the context of the children's own writing and should always be related to their function of making the writer's meaning clear to the reader. Once pupils can produce a printed style of handwriting fluently and confidently, they shoud be taught to develop a comfortable joined-up style.

**18**  Pupils should:

- use writing to learn, and to record their experiences in a wide range of classroom activities across the curriculum;

- undertake chronological writing, *e.g. reports of work in science and mathematics, instructions for carrying out a task, and accounts of personal experiences, as well as imaginative stories*;

- be helped to understand that non-chronological types of writing can be organised in a variety of ways and so, generally, require careful planning; this might include the presentation of information or imaginative prose;

- read good examples of descriptions, explanations, opinions, etc., and be helped to plan and produce these types of writing by being given purposeful opportunities to write their own;

- write personal letters to known recipients and be shown how to set them out;

- be helped to increase their control of story form, through their experience of the stories they have read and heard, recognising, for example, that the setting and the outcome need to be made explicit to the reader;

- have opportunities to write poetry (individually, in small groups or as a class) and to experiment with different layouts, rhymes, rhythms, verse structures, and with all kinds of sound effects and verbal play;

- have opportunities to create, polish and produce individually or together, by hand or on a word processor, extended written texts, appropriately laid out and illustrated, *e.g. class newspapers, anthologies of stories or poems, guide books, etc.*;

- write in response to a wide range of stimuli, including stories, plays and poems they have read and heard, television programmes they have seen, their own interests and experiences, and the unfolding activities of the classroom;

- be encouraged to be adventurous with vocabulary choices;

- be taught how to use a thesaurus;

- be introduced to the idea of the paragraph and encouraged to notice paragraph divisions in their reading;

- be shown how to set out and punctuate direct speech;

- be introduced to some of the uses of the comma and the apostrophe;

- be taught the meaning, use and spelling of some common prefixes and suffixes, *e.g. un-, in- (and im-, il-, ir-), -able, -ness, -ful, etc.*, in the context of their own writing and reading;

- think about ways of making their meaning clear to their intended reader in redrafting their writing;

- be encouraged and shown how to check spellings in a dictionary or on a computer spelling checker when revising and proof-reading;

- have opportunities to develop a comfortable, flowing and legible joined-up style of handwriting;

- consider features of layout, *e.g. headings, side headings, the use of columns or indentation*, in the materials they read, so that they can use some of these features to clarify structures and meaning in their own writing;

- be encouraged to find ways to reduce repetition in their own writing;

- be introduced to the complex regularity that underlies the spelling of words with inflectional endings, *e.g. bead-ing, bead-ed, bed-d-ing, bed-d-ed*, in the context of their own writing and reading.

## Detailed provisions

**19** For pupils working towards **levels 2 and 3**, see level-related and other relevant material in detailed provisions for key stage 1.

**20** In order to achieve **level 4**, pupils should be helped to recognise how Standard English has come to have a wide social and geographical currency and to be the form of English most frequently used on formal or public occasions and in writing. They should be helped to recognise any differences in grammar or vocabulary between the local dialect of English and Standard English, recognising that local speech forms play an important part in establishing a sense of group identity.

They should have opportunities to write for formal or public purposes so that there are valid reasons to use Standard English in their writing.

Pupils should discuss the history of writing and consider some of the ways in which writing contributes to the organisation of society, the transmission of knowledge, the sharing of experiences and the capturing of imagination.

**21** In order to achieve **level 5**, pupils should be helped to extend their range of vocabulary and to increase their awareness of what is suitable according to purpose and context, *e.g. the kinds of topics and situations in which slang is used; the need for specialist terms and the effects of their use outside the specialist group*. Discussion should bring out contrasts in how vocabulary is used in speech and writing.

## PROGRAMMES OF STUDY FOR KEY STAGES 3 AND 4

**22** During these two key stages, pupils' development as writers should be marked by:

- increasing conscious control over the structure and organisation of different types of text;

- the matching of form to subject matter and readership and a growing capacity to write independently and at length;

- a widening range of stylistic features more characteristic of writing than speech;

- an increasing proficiency in re-reading and revising or redrafting the text;

- an ability to reflect on and talk about writing;

- a widening knowledge of some of the main differences between speech and writing;

- a developing understanding of the range of purposes which written language serves.

**23** Pupils should be helped to recognise explicitly the different stages in the writing process;

- drafting (getting ideas on to paper or computer screen, regardless of form, organisation or expression);

- redrafting (shaping and structuring the raw material – either on paper or screen – to take account of purpose, audience and form);

- re-reading and revising (making alterations that will help the reader, *e.g. getting rid of ambiguity, vagueness, incoherence, or irrelevance*);

- proof-reading (checking for errors, *e.g. omitted or repeated words, mistakes in spelling or punctuation*).

In redrafting their work they should be encouraged to think of the first draft as tentative so that they are prepared to rethink their approach in the light of their own critical appraisal, or of their discussions with their peers or teacher.

**24** By building on the experiences of earlier key stages, pupils should be made aware of the following range of functions of writing:

- for communicating meaning to others: reporting, narrating, persuading, arguing, describing, instructing, explaining;

- for thinking and learning: recollecting, organising thoughts, reconstructing, reviewing, hypothesising;

- for aesthetic and imaginative purposes.

## General provisions for key stage 3

**25** Pupils should have opportunities to:

- write in a range of forms, including the following: notes, diaries, personal letters, chronological accounts, pamphlets, book reviews, advertisements, comic strips, poems, stories, play-scripts;

- build on experiences of a range of different stories which they have read and heard, and/or through discussion of their work with the teacher or their peers;

- handle the following elements of story structure with increasing effectiveness: an opening, setting, characters, events and a resolution;

- build on their experience of reading and hearing a wide range of poetry, and write, both individually and in groups, using poetic features such as rhythm, rhyme and alliteration in verse forms such as jingles, limericks, ballads, haiku, etc.;

- write for a range of purposes including describing, explaining, giving instructions, reporting, expressing a point of view;

- use writing to facilitate their own thinking and learning, recognising that not all written work will lead to a polished, final product;

- produce writing and proof-read on a word processor;

- record their first thoughts, capture immediate responses and collect and organise ideas so that they are available for reflection;

- write in aesthetic and imaginative ways;

- organise and express their meaning appropriately for different specified audiences, *e.g. their peers, their teacher, known adults, younger children, unknown but designated adults, such as a planning officer, a road safety officer, a novelist or poet*;

- organise subject matter into paragraphs in the context of their own writing, recognising that these enable readers to identify relationships between ideas, events, etc. and to follow the structure of a story, account or arguments, etc.;

- be enabled, through reading, listening to and talking about a wide range of texts, to use, in their own writing, those grammatical structures which are characteristic of written language and an increasingly varied and differentiated vocabulary;

- learn that the writer can indicate the relationship between essential and subsidiary information if parenthetical constructions are separated by brackets or pairs of commas or dashes;

- learn other uses of the comma, *e.g. around appositional constructions* and begin to use semi-colons and colons;

- consider explicitly the functions and possible structures of paragraphs;

- be helped to recognise, in the context of their own writing and reading, that words with related meanings may have related spellings and that this can sometimes be an aid in the spelling of words where the sound alone does not provide sufficient information;

- use appropriate methods of presentation for each piece of work, so that (a) notes and records may be more economical and useful to themselves and (b) finished work is presented or displayed clearly and attractively for other readers;

- learn, in the context of their own writing and reading, some of the words and roots which have been absorbed into English from other languages, so that they become familiar with the word-building processes and spelling patterns that derive from them.

## Detailed provisions for key stage 3

**26** For pupils working towards **level 3**, teachers should refer to level-related and other relevant material in the detailed provisions for key stage 1.

**27** For pupils working towards **levels 4 and 5**, see level-related material in detailed provisions for key stage 2.

**28** In order to achieve **level 6**, pupils should come to understand the functions of the impersonal style of writing such as might be used in academic – and particularly scientific – writing and to recognise the linguistic features, *e.g. the passive, subordination*, which characterise it. This should be done by reading and discussing examples.

Teaching should bring out the fact that as speech typically takes place in a situation where both speaker and listener are present, it can be accompanied by gestures and words like 'this', 'that', 'now', 'you', etc., whereas writing generally requires greater verbal explicitness. Pupils should be helped to recognise that because writers are not able to use the voice to emphasise key points in a sentence, they have to use a wide range of grammatical structures (such as the passive, or other alterations of word order) to bring about the desired emphasis. They should also recognise that writing is often more formal and more impersonal than speech: lexical and grammatical features of language both reflect and create these contrasts.

**29** In order to achieve **level 7**, pupils should develop a sensitivity to the different styles of vocabulary that are used in different types of writing.

Pupils should be taught about the different functions of written language: that writing can be for the writer alone; it can be addressed to a known reader; or it can be written for a large and unknown audience. They should be shown how it may primarily be either an artefact in its own right or a means of conveying information; how it functions as a tool of thought and as a creator of human relationships; how it can be stored and readily transmitted across time and distance. They should be helped to think of appropriateness in written language in terms of these functions and of the range of audiences that writers address, considering the effects, for example, of inappropriately formal vocabulary in personal letters or of colloquial expressions in impersonal writing.

**30** In order to achieve **level 8**, pupils should come to understand that, at its most characteristic, speech is interactive, spontaneous and informal which means that topics of conversation emerge in an unplanned and unstructured way; in contrast, writing needs a more tightly planned structure signalled by the organisation of topics into paragraphs and words and phrases such as *'meanwhile'*, *'in the same way'*, and *'on the other hand'*.

They should be helped to recognise the patterns of organisation of formal expository writing: *e.g. the introduction, development and conclusion of the academic essay; the use of illustrations and examples in persuasive writing and of comparison and contrast in argument.*

## General provisions for key stage 4

**31** Pupils should have opportunities to:

- write in a wider range of forms, including a number of the following: notes, diaries, personal letters, formal letters, chronological accounts, reports, pamphlets, reviews (of books, television programmes, films or plays), essays, advertisements, newspaper articles, biography, autobiography, poems, stories, play-scripts;

- learn through experience of a wider range of literature to produce stories which are more consciously crafted, for example, using detail in the portrayal of characters or settings or elements of suspense or surprise and a skilfully managed resolution;

- select verse forms appropriate for their own choice of subject matter and purposes through experience of a wider range of poetry;

- write for a wider range of communicative or informative purposes, including: describing, explaining, giving instructions, reporting, expressing a point of view, persuading, comparing and contrasting ideas, arguing for different points of view;

- use writing for private purposes, such as reviewing their own experiences, reflecting on their own ideas and formulating hypotheses;

- have continuing opportunities to write in aesthetic and imaginative ways;

- be given opportunities to write on topics that are demanding because of their subject matter;

- learn how to organise and express their meaning appropriately, not only for different specified audiences (as for key stage 3) but also for unknown audiences, *e.g. in producing instructions for a game, letters to a newspaper, publicity campaigns, etc.*;

- learn, in the context of their own writing, to construct different types of paragraph, *e.g. a general statement followed by examples, illustrations followed by a conclusion, cause followed by effect, etc.*;

- learn, for example by presenting the same material for different purposes or audiences, or in different forms, how they can achieve different stylistic effects in their writing by a conscious control of grammatical structures and lexical choices;

- extend and refine their competence in drafting, redrafting, re-reading and revising, and proof-reading and learn to judge the extent to which they need to use any or all of these processes in specific pieces of work;

- make their own decisions about the appropriate length for a piece of work and to recognise that there can be merit in brevity;

- craft their writing so that they can achieve a readable, pleasing style;

- learn about the uses (and misuses) of inverted commas for purposes other than direct speech, *e.g. enclosing slang or technical terms, or conveying an idea of falseness*.

## Detailed provisions for key stage 4

**32** For pupils working towards **level 3**, teachers should refer to level-related and other relevant material in the detailed provisions for key stage 1.

**33** For pupils working towards **levels 4 and 5**, see level-related material in detailed provisions for key stage 2.

**34** For pupils working towards **levels 6 to 8**, see level-related material in detailed provisions for key stage 3.

**35** In order to achieve **level 9**, pupils should be taught:

- how to recognise and describe some of the lexical, grammatical and organisational characteristics of different types of written texts, *e.g. letters, tabloid and broadsheet newspapers, teenage magazines, specialist hobby periodicals, holiday brochures, travel books, instructions, play-scripts*;

- about the nature and purpose of impersonal styles of writing, and the vocabulary and grammar characteristics of those styles, *e.g. the use of the passive voice and of other ways of depersonalising text – such as not using pronouns.*

**36** In order to achieve **level 10**, pupils should be taught, in the context of their own writing and that of a range of published writers, that, in evaluating the success of a piece of writing, different criteria need to be applied to different types; for example, a personal letter may be valued for its warmth and humour, a report for the clarity of its organisation, etc.

## NOTES

1 The statements of attainment at levels 1 to 3 are as specified by Order and published in the statutory Document entitled *English in the National Curriculum* (HMSO: ISBN 0 11 270682 7) on 31 May 1989.

2 The statements of attainment at levels 1 to 3 are as specified by Order and published in the statutory Document entitled *English in the National Curriculum* (HMSO: ISBN 0 11 270682 7) on 31 May 1989.

3 The statements of attainment at levels 1 to 3 are as specified by Order and published in the statutory Document entitled *English in the National Curriculum* (HMSO: ISBN 0 11 270682 7) on 31 May 1989.

4 The statements of attainment at levels 1 to 3 are as specified by Order and published in the statutory Document entitled *English in the National Curriculum* (HMSO: ISBN 0 11 270682 7) on 31 May 1989.

5 The statements of attainment at levels 1 to 3 are as specified by Order and published in the statutory Document entitled *English in the National Curriculum* (HMSO: ISBN 0 11 270682 7) on 31 May 1989.

6 Exceptions from the provisions of the National Curriculum with regard to the teaching of English in key stage 1 for pupils in Wales who are in a group where the medium of teaching to that group is wholly or partly in Welsh with regard to more than half of the subjects comprising religious education and the foundation subjects as defined in the Education Reform Act other than English and Welsh are set out in the Education (National Curriculum) (Exceptions) (Wales) Regulations 1989 – SI 1308/1989.

7 The programme of study for key stage 1, including references to levels 1 to 3, appears as specified by Order and published in the statutory Document entitled *English in the National Curriculum* (HMSO: ISBN 0 11 270682 7) on 31 May 1989.

8 The programme of study for key stage 1, including references to levels 1 to 3, appears as specified by Order and published in the statutory Document entitled *English in the National Curriculum* (HMSO: ISBN 0 11 270682 7) on 31 May 1989.

9 The programme of study for key stage 1, including references to levels 1 to 3, appears as specified by Order and published in the statutory Document entitled *English in the National Curriculum* (HMSO: ISBN 0 11 270682 7) on 31 May 1989.

# Appendix II: Approaches to the 'class novel'

# Approaches to the 'class novel'

●●●●●●●●●●●●●●●●●●●●●●●●●●●●●●●●●●●●●●●

The following table, from which we made selections, was produced by a Heads of English Group from Northamptonshire LEA.[1] The table outlines a number of approaches to the class-sharing of a novel. They are designed to reflect the purpose and nature of teaching literature in the shared context of the 'class-reader'. They concentrate on forms of response and interaction with the text that are characteristically different from forms that a reader might use in tackling a text privately. The overall purpose is to bring readers into *active* participation with the text, and to promote the text as a rich and vital source of meaning, which can be related to the needs, interests, purposes and motivations of the group as developing individual and social beings.

The approaches are framed in such a way as to recognise the levels at which a fictional text operates and to aid groups of readers in becoming aware of these levels, whilst accepting that in a mixed ability class there will be different degrees of appreciation and understanding:

> *narrative:* being aware of the story, particularly how it is sequenced; being able to follow the book at the level of its story;

> *symbolic:* being aware of what the story stands for – the universal meanings, and circumstances illustrated by the particular narrative; being aware of the metaphors and imagery used in the construction of the narrative and the descriptive passages;

> *stylistic/linguistic:* being aware of the 'crafting', particularly the structuring of the book, selection of literary devices and vocabulary, use of syntactic conventions; developing a critical awareness of the relationship between form and content.

It should be stressed that the approaches which follow should be seen as complementing other forms of reading activity, including pupils' independent reading and structured classroom discussion.

| Approaches | Methodology/ examples | Learning features |
|---|---|---|
| **1** **Author's visit** | Real visits arranged through 'writers in school' scheme, or imagined as in framing questions to ask the author or in correspondence with author. | Access to a professional writer. Seeing text in the writer's terms, readers communicating directly with writer, with texts as middle ground. |

| Approaches | Methodology/ examples | Learning features |
|---|---|---|
| **2** **Reading logs** | Exercise book or folder containing rough jottings, reflections, personal connections, reviews, in relation to books read in class and in private. | Developing personal responses. Valuing the reading's judgments and insights into text. Providing a cumulative record of reading experiences; developing learner's autonomy. |
| **3** **Cloze** | An extract represented with deletions in text in order to focus on author's style and vocabulary. In groups class make suggestions about deleted words by drawing on their understanding of style and language used in text so far. | Highlighting stylistic/ linguistic features of text, drawing attention to syntax. Encouraging hypothetical/ speculative talk as well as problem-solving activity. Developing reflective awareness of how a text is constructed, encouraging awareness of selection and alternatives. |
| **4** **Prediction** | Formal: extract is 'cut up' into sections, groups speculate on what's going to happen in next section by reference to text in section before.  Informal: breaking the reading in order to invite speculation on where the narrative is going. | Confirming and giving confidence in learner's existing sense of story. Developing logical sequencing skills. Encouraging close reading and awareness of contextual clues; to provide evidence from text. |
| **5** **Active com-prehension** | Groups frame their own questions about a passage and select key question to explore as a group or to offer to rest of class. | Developing ability to frame appropriate questions. Encouraging readers to adopt an active, interrogative attitude to the text. |

| Approaches | Methodology/ examples | Learning features |
|---|---|---|
| **6 Spider diagrams** | To map out ideas, further questions – relating to key question, or factors affecting a key event; or relationships between central characters and other characters; or relating events to central theme. | Finding patterns and relationships of meaning in a complete text. Drawing attention to structure and form; identifying themes and issues underpinning the text. |
| **7 Maps** | Representing journeys or a particular environment – building, street, etc. Whole wall maps with room for quotations, pictures, events to be pasted on to form spatial relationships. | Making the text 'concrete'. Visualising the text. Awareness of structure, developing sense of place. Tracking events. Matching events to places. |
| **8 Family trees** | Particularly when many characters are involved in narrative. 'Tree' may represent blood ties, may have theme to do with who knows whom; how people have met; what interests they serve or promote, etc. | Aiding the reader. Providing a structure to facilitate reader's progress with text. Holding the structure of the book; looking for relationships in the text. |
| **9 Storyboard for TV/film** | Series of drawings representing the way the camera would portray an event or passage from the book – camera angles, close-ups, long shots, etc. | Translating from one medium to another, working in familiar forms; selectivity of symbol. Matching images to event. Enabling reader to 'realise' perspective on the text. |

| Approaches | Methodology/ examples | Learning features |
|---|---|---|
| **10 Adver-tisers** | Promoting the book 'as if' the group were advertisers – choosing what to highlight about the book; target audiences, form of advertising, bookshop posters, jacket illustrations, blurbs, etc. | Developing critical awareness. Highlighting concepts of audience, register, writer's intentions, etc. selecting appropriate symbols, images, quotations, 'marketing' literature, providing motivation and sustaining interest. |
| **11 Illus-trators** | Working 'as if' illustrators to discuss or execute illustrations of text, jacket covers, etc. Emphasis on matching form of illustration to sense of text. | Working as 'experts' rather than as learners. Emphasis on style and atmosphere of text. Selecting events or moments to capture. Justifying and making decisions in relation to how the text should be represented. Close reading. |
| **12 Casting directors** | What sort of actor would have the right 'image' for the character in the book – tall/ short; assertive; young; deep voiced, etc.? | 'Filling out' characters. Making inferences. Stereotypic/original interpretations. Collective image of how a character would appear. Dwelling on aspects of character. |
| **13 News** | Incidents from the story written as news; front pages with a composite of stories relating to central event. Emphasis on reporting from outside the event; what should be selected as 'news'. | Translating events into familiar forms. Popularising the text. Reporting and journalistic conventions. Creating a distance between characters' perceptions of events and the readers'. |

| Approaches | Methodology/ examples | Learning features |
|---|---|---|
| **14 Investigative journalism** | In form of a documentary exposing an issue, or presenting an issue that is important in the book – maybe a number of related items drawing on background material beyond that offered in text; public inquiry, exposé, etc. | Emphasising issues in book. Relating text to other material dealing with same theme. Presenting, selecting, arranging material. Authorial intention and bias. Airing values, making judgements. |
| **15 Diaries or journals** | Written 'as if' by characters in book, reflecting their reactions to events of the narrative. Daily diaries, log of a journey, prison journals or extra instalments for journals and diaries that appear in the story. | 'Personalising' the characters and events. Imagining what people and events would be like. As an aid to reflection, filling out the text. Active participation with narrative. |
| **16 Time line** | Representing temporal relationships between events, places, characters, etc., as a linear sequence. Events in a character's life, frequency and proximity of events within time span of book. | Drawing attention to sequencing and structure. Establishing cause and effect relationships. Providing a framework of book's events for quick reference. |
| **17 Alternative narrators** | In groups, re-telling events from point of view other than that used by author – peripheral characters; third person, first person. Carrying on the re-telling in a variety of different registers, etc. | Highlighting characterisation. Offering fresh perspectives on story. 'Playing' with text. Demonstrating relationships between viewpoints and attitudes. Emphasising selectivity of style and language in the original form. |

| Approaches | Methodology/ examples | Learning features |
|---|---|---|
| **18** **Costume/ set design** | Deciding on how a character, or groups of characters, should be costumed, including personal props. Or how a set should be designed for a particular event or place in the text. Designs discussed, illustrated, made, or written as notes. | Dwelling on aspects of character and awareness of descriptive imagery. Making people and places more concrete and immediate. Attention to detail and contextual clues. Establishing a cultural context. |
| **19** **Corre- spon- dence** | Writing letters from characters to imagined people outside the text, or between characters, or between peripheral characters about behaviour or personality of a central character. | Becoming actively involved with the people and events in text. Demonstrating comprehension of aspects of characters. Commentating on text as a reader but from viewpoint of the characters. |
| **20** **Wax- works/ still images/ photos** | Group work to produce tableaux representing gesture, spatial relationships, body language at a particular moment, or to illustrate a quote; others can guess which moment or line is being presented and why. | Freezing action to allow time for detailed discussion and reflection on the significance of the selected moment. Allowing a greater variety of forms of communication to represent group's 'meanings', beyond verbal forms. Develops 'iconic' creativity and response. |
| **21** **Alter- native chapters** | Planning in talk or writing 'missing chapters' that fill out the original, or foreground peripheral characters not present in the central events. | Developing sense of alternatives and emphasising role of writer. Matching new material to existing forms in text – vocabulary, syntax, register, conventions, etc. |

| Approaches | Methodology/ examples | Learning features |
|---|---|---|
| **22 Spring-boarding** | Fiction is used as a starting point and focus for detailed analysis of an important issue. Fiction compared against factual material relating to the issue, or in comparison with other fiction which has an alternative bias on the issue. | Book used as starting point for issue-based teaching. Story helps to personalise the issues and allows for effective response to issue. Developing empathy for characters faced with an issue from a different perspective to reader's e.g. disability, race, gender, poverty, etc. |
| **23 Sound-tracking** | In groups, composing and performing sounds to accompany a sequence of action or to establish a sense of place. | Emphasising descriptive imagery. Matching non-verbal form to sense of text. Developing sense of 'atmosphere' and the 'environment' of the book. |
| **24 Thought-tracking** | Creating 'interior speech' for each character at critical moments or in crucial passages of dialogue. Contrasting inner dialogue (what is thought) with outer dialogue (what is said). | Encouraging reflective awareness of characters' feelings and thoughts. Recognising characters' relationships with others. Making inferences. Bringing readers into closer, more active participation with events and characters. Encouraging readers' insights into character. |
| **25 Visual interro-gation** | Drawing introduced as a means of making sense of a problematic passage. Building an image from clues in text. Accurately portraying textual description. Collective drawing. Representing negotiated consensus of how some thing, place, or person, would appear. | Using alternative iconic form to gain access to the text. Discovering from others as a result of mutual activity. Matching intuitions and hunches to what's actually represented in the text. Accessible form for less able reader. |

| Approaches | Methodology/ examples | Learning features |
|---|---|---|
| **26** **Starting in the middle** | As a way into book, or introduction to new section – a message, letter or fragment of text is presented and group asked to build speculations as to meaning, context, consequence. | Motivating readers' interest prior to reading of whole text. Encouraging intuitive speculation about narrative, characters, style. Extending range of possibilities offered by text. Looking for clues, problem-solving activity. |
| **27** **Cultural contexts** | Reconstructing and inferring a broader cultural context for characters or events, type of housing, likely occupations, cultural pursuits, class/ gender attitudes – how far are the events and characters socially constructed? How would a change of cultural context affect the effects? | Identifying social and cultural pressures and influences on characters and events. Identifying cultural and social assumptions underpinning book. Identifying authorial bias, purpose and intention. Filling out the world of the book. Testing credibility of book's context, examining stereotype and social cliché. |
| **28** **Meetings/ courts/ inquiries** | Improvised re-enactments of crucial meetings in story, or imagined meetings to deal with issues or events in story, or as post-mortem to events, or to establish motivations, consequences as in court case. | Bringing readers into active participation with text. Examining pressures and conflicts affecting decisions in book. Examining cause and effect relationships. |
| **29** **Hot-seating** | Individually, or collectively, taking on role of a character to answer questions posed by rest of group, who may also have a role, e.g. detectives, scientists, etc. | Highlighting character's motivation and personality disposition. Encouraging insights. Making readers participants in the action. Encouraging reflective awareness. |

# NOTE

1   Kate Buttler, Tony Buttler, Liz Gifford, Simon Langley, Clare Matthews, Brendan Mulcahy, Jonothan Neelands, David Pryke, Maurice Quirke, Mary Rich, Carol Sanderson.

# Select Bibliography

Adams, Anthony, and Pearce, John, *Every English Teacher* (OUP 1974).

Allen, David, *English, Whose English?* (National Association of Advisers in English 1988).

Bazalgette, Cary, ed., *Primary Media Education* (BFI Education Dept. 1989).

Benton, Michael, and Fox, Geoff, *Teaching Literature, Nine to Fourteen* (OUP 1985).

Britton, James, *et al.*, *The Development of Writing Abilities, 11 to 18* (Macmillan 1975).

Bruner, J. S., *The Relevance of Education* (Penguin 1974).

Crystal, D., *Who Cares About English Usage?* (Penguin 1985).

Crystal, D., *The English Language* (Penguin 1988).

Department of Education and Science [hereafter DES], *Children and their Primary Schools* [Plowden Report] (HMSO 1967).

DES, *A Language for Life* [Bullock Report] (HMSO 1975).

DES, *English from 5 to 16* (HMSO 1984).

DES, *Better Schools* (HMSO 1985).

DES, *The Curriculum from 5 to 16* (HMSO 1985).

DES, *Report of the Committee of Inquiry into the Teaching of English Language* [Kingman Report] (HMSO 1988).

DES and the Welsh Office, *National Curriculum: Task Group on Assessment and Testing: A Report* [and three supplementary reports] (HMSO 1987 and 1988).

Doyle, Brian, *English and Englishness* (Routledge 1989).

Eagleton, Terry, *Criticism and Ideology* (NLB 1976).

Edwards, V. K., *The West Indian Language, Issue in British Schools* (Routledge and Kegan Paul 1979).

Gannon, P., *Assessing Written Language* (Arnold 1985).

Gimson, A. C., *Introduction to the Pronunciation of English* (Allen and Unwin 1980).

Greenbaum, S., *The English Language Today* (Pergamon 1984).

Holmes, Brian, and McLean, Martin, *The Curriculum* (Unwin Hyman 1989).

Honey, John, *Does Accent Matter?* (Faber 1989).

Hughes, Ted, *Poetry in the Making* (Faber 1967).

Kermode, Frank, *An Appetite for Poetry* (Collins 1989).

Lodge, David, ed., *Modern Criticism and Theory* (Longman 1988).

Marsh, George, *Teaching Through Poetry* (Hodder and Stoughton 1988).

Nash, W., *English Usage* (Routledge and Kegan Paul 1986).

NATE, Lessons in English Teaching and Learning (NATE 1988).

Perera, K., *Children's Writing and Reading: Analysing Classroom Language* (Blackwell 1984).

Quirk, R., and Greenbaum, S., *University Grammar of English* (Longman 1973).

Quirk, R., and Stein, Gabriele, *English in Use* (Longman 1990).

Richmond, J., *The Resources of Classroom Language* (Arnold 1982).

Ricks, Christopher, and Michaels, Leonard, eds, *The State of the Language* (Faber 1990).

Steiner, George, *Language and Silence* (Faber 1967).

Strang, B. M. H., *History of English* (Methuen 1974).

Stubbs, M., *Language and Literacy: The Sociolinguistics of Reading and Writing* (Routledge and Kegan Paul 1980).

Stubbs, M., *Discourse Analysis: The Sociolinguistic Analysis of Natural Language* (Blackwell 1983).

Stubbs, M., 'What is Standard English?', in M. Stubbs, *Educational Linguistics* (Blackwell 1986).

Sutcliffe, D., *British Black English* (Blackwell 1982).

Tizard, B., and Hughes, M., *Young Children Learning: Talking and Thinking at Home and at School* (Fontana 1984).

Trudgill, P., *Accent, Dialect and the School* (Arnold 1975).

Young, D. J., *Introducing English Grammar* (Hutchinson Education 1984).